Dial "M" for Mother

Dial "M" for Mother

A Freudian Hitchcock

Paul Gordon

Madison • Teaneck
Fairleigh Dickinson University Press

New hardcover printing 2015 by University of Delaware Press
Co-published with Rowman & Littlefield
4501 Forbes Boulevard, Suite 200, Lanham, Maryland 20706
www.rowman.com

16 Carlisle Street, London W1D 3BT, United Kingdom

978-1-61147-358-2 (cloth: alk. paper)

Originally published by Associated University Presses
2010 Eastpark Boulevard
Cranbury, NJ 08512

Library of Congress Cataloging-in-Publication Data
Gordon, Paul, 1951–
Dial "M" for mother : a Freudian Hitchcock / Paul Gordon.
p. cm.
Includes bibliographic references and index.
ISBN 978-8386-4133-0 (alk. paper)
1. Hitchcock, Alfred, 1899–1980—Criticism and interpretation. 2. Motion pictures—Psychological aspects. I. Title.
PN1998.3.H58G67 2008
791.4302'33092—dc22

2007032749

∞™ The paper used in this publication meets the minimum requirements of American National Standard for Information Sciences—Permanence of Paper for Printed Library Materials, ANSI/NISO Z39.48-1992.

Printed in the United States of America

Contents

Acknowledgments

TO HENRY SUSSMAN, FOR HIS CONTINUED SUPPORT OF THIS AND all my other work. To the wonderful community of Hitchcock scholars who have made this book so difficult to write, but ultimately so much better. In particular, to Tony Williams, Professor of English at Southern Illinois University, Carbondale, who read the entire manuscript and offered many valuable suggestions, and to the "keeper of the gate" Ken Mogg, whose Web site has proven invaluable and who has been so generous with his time in answering my numerous queries. To Harry Keyishian, Julien Yoseloff, and their wonderful staffs at Farleigh Dickinson, and Associated University Presses respectively, with special thanks to the meticulous editing and support of Christine Retz and Jim Voss.

To my best friend and colleague, the extraordinary film scholar Ernesto Acevedo-Muñoz, who helped in countless ways, but perhaps most in encouraging the views of an outsider.

To Madigan, who makes everything better.

To my gifted Humanities students at the University of Colorado.

To my daughter Hilary, who will read this someday and understand it better than I ever could.

Dial "M" for Mother

1
Introduction: Dial "M" for Mother: A Freudian Hitchcock

1. Sebastian's mother (Leopoldine Konstantin) ominously greets the viewer and her son's new suitor (Ingrid Bergman).

"The libido has dwelt so long in its attachment to the mother, even after puberty, that the maternal characteristics remain stamped on the love-objects chosen later—so long that they all become easily recognizable mother-surrogates."
—Freud, A Special Type of Object Choice

"Our image of women is derived from our mothers"
Nietzsche, Human-All-Too-Human, #380

Dial "M" for Mother

In Hitchcock's *Notorious* (1946), a film in which the camera, as William Rothman has aptly noted, "expresses the full-bodied passion that vibrates in his greatest later films," there is a stunning sequence in which time seems to stop as the camera slowly moves from a medium shot of Alicia Huberman (Ingrid Bergman) "looking slightly frightened" to a long shot of Mme Sebastian (Mme Leopoldine Constantin), the mother of Alex Sebastian (Claude Rains) who moves towards the viewer and directly into the camera: "The appearance of Alex's mother, her descent down the giant stairway, as well as her meeting Alicia, make up the strongest scene in the film so far. . . . The main impact of the mother's appearance, almost brings a chill down the spine."[1]

Such momentous staircase scenes are frequent in Hitchcock, but so, I would argue, is the figure of the mother who is there to greet anyone entering the Hitchcockean oeuvre: "When, in *Notorious,* Ingrid Bergman investigates the house of spies, its uncanniness is confirmed, and personified, by the Hitchcockian figure of 'Mother.' "[2] George Toles even goes so far as to postulate a "law of the mother" in Hitchcock in which the other female characters "must first capture, in a metaphor borrowed from *Notorious,* all of the mother's keys."[3] This is not to disagree with the notion of Bellour and others that Hitchcock's films are ultimately all about Hitchcock (Bellour mentions this as the reason Hitchcock appears in all his films).[4] It is rather to agree with the notion of Kaja Silverman that the so-called "auteur" theory can be expanded to include the author's unconscious signature rather than just some authoritative notion of the author's presence.[5]

In arguing for the central role of the "mother" in Hitchcock it is important that the term (like that of the phallus in Lacan) be understood in an expanded sense which is linked to, but not limited by, its literal, biological significance. Elizabeth Cowie has pointed out that the maternal breast must be understood in Lacanian terms which are (in this case) completely compatible with the Freudian notion of the mother invoked here, as one example of the "objet petit a" which is never the original object of the drive to recover the original "lost love object."[6] As Toles has stated, the "mother" may even be linked to the celebrated movement of the camera for which Hitchcock is most famous: "When the camera's eye searches *for* mother, or searches *as if it were* mother, to whom does it belong? Are we not continually thrown back to the unmapped psychic territory of our earliest images and confusions?"[7]

More often than not the figure of the mother is replaced by one of her surrogates, one of the many women who, like Alicia Huberman, pose a threat to the mother's dominance over her son. The threat to the mother posed by such women, however, is ultimately unsuccessful, not least because the women who on a few occasions seem to succeed in wresting away the son, as Eve Kendall seems to in *North by Northwest,* or Melanie Daniels seems to in *The Birds,* only affirm the persistence of the maternal figure they, or their son-lovers, seek to replace. Moving some twenty years earlier to Hitchcock's films like *The Lodger* (1926), and some thirty years later to the underrated masterpiece *Frenzy* (1972), the mother figure and the other women who are her surrogates hover over the entire Hitchcock corpus the way, in *Psycho,* "Norman associates his mother with the deadly passivity of a monstrous bird of prey probably because she was the parent who hovered over him, watching his every move, threatening to pounce when he committed a mistake. In retaliation, he has removed her guts, the entrails of his mother. (Hitchcock did describe *Psycho* as a 'black comedy.')"[8]

The prevalence of M-names in Hitchcock, as Bellour states, runs "through too many films not to be deliberate," but Bellour fails to acknowledge the ultimate M-name which underlies all the others, a name which, moreover, is spelled out in the name of Hitchcock's own mother (and Uncle Charlie's motherly sister in *Shadow of a Doubt*): "M" "a," "Emma."[9] As Tania Modleski notes in her brilliant study of Hitchcock, "fear of the devouring, voracious mother is central in Hitchcock's work, even where it is not immediately apparent."[10] But it is not just fear of the devouring woman which is "central in Hitchcock's work," however much one might agree with Modleski, Rothman, and Creed that the "monstrous feminine" is one of the important ways the figure of the mother asserts itself in Hitchcock. There is also the desire for the mother, of which fear is merely a strategy of denial, as well as desire for the various other maternal-figures who populate—and I would argue dominate—Hitchcock's entire body of work. Psychoanalysis is frequently implied and invoked by writers, such as those just mentioned, who acknowledge the importance of the mother figure in Hitchcock. Yet an extended Freudian analysis of Hitchcock's films which would include other aspects both of the "original love object" and of the unconscious of which it is a part should help us to expand considerably on the important work of writers such as Rothman who, in comparing Sebastian's mother to an earlier figure in *The 39 Steps* (not, however, the earliest), touches too briefly on this important theme: "He [the Professor] appears to extend this stranger an extraordinary intimacy, presenting him with his secret view of his wife. She open the door, says, 'Lunch is ready, dear" in an icy voice, nods, and leaves. *Yet this view is enough to 'type' Louisa as a cold, overbearing woman, a nightmarish mother figure. . . .* [Rothman's note then adds:] *Perhaps the most chilling instance of this type is Claude Rains's mother in Notorious* (italics mine)."[11]

I am not saying that exploring Hitchcock psychoanalytically, and with particular reference to the figure of the Mother, is the only "key" to understanding these films: "One should not assume," states a recent writer on the uneasy relationship between psychoanalysis and film, "that either Freudian psychology or one singular version of psychoanalytical theory is the key to understanding a text."[12] There are of course many excellent analyses of Hitchcock, to which this book is enormously indebted, which either ignore psychoanalysis altogether or acknowledge its obvious relevance to Hitchcock without necessarily using Freud's ideas to analyze the films. There are many ways to enter the "house" of Hitchcock's genius, and many keys to many locks; the one thing all criticism can agree on is that, waiting inside this house, is the figure of Mother.[13]

A Freudian Hitchcock

In two important recent volumes of essays on Hitchcock numbering close to a thousand pages with some fifty contributors, there is not one Freudian analysis of any Hitchcock film, and only a handful of passing references to "Freud," the "Oedipus Complex," etc.[14] Indeed, in the lengthy introduction to *Hitchcock's America,* an important volume that focuses on Hitchcock's American films (many of the same films discussed here), there is no mention of Freud in the overview of critical approaches to the director, and when such brief mention of Freud is made it is usually disparaging, as in the comment that a Freudian reading would "rob [*North by Northwest*] of its aura of achievement."[15] Moreover, this dearth of Freudian readings of Hitchcock's films is also found elsewhere in the corpus of Hitchcock-criticism, whether one looks at the major books or the major journals in the field, and whether one considers works which openly disdain psychoanalysis or works which, like those of Cavell, Rothman, Walker, Wood, and others, everywhere imply the potential value of a psychoanalytic reading without, however, offering one. One can certainly speculate on the reason for these omissions, as I will attempt to do in various ways throughout this introduction. But, for now, it is important only to argue the need for the present volume (whether the volume fills that need is another question), which attempts to fill an obvious gap which has been left even after the "explosion" of critical interest in Hitchcock during the past four decades.

One reason for this neglect is Hitchcock's own frequent use of psychoanalysis within the "manifest" structure of his films. Many of Hitchcock's films themselves refer explicitly to Freud, as when, in *The Birds,* Annie Hayworth (Suzanne Pleshette) tells Melanie Daniels (Tippi Hedren) to ignore Freud and his "Oedipus Complex" when trying to understand the admittedly odd relationship Mitch Brenner (Rod Taylor) has with his mother Lydia (Jessica Tandy): "So what's the answer? . . . Clinging possessive mother? Wrong! With all due respect to Oedipus, I don't think that that was the case."

As Margaret Horwitz points out, such a warning is more, not less, susceptible to the very sort of approach Annie is denying.[16] Such references to Freud in Hitchcock's films will most often be critiqued as instances of either blatant misunderstandings of Freud—such as in the case of Annie Hayworth's wrongheaded comment—or as instances of readings which are at best inadequate—such as the psychiatrist's diagnosis of Norman's problems at the end of *Psycho,* which Donald Spoto argues is "mocked by what follows," or when Mark Rutland reveals the truth about his wife's frigidity in *Marnie* (an interpretation which is belied by his own questionable role in first raping and then curing his "patient"), or in *Spellbound* when Constance Peterson (Ingrid Bergman) solves the problem of Dr. Edwardes'/Ballantyne's (Gregory Peck's) fear of the "Rothmanian" parallel lines only to leave unsolved the latter's murder of his brother and the role of the various father figures which dominate the film.[17] Indeed, it might be said that Hitchcock is never less interesting from a psychoanalytic perspective than when he deals most directly with the subject, and never more interesting from a psychoanalytic perspective than when dealing with less explicit matters such as, for example, the anal-compulsive fixation on wrapping up things in *Psycho.*[18]

With regard to the actual references to Freud by Hitchcock himself and by others involved in the making of these films, such overt statements, which were influenced both positively and negatively by the vogue of psychoanalysis in Hollywood after World War II, should be taken with the proverbial "grain of salt," especially when dealing with such a notoriously guarded, playful, and idiosyncratic figure as Hitchcock was when discussing his own work: "Hitchcock, feeling himself suspected of being secretly an intellectual, rarely admits to anything incriminating. At question time he displays footwork of a nimble grace rivaled only by the steelier performances of Otto Preminger."[19] Nor do I believe that "We should take psychoanalysis seriously in Hollywood movies because Hollywood took psychoanalysis seriously."[20] The reason here for "taking psychoanalysis seriously" is neither the popularity of psychoanalysis expressed in the films themselves nor in the culture of the times, but rather as a particularly useful way of analyzing and interpreting the films themselves.

That being said, the particular use of Freud in the present work has yet to be defined. Even if one focuses on a Freudian approach to Hitchcock's films, as I do here, "Of course," in the words of André Green, "there are different Freuds."[21] Far from being the monolithic writer that his critics sometimes take him to be, Freud can be seen alternatively as someone who emphasized the pre- or post-Oedipal (or, as Kaja Silverman has argued, both simultaneously), the original Mother or the "Law of the Father,"[22] the theoretical or the practical, the cultural or the biological, the aesthetic or the historical, the structural, or the poststructural, etc. The "Freud" proffered here, like the Freud of Sarah Kofman, is largely the result of a reading of the numerous writings on art and art-related matters, the "aesthetic" Freud who understood art as resembling dreams in providing latent expressions of their own necessarily repressed, unconscious truths.[23] Although I do not think that the Freud one discovers when approached this way is incompatible or even inconsistent with the Freud that one understands in other terms, it is a Freud who is defined more by the aesthetic process of "close reading" than by the general assertion of what Freud "really meant." The approach here is to try to be guided first by the films themselves and then to utilize psychoanalysis to understand the work, rather than the obverse. This will result, I hope, in a work which is less technical and more faithful to the films themselves.

A Freudian Hitchcock argues for the "latent" meaning which is repressed or denied by the characters of the films in question, and even by the "manifest" meaning of the films themselves. Although this leads, as Mary Ann Doane has argued, to a certain "distrust of the visual" in Freudian psychoanalysis, this does not of course deny the latent significance of the visual itself.[24] Stunning analyses of Hitchcock's formal mastery, as in the superb studies of writers like Rothman, Bellour, and Sharff (for whom "Hitchcock is admired foremost as a master of cinematic form") abound, but it is the oft-neglected meaning of these films—such as the psychosexual significance of Uncle Charlie's murders of widows, the birds' attacks on Bodega Bay, etc.—that is the issue here.[25] And while there is ample discussion, when relevant, of matters such as "primary narcissism," "the uncanny," "anal-compulsive behavior," etc., it does turn out that most of the films discussed in *A Freudian Hitchcock*, starting with *Shadow of a Doubt* and ending with *Frenzy*, involve characters, both male and female, who are caught up in the impossible desire to recover the "mother" as the first love object.

While some post-Freudian writers, such as Samuel Slipp, have claimed that Freud himself neglected the "pre-Oedipal" and hence the pre-paternal period in his work ("Freud had not acknowledged the role of the mother and emphasized the relationship to the father in the child's personality development. . . . The mother's role in child development was generally ignored in psychoanalysis until the 1920s), it is the view of this writer, and of D. N. Rodowick's attempt to reclaim a Freud who is less "binary" than even subsequent Lacanian reinscriptions, that this "neglect" is more a matter of the interpretation of Freud's works than of the works themselves.[26] The history of psychoanalysis is of course replete with examples of official and unofficial "breaks" with Freud, but it would be hard to imagine Freud disagreeing with those who would emphasize the pre-Oedipal role of the mother when the founder of psychoanalysis himself wrote:

"This [sensual] sucking involves making the mother's breast the first object of the sexual instinct. *I can give you no idea of the important bearing of this first object upon the choice of every later object, of the profound effects it has in its transformations and substitutions even in the remotest regions of our sexual life* (italics mine)."[27]

Just as it would be legitimate to emphasize more than Freud did himself the period, for example, of primary narcissism and its subsequent effects without deviating in any fundamental way from Freud's "libido-theory," so it would be entirely within the scope of psychoanalysis as defined by Freud to stress the role of the mother when applicable, as I believe it is in the case of Hitchcock. My use of the notion of the "mother" here is thus consistent with Freud but, as mentioned earlier, the notion must be understood as both the figure associated objectively with the mother as well as with the pre-Oedipal figure which Kaja Silverman refers to as "an emblem of infantile plenitude and bliss," "that "all" which has been sacrificed to meaning."[28] While the "object-relations" theories of later psychologists like Winnicott expands on Freud's (and Melanie Klein's) theory of the child's problematic relation to the mother as the "first love object," these later developments serve to confirm Freud's thesis about the underlying importance of this stage of the child's development.[29]

It has long been commonplace for poststructuralists like Deleuze, Foucault, Derrida, Baudrillard, and others to dismiss Freud's so-called essentializing tendencies as incompatible with their own hyper-mediated deconstructions: "Neither [Freud nor Marx], Baudrillard has argued, was able to escape the mirror; that is, neither was able to avoid the modernist error or representation—the beliefs that, at bedrock, there is some referent, some principle of truth, and that one's purpose is to reflect it accurately."[30] The view of Freud offered in this book is that psychoanalysis, while certainly grounded in a "biological" sense of human needs and desires, is not essentializing insofar as it follows the unconscious traces of meaning left by those same desires. I agree with D. N. Rodowick that "Rather than following the 'law' of unity and identity, is Freud among the first to understand the possibilities of individuations without 'subject' and a minority language of sexuality? . . . *Freud's lifelong reflections on femininity and female sexuality led him to profoundly question the biological or instinctual determination of sexual difference*" (italics mine).[31]

The "mother," for example, whom Freud identifies in the passage quoted above as the "first love object," is in reality a figurative term which may also refer to the breast, the milk, the nipple, the original state of narcissistic "oneness" just referred to by Kaja Silverman, and, most importantly, to the secondary love objects who continue to represent this original love object.[32] In other words, when we speak of the "mother" in the films discussed here we mean an "original love object" to whom the continued attachment of Hitchcock's protagonists—male and female—helps us to understand the hidden, "latent" meaning of these characters and the films in general. I would not, then, consider the readings of Hitchcock in this book essentialist, although they are certainly grounded in a "poststructural" understanding of Freud's "biological" grounding in the figure of the mother.

In *Shadow of a Doubt* the return of the "Merry Widow Murderer," Uncle Charlie, to the home of his motherly sister Emma can be seen as the cause, and not merely the effect, of his Oedipal murdering of already-married women, i.e. mother figures. In *Rear Window* L. B. "Jeff" Jeffries' preference for satisfying his perverse, voyeuristic desires over that of marrying the socialite Lisa Fremont (Grace Kelly), and the violent reenactment of this preference in the protagonist's obsessive spying on his neighbor Thorwald's murder of his wife, is seen as the result of the male's "cast-ration" by the "perfect woman" (for thus is Lisa Fremont described), a woman whose perfection is seen as stemming from a "mother complex" which elevates as well as denigrates Jeff's desire for the original mother.[33] Similarly, in *Vertigo* the Freudian notion of repressed maternal desire will be seen as explaining the protagonist's neurotic fixation on an imaginary woman—the fictional "lost mother" Carlotta Valdez—who is then split between the "Madonna" figure of Madeleine Elster and the "Harlot" figure of Judy Barton. This replication in this film of the same woman into three different mother figures (four including the "motherly" Midge, who literally tries to paint herself into the figure of Carlotta) explains, as the film does not otherwise explain, Scottie's vertigo as the result of an impossible desire to recover the lost mother. In understanding, as we shall attempt to throughout this volume, the various "Madonna/Harlot" figures in Hitchcock's films as all functions of the original mother we will avoid the mistake of taking either their innocence or their guilt too literally, as does Michael Walker when he argues that Grace Kelly's Margot in *Dial M for Murder* "has been unfaithful, but this is in the past, and all the signs are that she is now perfectly loving with her husband Tony."[34]

One might object that, in films like *North by Northwest*, this pattern of an impossible return to the original object of desire is ultimately resolved by the "happy endings" that occur often enough at the end of Hitchcock's films. In this respect *A Freudian Hitchcock* takes a strong and somewhat controversial stand in declaring that such endings are nonexistent, and when they do seem to occur they are at best ironically "happy" because the mother complex which underlies these films is never—indeed can never be—really resolved.[35] (I would apply Rothman's declaration regarding *The Lodger*, "Do we really know that this ending is a happy one?" to all the films discussed here.)[36] In *Rear Window* the hero's double cast-ration at the end of the film is seen as confirming Jeff's earlier statements of feeling entrapped by the "perfect woman" rather than as resolving this complaint. In *North by Northwest* I argue that the initial "slip" which occurs when Roger Thornhill is mistaken for the spy George Kaplan is not coincidentally the result of his beckoning a waiter for a phone in order to confirm a dinner-date with his mother. Indeed, the important relationship between Thornhill and his mother which occupies the first part of the film functions like a "parapraxis" in only seeming to be unrelated to the rest of the film. It is, I argue, its cause, for the absurd MacGuffinesque plot is merely the "screen story" of a character whose decidedly strange relationship to his mother (a relationship made all the more strange by Hitchcock's insistence on casting a woman who was younger than her "son" Cary Grant) leads to his "fugue state," and to his subsequent relationship with yet another "Madonna/Harlot" figure. It is because Eve Kendall fits both these roles so perfectly in first attempting to kill and then attempting to save Thornhill, in first seducing him and then attempting to marry him, that one can legitimately question whether the complex which drove Thornhill away from his mother in the first place has been successfully resolved by the film's so-called "happy ending."

It is remarkable that just one year after the lush Technicolor "epic" of *North by Northwest* Hitchcock made *Psycho*, a film which might be seen as *North by Northwest*'s cadaverous, nightmarish reflection. For in *Psycho* the "rot" (the initials inscribed on Roger O. Thornhill's matchbox) of Cary Grant's relationship to his mother is actualized in Norman's relationship to his mother—a relationship which, I argue, is more the rule than the exception in all the films studied in this book. But it is just as important to establish, as I try to do in my chapter on "'Disrespectful Respectability' in *Psycho*," that the first half of the film in which Marion steals forty thousand dollars in order to attain the "respectability" of marriage is fundamentally the same problem Norman is dealing with in coping with a mother whose insistence on respectability can be seen as a way of covering up Norman's illicit incestuous desires.

While many of Hitchcock's critics have insisted that the symbolic significance of *The Birds*—especially that of the birds' attacks—is deliberately incomprehensible and uninterpretable, I argue that the meaning of *The Birds* is inseparable from the film's double plot in which the relationship between Mitch Brenner and Melanie Daniels leads the latter back to the family home of a grown man who is still living with his mother and who has a "sister" young enough to be their daughter.[37] The birds' attacks, which follow Melanie to Bodega Bay, are not essentially different from the similar bird-like attacks on women like Marion *Crane* in *Psycho*; they present the persistence of an Oedipal conflict which turns the beauty of a mother's love—and the maternal breast—into its hated antithesis, the castrating beak of a persecuting bird.

Notwithstanding Tania Modleski's important work in redeeming the privileged position of the "women who knew too much" in Hitchcock, the protagonists in these films represent the bisexual unconscious in its relation to a genderless infantile substratum of maternal desire, and the "all-knowing" mothers, to the extent that they are present, are merely phantasms of this infantile desire.[38] Marnie's screen-memory in which she protects her mother from one of her "clients" is not, I argue, the real story of *Marnie*. Rather, Hitchcock's film is a model of the same problematic attachment seen in all of the films discussed here, and it is based, not on the incident described in the film's "recovered memory" but on the impossibility of recovering the mother's love—even at the film's end Mrs. Edgar continues to push Marnie away. For this reason Mrs. Edgar, like Mme Sebastian, Mrs. Thornhill, Mrs. Bates, Mrs. Brenner, and other such maternal figures, is not really the nightmarish figure the film makes her out to be, but is rather the product of a "return of the repressed" which disguises illicit desire by its hated opposite. Because of this, Marnie's halfhearted commitment to her husband Mark at the end of the film ("Oh Mark, I don't want to go to jail, I'd rather go with you") is indicative, like the endings of all these films, of the inevitably unsuccessful resolution of this conflict in Hitchcock. (I do not mean, of course, artistically unsuccessful.)

In Hitchcock's penultimate film *Frenzy,* which Rothman referred to as a "self-conscious return to Hitchcock's origins," the director returned not only to the England of his earlier career in cinema but also to the England of his childhood—the England of his Jesuit education as well as of his father's "green grocer" occupation.[39] In recounting the story of a modern Jack the Ripper once again stalking the streets of London the film will return to the important theme of the serial murderer, a theme which was of course never far from the director's oeuvre. The film also utilizes another staple in Hitchcock (also found in *The Lodger*), the "wrong man" plot which, in psychoanalytical terms might be better understood as a wrong man *ploy* insofar as the device reminds the viewer of her—and the "wrong man's—complicity with our darker, unconscious desires. The murderer's mother has an important role in *Frenzy,* but the other, more prominent women in the film—the objects of both the protagonist Blaney's as well as of the murderer Rusk's "affections"—also confirm Hitchcock's return to a mother complex that makes any romantic relationship at best unhappy, and at worst, deadly.

Hitchcock and Psychoanalytic/ Feminist Film Studies

Comparing the Freudian approach offered here with other works on Hitchcock, particularly those which have made a certain use of psychoanalysis or have, on the other hand, openly declared its irrelevance to Hitchcock will help to clarify the intention of the present volume. This will exclude for the moment important writers on Hitchcock like Rothman, Cavell, Toles, Pomerance, Wood, Bellour, and others whose unpsychoanalytic views of the director are nonetheless "psychoanalytically unpsychoanalytical" in proffering numerous statements which attest to the potential relevance of reading Hitchcock with Freud:

> Hitchcock calls upon us to acknowledge film's ordinary avoidance of intimacy, and our own in our ordinary lives. *Is it that we are fearful that our appetite for love is so voracious that we do not dare give in to it at all?*
>
> —William Rothman, *Hitchcock: The Murderous Gaze*[40]

> *Vertigo* seems at first to be about a man's impotence in the face of, or faced with the task of sustaining, his desire; perhaps, on second thought, about the precariousness of human verticality altogether. But it turns out to be about the specific power of a man's fantasy to cause him not merely to forgo reality . . . but to gear every instant of his energy toward a private alteration of reality.
>
> —Stanley Cavell, *The World Viewed (Reflections on the Ontology of Film)*[41]

> There is something wrong—pervasively wrong and violating—about Hitchcock's way of representing women on screen.
>
> —George Toles, *A House Made of Light*[42]

> I don't believe it [psychoanalysis] solves all the riddles of film, especially since the very few (and very precise) essays Freud actually wrote about creative work, such as "The Poet and Daydreaming," almost never get quoted or used as the basis of filmic analysis.
>
> —Murray Pomerance, *An Eye for Hitchcock*[43]

> She [Eve Kendall in *North by Northwest*] helps him remove his jacket to have it cleaned, and he [Roger Thornhill] says, "When I was a little boy I wouldn't even let my mother undress me"; she tells him that he is a big boy now. It is one of those unobtrusive, almost offhand exchanges that reveals a great deal.
>
> —Robin Wood, *Hitchcock's Films*[44]

> They [Strutt and Mark Rutland in *Marnie*] are nothing but doubles, irregularly distributed along a trajectory at whose origin is Hitchcock, the first among all his doubles, a matrix that generates them as well as his own representation as duplicate image of himself.
>
> —Raymond Bellour, *Analysis of Film*[45]

When one speaks about "psychoanalytic film studies" one often thinks of Jacques Lacan and Christian Metz, writers whose popularity has led one writer to declare that "Psychoanalysis, once the dominant theoretical paradigm in cinema studies, has not fared well since the mid-1980's."[46] While Metz's particular use of psychoanalysis, which is far less Freudian than Lacanian in its study of the process whereby the screen functions as a mirroring of the spectator's desires and identifications, was once film studies' "dominant paradigm," the application of Freud proper to the study of film, with the important but qualified exception of the field of "feminist film studies" which will be discussed later in this introduction, has been considerably less successful.[47] As the editor of an important volume on *Psychoanalysis and Cinema* observes, "Freudian film analyses have not been at the center of film research."[48] Indeed, as Robin Wood, in the introduction to a recent collection of essays on *Horror Film and Psychoanalysis,* describes it, "Few today appear to read Freud or Marx with a view to sorting out what is still valid," while Murray Pomerance argues that, within film studies, Freud was never really read closely to begin with.[49]

According to the various contributors to the recent *Horror Film and Psychoanalysis* volume, and to the editor of the same text, the main reason for this complaint is that Freudian readings are too reductive, too unconvincing, and "fail to account for the artistic function of the film."[50] Yet reductive readings, those which see, for example, the psychoanalytic study of film as a simple matter of noting the "return of the repressed," of the "beast within," are indictments, not of psychoanalysis, but of superficial applications of Freud. To avoid this problem many of the essays in *Horror Film and Psychoanalysis* proclaim the value of a "cognitivist" psychology over that of psychoanalysis because it rejects the idea of the unconscious as the latent infantile explanation of manifest content. But, again, I would claim that this argument, which has been made as far back as the debate between Freud and Jung, and between psychoanalysis and "ego-psychology", should serve only as a well-advised warning to eschew the "sickening banality of psychoanalytic readings which repress rather than generate meaning."[51] If the editor of *Psychoanalysis and Cinema* can dismiss Freudian interpretation as more of a "violation" of the text than Lacanian psychoanalysis, that is because she associates the former with a kind of "psychobiographizing" ("the Freudian method is ultimately biographical") with which it is by no means synonymous.[52] As Mary Ann Doane explains:

As Freud pointed out with respect to the dream, "To explain a thing means to trace it back to something already known, and there is at the present time no established psychological knowledge under which we could subsume what the psychological explanation of dreams enables us to infer as a basis for their explanation." This destabilization of theory with respect to its object has frequently been noted. Samuel Weber describes psychoanalytic theory as "the struggle to wrest meaning from a process that entails the deliberate dislocation of meaning."[53]

If the current state of film theory eschews the "top-down theorizing" of earlier decades in which the influence of Lacan on film studies was dominant, then it is to be hoped that the false argument of the "excluded middle" would not require, as the editors and contributors to a recent volume of essays on *Post-Theory: Reconstructing Film Studies* argue it must, a turn to empirical, "cognitivist" studies of film which would meet the "burden of proof" which is supposedly lacking in theory.[54] Theory, and that includes the sort of Freudian theory practiced here, is not exempt from the "burden of proving" the truth of its assertions to its readers, although that truth is not just a matter of observation, but also one of interpretation.

The view of the Freudian "paradigm" discovered in the films discussed here would seem to preclude Žižek's Lacanian (versus Freudian) reading of the Hitchcockean hero as "the man who knows too much," agreeing instead with Modleski's view of the typical Hitchcock hero as knowing far too little about his or her own unconscious motivations.[55] Indeed, Žižek's Lacanian reading of Hitchcock is not, I would argue, really even Lacanian given that Žižek uses some of the terms and structures of Lacan's thought without maintaining their distinctive grounding in psychoanalysis. This is both the strength and weakness of Žižek insofar as his readings are meant to incorporate a number of different methodologies rather than to adhere to any one of them. Regarding his particular readings of Hitchcock, because there is even less connection to Freud than to Lacan there is correspondingly little connection between his and the readings offered here. I discuss my particular disagreements with these interpretations at a number of points in this book, but would mention here that in his insistence on applying a supposedly Lacanian structure to Hitchcock Žižek misleads the reader into thinking, for example, that the relationship to Lisa in *Rear Window* is normal when compared to the relationship between Thorwald and his wife; that Scottie in *Vertigo* is a healthy version of Norman in *Psycho*, and that the mother at the end of *The Birds* ultimately proves benign in her supposed acceptance of Melanie.[56] The Freudian readings offered here argue instead for a Hitchcock who is unrelentingly faithful to the impossibility of normalcy given the inherent impossibility of reconciling consciousness with an infantile unconscious (there is no other kind) which, I argue, it is the goal of all these films to reveal.

The relationship of this work to the important field of "feminist psychoanalytical film studies" is, on the other hand, a very different story. It is no small statement to say that much of the best theoretical work of the past thirty years has been done within the field of "feminism and psychoanalysis," work which often includes, if not being squarely based within, film studies. The work of writers like Laura Mulvey, Tania Modleski, Kaja Silverman, Mary Ann Doane, Gaylyn Studlar, Barbara Creed, and others clearly demonstrate the critical importance of women's studies for all aesthetic, humanistic studies.

And yet, within the field of feminist film studies attempts to adopt a Freudian approach are almost as rare as attempts to ignore its validity. Indeed, there seems to be an almost mandatory disclaimer with which books and articles in the field of "feminism and psychoanalysis" begin, declaring that the very Freudian method which is largely responsible for the analysis in question is itself of questionable importance. Typical of such ambivalence is Jane Wager's introductory statement in *Dangerous Dames* that "This view of cinematic identification as a series of shifting positions is reiterated in the psychoanalytic reassessment of fantasy. . . . *While these original fantasies reinscribe a psychoanalytic view of sexuality that I am not necessarily willing to perpetuate here*"[57] (italics mine). Similarly, Gaylyn Studlar (following Deleuze) makes ample use of Freud's writings in her own attempt to redefine cinematic pleasure as masochistic but states (wrongly, I think) that "He [Freud] looked upon masochism, with its self-punishing ego activity, as a tremendous danger to humanity," and many forget that Laura Mulvey's classic denunciation of the male gaze is also "the best and most brilliant exposition of the reading of Freud produced by Anglo-American film theory in the seventies."[58] It is tempting to explain such ambivalence and its related hostility in psychoanalytical terms, but to do so would be to assume knowledge and acceptance of the very methodology that it is my goal here to describe, and to further frustrate critics like Michael Grant who decry "the use standardly made of psychoanalysis in theoretical studies of Hollywood cinema . . . [in which] such theories necessarily presuppose the very condition they are trying to explain."[59] In the introduction to one of a number of important volumes on "feminism and psychoanalysis," introductions that always, it seems, begin with the aforementioned obligatory restatement of the hostility between the two camps joined in their title, the editors argue for a Lacanian "third term" between the two: "In a figurative sense, this missing term is broadly analogous to Jacques Lacan's notion of the 'third term' as that which destroys the symmetry of binary oppositions postulated in both early feminist and early psychoanalytic theory."[60]

Such a third term is obviously not the Hegelian *tertium quid* but, rather, a denial of the "violence of the binary," i.e., of the binary altogether. Feminism is not, either in theory or in practice, opposed to psychoanalysis. One might even go so far as to claim, with Elizabeth Wright and Juliet Mitchell, that "the rejection of psychoanalysis and Freud's works is fatal for feminism."[61] With regard to the present volume of Freudian essays on Hitchcock, a volume that relies heavily on the work of feminist writers, the "third term" is, simply put, the equation between the two. That is, psychoanalysis *is* feminism, and feminism *is* psychoanalysis, insofar as the women in Hitchcock's films are all understood in term of the male characters'—and male director's—obsessions with an unconscious, maternal prototype. To understand this pattern is to understand both the importance of Hitchcock as well as the importance of the women who form the "matrix" of his works. It is, moreover, to avoid the tendency decried by Mary Ann Doane to revalorize the maternal "woman who knows too much" through Hitchcock's (and Freud's) constant contextualization of this desire within the infantile unconscious.[62]

In exposing the mother fixations of these films the present work will hopefully be seen as relevant to the important field of "feminism and psychoanalysis" in general, as well as to the study of Hitchcock in particular. Mulvey's now famous notion of the "male gaze" as possessing an authorial power of controlling the narrative point-of-view "with all the attributes of the patriarchal superego" has been rightly criticized by subsequent criticism—including that of the author herself—as insensitive to the richness and complexity of the Hitchcockean oeuvre (and, according to Elizabeth Cowie, Joan Copjec, D. N. Rodowick, and others, of the cinematic experience in general) on which her argument is in part based.[63] Toles, Modleski, and other critics have called attention to the obvious critique of such patriarchal authority in Hitchcock's films as evident, for example, in the failure of Scottie Ferguson (in *Vertigo*) to succeed in his intentions of controlling Judy Barton, Madeleine, or for that matter anyone or anything in the film: "Norman's and Scottie's gaze, far from being stable power positions, are, almost from the moment these figures enter their narratives, marked by an obscure ailment that that threatens to recur. Their seeing disorders, when they 'erupt,' have the capacity to unman them, quite literally in Norman's case."[64]

Modleski's notion that "Hitchcock's films remain resistant to patriarchal assimilation" in "subverting the claim to mastery and authority not only of the male characters but also of the director himself" certainly comes closer to the view of Hitchcock's films offered here, but my view, like that of Bellour, sees the "women who know too much" in Hitchcock as largely phantasms of their protagonists'—and their director's—unconscious.[65] This might seem to push the present volume back in the direction of Mulvey's view just discussed, except that, according to the view offered here, infantile mother complexes such as that of Scottie in *Vertigo* do not necessarily imply anything patriarchal or authoritative, and they allow for a certain "middle ground," also argued for by Kaja Silverman, in which Hitchcock's "own authorial system . . . may in fact contain a female voice as one of its constituent although generally submerged elements."[66] Thus the Freudian interpretation of Hitchcock's films contained here falls somewhere between Mulvey and Modleski in exposing a decidedly infantile, if not neurotic, attitude toward women based ultimately on a deep-seated mother fixation which, in the final analysis, is never resolved in any Hitchcock film.[67] As such, my position is also somewhere "to the left" of Molly Haskell's largely correct view, in her classic critique of cinema's exploitation of women, of Hitchcock's misogynistic need to destroy the "icy self-possession" of the ideal Hitchcock woman, a view which nonetheless (like that of Mulvey) fails to account for the films' clear indications of a mother complex underlying this misogyny, as well as the corresponding complexity of the "Madonna/whore" complex which Haskell also correctly perceives in the films.[68] To understand the psychological underpinnings of Hitchcock's protagonists is to understand why Haskell's statement that "Hitchcock's women must be tortured and punished" (351) is true, and why, for so many women in so many of the films, it is not.

I aim to develop at some length Modleski's claim that "fear of the devouring, voracious mother is central in much of Hitchcock's work" (107), but, again, I would not go so far as to claim that "Hitchcock's fear and loathing of women is accompanied by a lucid understanding of—and even sympathy for—women's problems in patriarchy" (112). In Barbara Creed's study of *The Monstrous Feminine,* which has been referred to as "one of the most influential uses of psychoanalytic reading in film theory," the author's thesis is that "the presence of the monstrous-feminine in the popular horror film speaks to us more about male fears than female desire or female subjectivity."[69] This fits perfectly the notion here that the mother and her surrogates in Hitchcock are projections of the director and his protagonists, although the fact that many of Hitchcock's protagonists are female, as are the protagonists of many of the films Creed herself analyzes (e.g., *Carrie* and *Alien*), suggests that such projections *of* the female may also be *by* the female. Nonetheless, in Creed's analysis as in mine, the figure behind such "monsters" is the mother:

> Suddenly, Carrie calls on her powers of telekinesis to send a barrage of knives sailing though the air, pinning her mother to the wall. Mrs White dies in a pose which imitates that of Christ on the cross in the statue she keeps in the prayer cupboard. There is no doubt that Carrie's knife has sexual connotations. As Mrs White dies she utters orgasmic moans, which suggest that her release has been brought about by a symbolic form of phallic penetration by her daughter. *This scene suggests that the doomed mother child dyad is marked by repressed sexual desire—a theme also explored in Psycho.* (82, italics mine)

Creed's analysis of horror films, which draws heavily on Freud as well as on Kristeva's notion of the maternal female as "abject," is certainly relevant to a study of Hitchcock which explores, as I do here, the mother as the fantasmatic source of the protagonist's projected fears and desires. "Monstrous women" are central in such horror films as *Psycho* and *The Birds* (Creed's analysis of the latter film notes the connection between the castrating birds and such mythological winged female monsters as the striges and the gorgons), but they are also, as Modleski noted, "central in much of Hitchcock's work."[70]

"Freudian mother theory" is also central to E. Ann Kaplan's work on cinema, and on Hitchcock.[71] Although she is critical, as am I, of Hitchcock's view of motherhood in films such as *Marnie* as supporting the patriarchal (and, according to Silverman, Kristevan) view of the maternal as abject, Kaplan acknowledges that the terror of the abject mother, also described by Creed, is accompanied by "a desperate need for the mother . . . felt also by Hitchcock" (137).[72] It is worth noting in this regard that, unlike films like *Carrie,* the mother in Hitchcock kills, she is not killed. (The murdered Mrs. Bates, whose voice haunts *Psycho,* is not really an exception to this rule.) Kaplan goes on to suggest that Hitchcock's obsession with this dominant, immortal mother anticipates her idea of a "postmodern mother," that is, a mother who is "unrepresentable" within a patriarchal system of values, hierarchies and epistemological certainties. This would support Tom Cohen's recent two-volume opus on Hitchcock's *Cryptonomies,* which argues strongly for a postmodern Hitchcock who is not at all subject to any "classical" system of values and meanings.[73] My own sense, which I think is also that of Kaplan, is that while Hitchcock anticipates a postmodern rethinking of motherhood's challenge to patriarchy, his "p.o.v.," like that of most "infants [who] move towards differentiation and separation to the mother's attempts to retain synthesis," is still that of the child who is desperately—indeed, neurotically—trying to move toward a differentiation from the mother which would serve to put mother back in her "proper" place.[74]

Following Deleuze's reevaluation of masochism in *Coldness and Cruelty,* Gaylyn Studlar attempts to oppose the notion, standard since Mulvey, of the sadistic, masculine "gaze" with an alternative theory of the "masochistic basis of cinematic pleasure" which would feminize (as it were) the role of the spectator and thereby undermine the traditional view of the way gender roles are represented.[75] Although Studlar sometimes chides Freud for his "neglects" and "failures," much of what she says about a primary, prephallic, bisexual masochism is ultimately derived from Freud and thus consistent with his views, and with the view of the "original mother" proffered here. While it is arguable whether Freud "fail[ed] to adequately acknowledge the role of the mother as a . . . powerful and even threatening figure" (15), and Hitchcock may well have "written the book" on the subject, Studlar's notion that "the oral mother could be the primary figure in a construct that centralizes scopic pleasure and fetishism" (30) confirms the "ground zero" of the present work, despite the fact that, for Hitchcock, the denial of that "primary figure," and her subsequent conversion into the aforementioned "powerful and even threatening figure," is everywhere apparent.

Despite the tendency, even after Deleuze's *Cinema* I/II, to see film as primarily a visual medium, Kaja Silverman's *The Acoustic Mirror* is informed by the author's notion of cinema as "a loss which both threatens and secures the viewing subject" (2). In a dialectical move which is not uncommon in psychoanalytical/feminist writings (and in Barthes's paean to the "powers of castration," *S/Z*), it is the female who, by virtue of "always already" having been denied the illusion of mastery, can claim to represent the very essence of this castrated, cinematic power. The female for Silverman thus represents the paradox of a maternal plenitude which, because it can not exist within the limits of male subjectivity and "phallogocentric" discourse, is rendered inadequate because of the very "infantile plenitude" which the male is lacking.

> The fantasy of the maternal-voice-as-sonorous-envelope takes on a different meaning depending upon the psychic "lookout point": viewed from the site of the unconscious, the image of the infant held within the environment or sphere of the mother's voice is an emblem of infantile plenitude and bliss. Viewed from the site of the preconscious/conscious system, it is an emblem of impotence and entrapment. (73)

In other words, women are rendered impotent, castrated beings in cinema as a way for men to regain a power which is as false as the lack of power over which it triumphs: "At the level of sound, as of that of the image, Hollywood protects the male subject from unpleasurable self-knowledge by requiring woman to stand in for him" (71). This is, I would argue, exactly the role of women in Hitchcock's films, women who represent a maternal prototype which must, like Judy Barton at the end of *Vertigo*, be destroyed precisely because they represent a figure whose very perfection implies a loss of the male protagonist's ability to triumph over her. Recall how, in *Rear Window,* Jeff Jeffries (James Stewart) complains to the maternal figure who is nursing him that he can not marry Lisa Fremont (Grace Kelly) because she is "too perfect." In an obvious allusion to *Marnie,* Silverman notes how this need to castrate the woman (in my terms, the mother) who will otherwise castrate the child results in "The female subject's gaze . . . as partial, flawed . . . she bumps into walls, *or loses control at the sight of the color red*" (31, italics mine).

Unlike these feminist critics, whose measured objections to Freud are often belied by their frequent use of psychoanalysis as the very groundwork of their readings, Tom Cohen is one of a number of important critics of Hitchcock who is adamant in his rejection of psychoanalysis as a way of reading the films. For Cohen, Freud is simply too reductive (a criticism we have encountered before) relative to his postmodern insistence on a much more "free-floating signifier":

> To speak of a "passing" or overpassing (in a Nietzschean sense) of the "Oedipus" by Hitchcock is to redirect our attention away from the auteurist, psychoanalytic, culturalist, film theoretical, surrogate, and gender-political Hitchcocks toward a mnemonic field of teletechnics, a sensorium that is being disassembled and reassembled as a mnemotechnic of passage, marked across these films in figures of ports, bridges, aporetic border crossing, and so on, from the earliest works on.[76]

As one would expect, Cohen steadfastly eschews any Freudian readings of Hitchcock, and agrees with Annie Hayworth's comments quoted above regarding the irrelevance of Mitch Brenner's attachment to his mother. Elsewhere he notes that the comment by Mitch's young sister Cathy about "No touching" during the game of blindman's bluff at her birthday party "has no bearing on the sexual frigidity at issue elsewhere, itself a MacGuffin" (2:125). Above all, the birds' attacks, we are told, "are causeless" (or, rather, they are "teletechnic agents"; 2:151). While I share Cohen's deconstructive distrust of univocal readings, it remains for the reader, and the viewer of the film, to decide whether the "causelessnes" of the birds' attacks is more or less univocal than the notion of Creed, and the psychoanalytic interpretation of *The*

Birds offered here (chapter 7), of the birds' identification with the female figures of the film (Melanie, Lydia, and Annie Hayworth), and of Mitch's (and Melanie's) "mother complex" that underlies them.

Richard Millington also rejects a psychoanalytical approach as potentially "robbing the film [*North by Northwest*] of its aura of achievement," although he does so on very different grounds than Cohen.[77] Millington notes that "for Robin Wood, for Stanley Cavell, for Leslie Brill, the film is a work of considerable moral beauty . . . [in which] Roger Thornhill and Eve Kendall move from inner emptiness to a fully achieved selfhood." Millington himself sees the film in slightly less glowing terms as an "ironic meditation on the condition of American character," but according to the Freudian view proffered here "moral beauty" is not only utterly lacking in the film (as it is, I would argue, in all the films discussed here), it is expressly subverted. The silent "founding fathers" represented in the film by the faces on Mt. Rushmore, as well as the present authority figures represented in the film by the CIA, are not in the least concerned with the lives of Roger Thornhill or Eve Kendall, both of whom have been deemed expendable earlier in the film, but are rather concerned with the microfilm contained in the statue that Leonard is holding. Indeed, in an earlier scene Thornhill roundly condemns the CIA for the lack of morals shown by its callous indifference to the life of one of its agents (Thornhill doesn't realize that they had, earlier, similarly written him off). And if one tries to find the "moral beauty" of the film in the way Roger Thornhill and Eve finally find "fully achieved selfhood," the thesis itself suggests that what the film is mostly about, notwithstanding the patent Hitchcockean ironic ending, is its preceding "inner emptiness."[78] It is this "inner emptiness" which a psychoanalytical interpretation of *North by Northwest* reveals to be the core of Hitchcock's film: Roger Thornhill's problematic relationship with, first, a mother who laughs at his life and death predicament, and then a woman, the new "Mrs. Thornhill," who also had earlier tried to have him killed. It is, as I argue in my chapter on *North by Northwest* and throughout this book, anything but "moral beauty" or "fully achieved selfhood" that constitutes the greatness of the Hitchcockean oeuvre, despite the tendency in a great deal of excellent Hitchcock criticism to insist on such a positive recuperation of meaning at the end of films such as *North by*

Northwest and *Rear Window*. Nor do I do think that arguing for a lack of such moral beauty in Hitchcock diminishes the greatness of the Hitchcockean oeuvre. As Maurice Yacowar states:

> Hitchcock's justice is tricky, poetic rather than legal. For his world is full of uncertainty. *Shadow of a Doubt* may seem to have a happy ending, but the killer is eulogized by the small town, and an innocent man was fed to an airplane propeller by mistake. . . . No simple justice, no simple psychology, can be sustained in Hitchcock's world of quicksand insecurity. So almost all Hitchcock's films end on an uncertain image, from the new lovers in *The Pleasure Garden* to the mass of abiding doom at the end of *The Birds*.[79]

If one is to use the notion of morality at all, I would argue that it is in the films' "immoral beauty," their unrelenting grasp on their "heroes'" immoral, unconscious desires which constitutes the fascination and power—the "aura of achievement"—of these films. In this respect we may indeed take the famous scene on Mt. Rushmore, in which Roger Thornhill and Eve Kendall are hanging precariously from the President's face, as emblematic, not of moral beauty, but of our tenuous grasp on it—our vertigo, if you will.

Which Hitchcock?

The present work will focus largely on the "widely acknowledged canonical works" and "masterpieces" from Hitchcock's so-called golden age, that is, films from the mid-1950s (beginning with *Rear Window*) through the mid-1960s.[80] Everyone is free to argue for their own choices of Hitchcock's most important films or "periods" (and argue they do), but there seems to be a general consensus among critics that the films of this period are Hitchcock's finest. Richard Schickel agrees that "such great works of the 1950's and 1960's . . . and, climactically, *Psycho* and *The Birds*, were much more ambiguous, pessimistic, and richer in meaning than most of what had gone before. (*Shadow of a Doubt would be the one film of his earlier career that I would rank with these in complexity and ambition*)"[81] (italics mine). Rothman refers to Hitchcock's "masterpieces of the fifties and early sixties such as *Rear Window, The Wrong Man, Vertigo, North by North-*

west, Psycho, The Birds, and *Marnie.*"[82] The two exceptions to the period of Hitchcock's "masterpieces" studied here are the inclusion, in the first chapter, of *Shadow of a Doubt,* and, in the final chapter, Hitchcock's *Frenzy* (1972). Although I discuss, in an afterword, the relevance of my thesis to a number of other Hitchcock films (*Rebecca, Notorious, Dial M for Murder, The Man Who Knew Too Much*), the inclusion here of separate chapters on *Shadow* and *Frenzy* deserves some comment. First, I thought it important to include studies of two films that fall outside the so-called "golden age" in order to show that such a notion, when dealing with Hitchcock, is useful but artificial, more "plastic" than "golden." While dating from the early 1940s, Hitchcock regarded *Shadow of a Doubt* as his favorite film long afterward, a judgment confirmed by many of his critics.[83] *Frenzy,* on the other hand, is not as often viewed as part of the Hitchcock "pantheon," although I am certainly not alone in placing it there (Sharff refers to it as a "showcase for cinema art.")[84] *Shadow of a Doubt* and *Frenzy* are both compelling examples of how, as was stated earlier, Hitchcock can be most interesting from a psychoanalytic perspective when he is least explicit about it. Both films deal with serial murderers of women who, significantly, are juxtaposed with "normal" families and individuals who turn out, on closer examination and at many levels of their respective narrations, not to be so "normal" after all. In short, *Shadow of a Doubt* establishes, and *Frenzy* concludes, a certain "typology" which we will observe throughout this work as well as in the various films discussed in the afterword, where I adopt Yacowar's thesis that "the early films show the same thematic concerns for which his later work is known."[85]

The selection of many of Hitchcock's best-known and most commented-upon films of his "major period" in *A Freudian Hitchcock* is also justified by the surprising paucity of Freudian interpretations of these same films mentioned earlier. Theodore Price is one of the few critics to try and deal with Hitchcock at a consistently "latent" level, but Price's own insightful analysis is belied somewhat by its own brilliant quirkiness.[86] His thesis of an undercurrent of homosexuality running through the films is important (consider, for example, *Rebecca, Rope, Strangers on a Train,* and other less obvious examples, such as *The Paradine Case*), and although I do not deal with homosexuality at any length in the present work, I think the notion which is developed here of a deep-seated mother complex and subsequent fear of women is completely congruent with Price's analysis. Among other critics there is most often a passing acknowledgment of the relevance of Freud to Hitchcock, such as Schickel's comment that Hitchcock's protagonists are all "guilty" even when they are not guilty of what they are accused of.[87] Not infrequently, however, one encounters a passing *rejection* of psychoanalysis' usefulness in understanding Hitchcock's films, such as in Douchet's statement that "I do not, however, believe that psychoanalysis suffices to explain the invention of forms and their internal dynamics."[88]

This lack of Freudian interpretations of Hitchcock is surprising, because these films would seem to require an analysis of the persistent patterns of mother complexes, male perversions, narcissism, "Madonna-harlot" complexes, neuroses and psychoses, etc. which are often their very subject matter and which are also evident even when they are not so obvious. If ever there was a director whose works respond to—if not require—a Freudian perspective it is Hitchcock, and it is the purpose of the present study to help to fill a gap which can perhaps only be understood from the very psychoanalytic perspective that is being avoided. For Hitchcock is telling a story in all these films that is unparalleled in its unrelenting adherence to the "darker side" of our unconscious' fears and fascinations, and in its unwillingness to veil this exploration of the Freudian Unconscious with Hollywood's—and society's—denial of such truths. Although he is speaking specifically about *Spellbound,* Murray Pomerance's acknowledgment of the affinity between Hitchcock's and Freud's mission of exploring the "inner light" of humanity's darkest truths might be applied to the entire oeuvre: "The real search for the light of meaning had to reject false pathways . . . and head toward what had not yet been seen. Or, better: toward what had once been too powerfully seen, and was repressed. . . . This was the message of Freud . . . [and] this was the message of Hitchcock."[89]

2
Sometimes a Cigar is Not Just a Cigar: Shadow of a Doubt

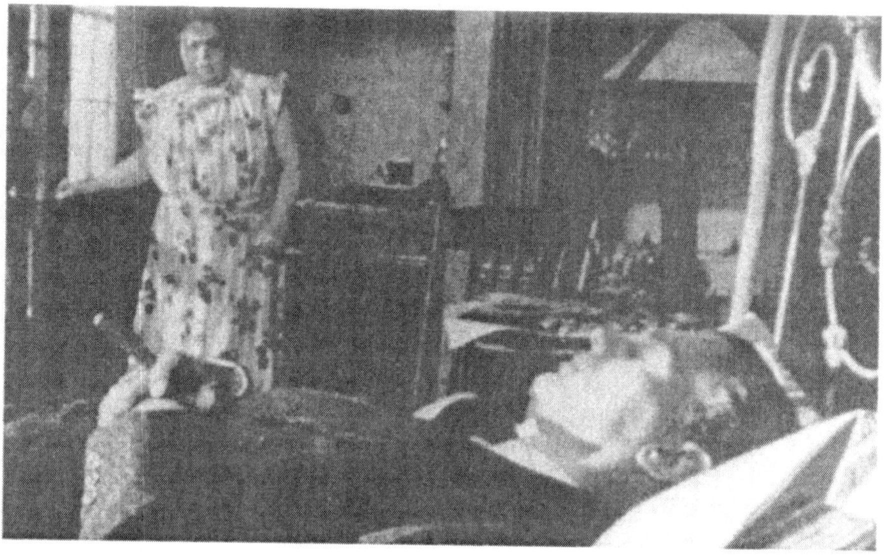

2. Uncle Charles (Joseph Cotten) shows his world-weariness.

IN HIS CLASSIC STUDY OF *HITCHCOCK: THE MURDEROUS GAZE*, William Rothman refers to *Shadow of a Doubt*, one of Hitchcock's first American films of the early 1940s, as "the equal of his greatest British work."[1] Among the many important elements Rothman acknowledges as distinguishing Hitchcock's "favorite film" is Patricia Collinge's "magnificent" performance of Emma as a "figure of great originality and power."[2] Although Rothman lavishes considerable praise and attention on Emma throughout his analysis he does not recognize that Uncle Charlie's sister, the figure to whom Charlie periodically returns, is in many ways the central figure of the film. First, she—and not young Charlie—is the reason Charlie is returning to Santa Rosa. She is also the figure with whom, as George Toles notes, young Charlie's "real struggle" is concerned, and not with "her deranged, homicidal uncle."[3] Indeed, one could also argue that the struggle between the two Charlies is over the life and death of Emma, a figure whom Toles refers to as "the woman that all of his victims resemble but who is herself mysteriously exempted from his rage and retribution." Robin Wood comes closer to the Freudian interpretation of *Shadow of a Doubt* offered here in stating that "In *Shadow of a Doubt* it is above all sexuality that cracks apart the family facade. As far as the Hays code permitted, a double incest theme runs through the film: Uncle Charlie and Emmy, Uncle Charlie and Young Charlie. Necessarily, this is expressed through images and motifs, never becoming verbally explicit; certain of the images depend on a suppressed verbal play for their significance."[4]

But Wood does not make the connection between this "double incest theme," Charlie's mother fixation, and his murder of widows. Emma, the mother figure of a film made when Hitchcock's own mother Emma was dying, the woman whose very name spells out the essence of the maternal, is our first example (but by no means the first in Hitchcock) of a mother fixation that underlies the rest of the film just as it does much of the Hitchcock oeuvre.

A Special Type of Object Choice

In his essay "A Special Type of Object Choice Made by Men" Freud talks about men who prefer a particular kind of woman, specifically those whose loose morality results in flirtatious behavior or even prostitution.[5] Also characteristic of this group of neurotic as well as "ordinary healthy" men is an elevation of the same degraded love object into someone with redeeming virtues, as well as a preference for the added involvement of a "wounded third party," such as a husband or rejected lover. Underlying this seemingly unrelated amalgam of conditions, particularly the paradoxical elevation of a "fallen woman," is the Oedipus complex. The surfacing of illicit sexual feelings for the mother makes her into a "prostitute" while the denial of those same feelings makes the mother into a sexless Madonna figure who possesses a high moral character. Finally, the "injured third party" is identified by Freud as a version of the original father from whom the child must woo away the mother:

> The choice of an object complying with these peculiar conditions and this strange way of loving her have the same source as the normal attitude in love; they are derived from a fixation of the infantile feelings of tenderness for the mother and represent one of the forms in which this fixation expresses itself. In the normal attitude there remain only a few traces unmistakably betraying the maternal prototype behind the chosen object, for instance, the preference young men show for mature women; the detachment of the libido from the mother is accomplished comparatively swiftly. *In our type, on the contrary, the libido has dwelt so long on its attachment to the mother, even after puberty, that the maternal characteristics remain stamped on the love-objects chosen later.* . . . Moreover, the fact of the mother belonging to the father might easily come to be an inseparable part of the mother's nature to the child growing up in the family circle, so that the "injured third party" mentioned by Freud is none other than the father himself. (166–67, italics mine)

Although the main character of Hitchcock's *Shadow of A Doubt* (1943) murders widows rather than courting women of dubious moral character, the pattern of expressing and repressing one's childhood love for the mother is apparent all the same. The widows Uncle Charlie seduces, marries, and then kills are all identifiable as "mother surrogates"; not only are they significantly older than Charlie but also because as widows they are in a sense still married to the father figure. The "injured third party" that represents the father in Freud's paper is thus represented in *Shadow of A Doubt* by the dead husbands whom Charlie is replacing by seducing their wives. Finally, just as repression of the desire for the mother figures in Freud's patients results in their being seen as fallen women engaged in illicit sexual practices, Charlie will justify murdering the widows he seduces by complaining—without any justification—that they are morally bankrupt and so deserving of death. And while, in "A Special Type of Object Choice Made by Men," Freud notes that the rejection of sensual desire for the parent takes the form of the opposite tendency to regard the mother as a personification of impeccable moral purity ("Few suggestions from without are so insulting, or from within so painful, as those which cast doubt on the mother's character" 168), this too fits perfectly Uncle Charlie's statement that, in reference to the period when his parents were alive, "everyone was sweet and pretty," whereas now "the world's a hell, what does it matter what happens in it." This chapter will analyze these and other ways that Hitchcock's film supports the Freudian notion that Charlie is murdering widows because of an obsession with his own childhood and, particularly, with his own mother.

Uncle Charlie

Our first indication of the relevance of Freud's essay occurs in the film's celebrated parallel openings, where we are introduced to the two main characters, Uncle Charlie (Joseph Cotten), and young Charlie (Teresa Wright), each of whom is lying in bed brooding before being interrupted by parental figures of the opposite sex.

In one of the most often cited studies of *Shadow of a Doubt* Francois Truffaut attempts to prove Hitchcock's awareness of a pattern of weaker and stronger personages that runs throughout the latter's films. Truffaut is thus careful to point out the important symmetry of these two opening shots which introduce us to the two main characters of the film, although he does not mention that this symmetry includes two parental figures who both want to know if "everything is all right": "the head (of Uncle Charlie) is towards the right of the screen. . . . [Whereas, in the second opening] the direction of the sequence is identical with that in which Cotten was first presented to us, but it is reversed: Teresa Wright's head and the door at the back are on the left of the screen."[6]

Like a number of protagonists in Hitchcock's films, such as the Rod Taylor figure in *The Birds,* young Charlie immediately strikes the viewer as too old to be living at home (the character is eighteen, but Wright was twenty-four when *Shadow of a Doubt* was made), and her boredom is a sign that the sexual maturity and independence to be acquired in the course of the film are long overdue. Young Charlie herself explains this depression to her father as result of the family's lack of vitality, but she is clearly projecting onto them her own lack of excitement. For Charlie's

3. A concerned father's inquires about his daughter Charlie's (Teresa Wright) malaise.

family is not nearly as unhappy as she describes, and her focusing on Emma to the exclusion of her father Joe, who is as burdened as anyone in the family, is equally unjustified. Young Charlie is in a state of "arrested development" in which she is directing back toward her family, and especially towards her mother Emma, the need to gratify desires that should be directed elsewhere. Although Toles might overstate matters somewhat when he declares that "Charlie takes the darkness of her own unavoidable killing of her uncle inside herself so that her mother can be permanently spared," he is certainly right in arguing that the mother figure is a central figure for *both* Charlies.[7] Moreover, if he is right about the ending of the film, then it would be good reason to doubt the notion that young Charlie has progressed beyond her mother fixation—something which I will argue throughout this volume that Hitchcock's characters never succeed in doing.

If young Charlie's bedroom scene suggests that she is stifled by desires which she is unable to direct outside the family, the same can be said of Uncle Charlie as he lies in bed, half-conscious and motionless except for the stroking of his cigar. The bed, the cigar, and the soporific manner in which Charlie answers his landlady's kindly solicitations all signify Uncle Charlie's similar narcissistic withdrawal from the "real world" as he plans his return to his family in Santa Rosa. Likewise, the money carelessly scattered on the floor also symbolizes, not any untidiness on the part of the usually fastidious Uncle Charlie (and typically fastidious Hitchcock villain), but his contempt, like that of his niece, for the conventional attitudes toward money of those around him (young Charlie's father is, after all, a banker). And, added to these parallels is the fact that, if young Charlie is thinking about her mother when she should be thinking about sex, the same can be said about her uncle. For Charlie has recently seduced and murdered another "merry widow," and so we assume that his thoughts too concern sexual drives redirected at either this surrogate mother figure or the motherly sister whom he is about to revisit. The cigar which Charlie is stroking as he lies in bed thus symbolizes, as Freud suggested it might, the sexual nature of both young Charlie's and Uncle Charlie's thoughts as they lie in bed and plan, respectively, how to save and/or murder their mothers.[8] The fact that both characters seem linked to each other "telepathically" (as young Charlie explains to the telegraph operator) is another indication of their being "of one mind." As young Charlie later says to her Uncle, "You can't hide anything from me."

Uncle Charlie makes a number of strange, general statements about women throughout the film which may at first seem inconsequential: "Women are fools. They'd fall for anything." "[Widows are] faded, fat, greedy women." "[They are] fat, wheezing animals". James McLaughlin is one of the few critics to focus on such remarks, but he nonetheless fails to follow through with his own important observation that Charlie's comments demonstrate a typical fear of powerful women which runs throughout Hitchcock's films.[9] The question he leaves unanswered is *why* characters like Charlie Oakley fear independent women. While it will remain for the rest of the chapters of this book to provide an understanding of Hitchcock's male protagonists and their attitude toward women, a better understanding of Uncle Charlie's motivations in marrying and then murdering already-married women is our first important step in that direction. As Charles himself says to young Charlie, "There's so much you don't know [about the world] . . . you're a sleepwalker, blind." This, as it turns out, is less true of the state of the world than it is about young Charlie's eagerness to believe in a goodness, and a state of "normalcy," which neither Hitchcock nor his villainous protagonist can share.

The widows like Mrs. Potter (the woman Charlie meets in the bank and plans to pursue next) whom Charlie seduces are not really shown to be "fat, wheezing animals," nor are they "fools" who would "fall for anything." True, Mrs. Potter and the other unfortunate victims "fall for" Charlie Oakley, but to blame them for that is like kicking someone in the shins and then blaming them because it hurts. Women's intelligence is not the real issue here; rather, it is Charlie's interest in such women, and the violence with which he resists that interest. Indeed, if the widows were really the "fat, wheezing animals" Charlie depicts them as being, no amount of money would induce him to seduce them. Moreover, if Charlie only desired money he wouldn't have to murder his companions. His *modus operandi* does make sense, however, if his real desire is not money but murder, and if his hatred is really a repressed form of sexual desire which underlies fifty years of Hitchcock films from *The Lodger* to *Frenzy*. As William Rothman states regarding Charlie's murder of these widows: "It is fundamental to *Shadow of a Doubt*, as I read it, that Charlie's killing can be viewed as expressing either contempt for his victims or compassion, indeed love, for them. Failure to acknowledge this ambiguity, and to appreciate its implications, is a failure to comprehend the film."[10] I agree with Rothman, but this rather strange form of love also needs to be more fully understood in order to "comprehend the film."

If one were to object that Charlie could not possibly be attracted to the older women he seduces, this could be countered by the simple fact that he does seduce such women, and the objection viewed as further evidence of the powerful taboo against just such a desire. Moreover, the image of the mother which the Oedipally fixated child retains owes more to past associations than to any present consciousness. This is supported by Uncle Charlie's statement that "I think about them, those [childhood] days, all the time," as well as by the recurrent "Merry Widow Waltz" sequence which figures so prominently in the film.

Despite its prominence, the "Merry Widow Waltz" sequence has eluded critics' grasp—indeed, most fail to analyze it at all.[11] Even William Rothman, who devotes a highly insightful chapter

4. One of many dissolves into the mysterious "Merry Widow Waltz" sequence.

to the film in *The Murderous Gaze,* refers only to the "mystery" of the enigmatic waltzing couples.[12] When interpreted (Durgnat, Scheib), the "Merry Widow Waltz" sequence is usually seen as the recollection of a beautiful world (Scheib's Eden), which is opposed to the modern urban jungle inhabited by Uncle Charlie. This is compatible with the Freudian analysis offered here, but it fails to explain *why* Uncle Charlie is intent upon destroying the very world he professes to admire.

The film itself takes place in 1941, and so this anachronistic sequence, which seems to come out of another movie altogether, only makes sense when seen as belonging to the generation of Uncle Charlie's victims, as well as to the generation of his own parents. One thinks of Welles's *The Magnificent Ambersons,* which was released only one year before *Shadow of a Doubt* and which has much in common with it, including a prominent Oedipal conflict.[13] That the sequence belongs to the period of his victims is evident from the newspaper clipping young Charlie finds, which describes the woman Charlie has recently strangled as "the beautiful Thelma Schenley," who was "known to audiences at the beginning of the century." That the sequence belongs to the period of Charlie's parents' early years together is evident from the fact that the photo Charlie gives to Emma dates from 1888. "The beautiful Thelma Schenley" and Charlie's mother, then, are practically contemporaries, and so Charlie's obsession with the widows he seduces and then kills can be seen as a continued mother fixation stemming from his early childhood.

George Toles writes of the "secret but urgent quest to escape maternal law" that informs a number of Hitchcock's films, including *Shadow of a Doubt:*

> Read in the light of a secret but urgent quest to escape maternal law, young Charlie Newton's real struggle in *Shadow of a Doubt* is less with her deranged, homicidal uncle than with his sister, Emma—the woman that all of his victims resemble but who is herself mysteriously exempted from his rage and retribution. In his mind, she is the one surviving remnant of an all-but-vanished world of female gentility, delicacy, innocence.[14]

Emma does indeed resemble Charlie's other victims, and she does indeed belong to the beautiful world he seems both to revere as well as to deny. Emma, whose name, as we have said, is the ultimate maternal signifier (not to mention the fact that it is also the name of Hitchcock's mother), is thus not only a mother figure but one who is associated with his actual mother in that she is now the age his mother was when he was a boy the age of Roger. Her "exemption" from Charlie's murderous plans, which is not in fact total in that young Charlie repeatedly says that the discovery of the truth about him would kill Emma, is not mysterious when one considers that she is the "original love object" from which he frequently escapes and to which he just as frequently returns, and that her status as his sister protects her from their getting too close. Charlie murders women who look like Emma, but since he marries them they must, as maternal figures, be killed. The fact that Charlie does try to murder his niece Charlie, with whom he is incestuously "married" in the ring ceremony we shall discuss later, is further evidence of this pattern.

Charlie's obsession with the past is made apparent in the bedroom scene where Emma and young Charlie dutifully serve the returned prodigal his breakfast in bed. (This tendency to allow his niece and sister to wait on him hand and foot, as when Charlie smiles smugly as young Charlie carries off his rather large suitcase from the railroad station, will be discussed shortly.) One

5. Again in bed, Uncle Charlie expresses contradictory views about his childhood and the past.

of the most striking visual aspects of this scene is the way Hitchcock plays everything off against a thick sfumato of shadows.

The lighting of this scene corresponds, I think, to the lively interest Emma and young Charlie express in the past, about which their "shadowy" Uncle Charlie can only brood silently. Indeed, Charlie himself refuses to acknowledge his past, as when he wrongly insists that there are no old photographs of himself in existence anywhere. At the end of the scene Charlie declares: "What's the use of looking backward, what's the use of looking forward, today's the thing." But, as evident from his earlier statement that "I think about them, those days, all the time," as well as from the photographs of his parents that he gives to Emma, Charlie's denial of the past is contradictory at best. This contradictory obsession is made even more evident, and perhaps explained, as Emma tells the story of Charlie's boyhood accident while her brother listens in rapt, even hypnotic attention.

"Mama wondered if he'd ever look the same. Mama wondered if he'd ever be the same." Disregarding the simplistic attempt to explain Uncle Charlie's changed personality from a sweet child into a serial killer as a result of the concussion he received from a bicycle injury, we nonetheless learn that Uncle Charlie's relationship to his mother underwent a profound, disturbing change. A fundamental change in Charlie's relationship with his mother did in fact occur about this time, for Charlie's later obsession with seducing and killing mother figures first manifested itself upon sexual maturation (symbolized by Charlie's first experience riding a bicycle!) as a powerful expression and equally powerful repression of his Oedipal desires. Robin Wood agrees that this story of the bicycle accident "can be read as elementary Freudian metaphor for the trauma premature sexual awakening," and he goes on to suggest that this "awakening" is related to his relationship to his sister, while William Rothman notes the important reference in this story to the fact that "it is the father who is to blame" for Charlie's accident, a fact which is certainly compatible with the Oedipal interpretation of Charlie's boyhood accident proffered here.[15] Emma's son Roger, who cuts a very curious figure in the film, may be another way that Hitchcock is addressing this peculiar mother/son relation, a possibility underscored by young Charlie herself when she says of Uncle Charlie that "He's her [Emma's] younger brother just like Roger is mine." Unlike his two sisters, Roger is given almost no attention throughout the film, a fact which suggests a possible source for Uncle Charlie's own ambivalence toward women. In the scene where Uncle Charlie is bestowing gifts upon the whole family he gives Roger a toy gun, a particularly significant gift given Charlie's identification with his neglected nephew.

Charlie's rigid, hypnotic state while holding the only photograph of himself as a boy and listening to the story of his past is evidence that he is still immersed in the past, still anachronistically connected to the period of the "Merry Widow Waltz" sequence when he was the age of his photo and his mother was an object of his sexual desire. Spoto discusses this scene, which Hitchcock wrote himself, as referring to Hitchcock's own childhood, and his own mother who died during the making of this film.[16] This explains why Hitchcock chose to engulf the scene, and particularly Charlie, in shadows, for Charlie is the "shadow of a doubt" that accompanies the seemingly "bright and sunny" family through bright and sunny Santa Rosa. Charlie's obsession with the past also explains why he is so comfortable having his family work for him. The same ambivalent impulses that lead Charlie to pursue mother figures and then to murder them are also evident in his relationship with his family, who are being punished by having to work for him as well as by the more overt violence he later demonstrates.

When the two Charlies enter the bank where Joe works to deposit forty thousand dollars of Uncle Charlie's ill-gotten gains, young Charlie is beaming with delight at being accompanied by her dashing uncle, while Uncle Charlie seems equally delighted but noticeably unresponsive to the compliments proffered by his niece.[17] As in other scenes, Uncle Charlie basks in the glow of his family's attention while, at the same time, he seems intent upon punishing them for the love which we have suggested he did not receive as a child in the past. This ambivalence is also evident from the sudden shift in mood when Uncle Charlie strides boldly up to Joe's window and then abruptly blurts out:

> UNCLE CHARLIE. Can you stop embezzling a minute and give me your attention?
> JOE. Charlie, we don't joke about such things here.
> YOUNG CHARLIE. Uncle Charlie, you're awful, everyone can hear you.

What does Uncle Charlie mean by this strange, offensive remark? Charlie himself offers some important clues in the exchange which immediately follows: "We all know what banks are; look alright to an outsider, but no one knows what goes on when the doors are locked . . . forty-thousand is no joke to him [the bank president], I'll bet, but it's a joke to me; the whole world's a joke to me. . . . I wasn't teasing him [Joe]; I just don't like this stuffy atmosphere."

Charlie refuses to allow the seriousness of the bank to intimidate him. Instead, he attacks it head on by labeling large sums of money a big joke and by calling Joe an embezzler, not because he thinks that Joe really is one, but because, like Marion Crane and Marnie, he feels the need to defuse the bank's "stuffy" atmosphere" by impugning its credibility. This may explain what Uncle Charlie is trying to accomplish through his outrageous behavior, but not *why* he is acting this way. Uncle Charlie is trying to break through the stuffy atmosphere of the bank precisely because it weighs on him so heavily, and it weighs on him so heavily because he is so hostile to the kind of paternal authority which the bank represents. It is the father, and parental authority in general (this can also take the form of the "maternal superego"), who blocks the son's desire for the mother in Freud's description of the all-important Oedipal triangle. A later scene has Uncle Charlie and Emma laughing giddily at the dinner table while, at the same time, offending the father Joe's sense of propriety, reveals that Uncle Charlie's contempt for the masculine figures in the bank is only part of his more general contempt for all the male figures in the film—not only Joe, but Charlie's love interest Detective Graham as well as all the other men in the film. As in the case of Charlie's childish behavior in the bank, his attempt to laugh at the various male figures of paternal authority in the film is still more evidence that his desires go all the way back to his childhood, all the way back to the time of the "Merry Widow Waltz" sequence we discussed earlier.

The Two Charlies

Uncle Charlie and his particular pathology are thus, according to the interpretation offered here, the central issue of the film. Because most studies of *Shadow of a Doubt* have focused more on young Charlie they have left unexplained the motivation of her uncle and also thereby misunderstood the true nature of the "doubling" between the uncle and his niece. Samuels, in *Mastering the Film,* argues that Hitchcock "ruins the subtle equation" between the two Charlies because the film devolves into mindless manipulation: "A critic like Susan Sontag," Samuels writes, "wouldn't be caught dead discussing Hitchcock because he is so relentlessly lowbrow and frivolous about meaning."[18] Gavin Millar also attacks Hitchcock's supposed shallowness in his "deceptively simple" vision of small town America and in his exaggerated, melodramatic portrait of evil, while LaValley, in the introduction to his edition of essays on Hitchcock, says that the pattern of doublings in Hitchcock's films, "which the French critics have made so much of, is just a way for Hitchcock "musically" to organize his "narrative line."[19] These criticisms of Hitchcock are easily dismissed when the familial nature of Uncle Charlie's crimes is taken into account, and when young Charlie and the rest of the Newton family, as well as the "bright and sunny" city of Santa Rosa, are understood as the very shadow of Uncle Charlie's shadowy persona. In the remaining pages of this chapter I will examine the relationship between the two Charlies as a function of the Oedipal conflict of Charlie's uncle examined thus far.[20]

Objects in films often have a potency which belies their usual status, and the object in *Shadow of a Doubt* that stands out most clearly in this respect is surely the wedding ring which Uncle Charlie gives to young Charlie. Few critics, whether inclined toward a psychoanalytic interpretation of the film or not, have failed to note the incestuous implications of this scene: Uncle Charlie places the ring on Charlie's finger just after she has declared that they're more than "just an uncle and a niece." But how does this proposal fit with our hypothesis that Charlie is fixated on older women who are mother figures, and what is the explanation of young Charlie's involvement in this symbolic marriage?

How is it that Charlie happened to forget to check to see if the ring had been inscribed to his last victim, a curious oversight for someone who insists that "it's the little things that matter"? Charlie does not check the ring, I would argue, because he does not want to; that is, he wants to marry the same woman he has just murdered. Charlie gives Charlie the wedding ring he has taken from Thelma Matthews (again, the familiar "M"-name) because both she and young Charlie—like the equally maternal and sisterly figure of Emma—are all surrogates for Charlie's inces-

6. Uncle Charles (Joseph Cotten) "proposes" to his niece (Teresa Wright).

tuous desires. For Charlie is fixated, first, on his mother, and then on the period when he was a boy and she was youthful like young Charlie—the only time, according to a statement Charlie made before putting the ring on his niece's finger, when life was beautiful. If Charlie also turns against young Charlie and Emma so quickly, it is because his attraction to both of them as mother/sister figures is so powerful that it must also be repressed just as violently. For her part, young Charlie's initial reluctance to look at the emerald ring, as well as her later discovery of the inscription that reveals its illegitimate origin, demonstrate her own unwillingness to accept Uncle Charlie's proposal. In bestowing the same name upon the two characters Hitchcock wants us to realize the familial origin of Uncle Charlie's crimes, but this does not mean that young Charlie is trapped by childhood fixations the way her uncle is. Quite the contrary; although the relationship between the two Charlies does at times suggest a kind of doubling, throughout the film young Charlie is in the process of asserting her independence through her relationship with detective Graham, whom we must assume she eventually marries. (I agree, however, with Rothman's assertion that the ending of the film is decidedly ambiguous in this regard.)[21]

A frequent interpretation of the climactic scene of the film, when Uncle Charlie tries to murder young Charlie by luring her onto the departing train but is then thrown off himself, tends to view the niece as demonstrating some of the murderous qualities of her uncle.[22] The fact that Charlie doesn't turn her uncle in to the police after she begins to believe her suspicions is also seen as evidence of her complicity. But young Charlie's reasons for not turning her uncle in are actually more virtuous than blameworthy, first, because she is still struggling with the fact, if not the question, of his guilt, and, second, because she wants to protect her mother from a recognition that she says would kill her. As to Charlie's role in Charlie's death, that too has been overplayed by critics anxious to equate the two Charlies. As I have suggested, young Charlie is in the process of growing out of her own Oedipal conflict, and so it would be a mistake to push her identification with Uncle Charlie too far, particularly into the latter part of the film. Although young Charlie does tell Charlie to "leave [Santa Rosa] or I'll kill you myself," such an open declaration means little compared to the genuine evil of Hitchcockian villains like Uncle Charlie, or Rusk in *Frenzy,* who almost never declare their murderous intentions outright. Not that young Charlie doesn't mean what she says, only that she could never have acted upon it.

Despite attempts to prove her complicity in her uncle's death, young Charlie does not push Charlie into the path of an oncoming locomotive. The sequence of movements can be reduced to the following: a) Charlie says "Now" and pushes young Charlie toward the open door; b) Young Charlie grabs the doorway for support; c) she uses Uncle Charlie to push herself away from the open door, and only inadvertently pushes him back toward the door. This scene does indeed raise a number of interesting questions, but the idea of young Charlie murdering her uncle symbolically or otherwise is not among them. The reason, I would add, that Hitchcock does not have young Charlie throw Charlie from the train is that such relatively benign figures as young Charlie, like Blaney in *Frenzy,* or Jeff in *Rear Window*—all characters, to be sure, with a "dark side"—are part of a Hitchcockean "type," which is more often than not impotent in the face of their more powerful alter-egos. In all these cases the supposedly innocent protagonists are too contaminated by their own potential neuroses to oppose with any real force their more evil counterparts.

When Uncle Charlie is leading Charlie onto the train he waves to Mrs. Potter, who is at that moment entering her own compartment. Evidently Charlie and she have arranged a trip together, and we can also assume that Mrs. Potter is to be Charlie's next victim. But, oddly enough, Charlie then tells the porter to bring a bag of his that has been taken to Mrs. Potter's compartment back to his own. A small point, but one that can be understood in terms of the interaction between the two Charlies. Bringing young Charlie into his compartment, where the bag destined for Mrs. Potter's compartment is to be returned, is only the first of a number of mixed signals that suggest that the struggle that follows can be seen, as Rothman argues, as both as a seduction as well as a murder. When the two Charlies join hands what is meant to appear at first as a token of his affection turns, according to Rothman, into a "conventional Hollywood image of a lovers' clinch" in which Charlie has gained the upper hand and is waiting for the moment of climax: "Not yet, Charlie, let it get a little further."[23] Indeed, just moments before Uncle Charlie was holding Emma's hands in exactly the same benignly murderous way as he bade her farewell. As Young Charlie realizes that Uncle

Charlie's hands are locked onto hers she begins backing away as he continues to approach her. I would not go quite as far as Rothman in saying that Charlie's murderous intention is in reality sexual, but rather maintain that the two intentions are simultaneously present. Young Charlie is, as Uncle Charlie earlier claimed, "the thing I love most in the world," and in this third and final attempt to kill his niece Charlie is continuing to manifest the same love/hate relationship he has with all his family, as well as with the widows who are their surrogates. Indeed, the "Merry Widow Waltz" sequence reappears for the final time immediately after the two Charlies struggle and Uncle Charlie falls from the moving train, thus suggesting that we view their "embrace" as a continuation of the same dance, with Charlie's fall representing the inevitable impossibility of attaining the recurrent dream image of a time when "Everybody was sweet and pretty. . . . The whole world . . ." [including] "the beautiful Thelma Schenley."

3
Cast-ration by the *Rear Window*

> The attitude towards marriage is remarkably bleak and skeptical. This may account for the perfunctory nature of so many Hitchcock happy endings . . . without much evidence of enjoyment or conviction.
>
> —Robin Wood, "Plot Formations," in *Perspectives on Hitchcock*

L. B. "JEFF" JEFFRIES (JAMES STEWART) HAS A VERY CONSPICUOUS "hard-on" throughout Hitchcock's *Rear Window* (1954), but it is not at all clear what has aroused him.[1] So unclear is the object of Jeff's desire that many of the film's critics disagree as to whether his leg is symbolic of an erection (Modleski considers that "The first image of Jeffries . . . is quietly masturbatory") or of castration (Fawell describes Jeff as an "emasculated hero"), and whether his spying on his neighbors across their adjoining courtyard is less a symbol of perverse desire than of the repression of those same desires.[2] As we shall see, Jeff's leg is both, both a cast-ration as well as an erection, and identifying the object of Jeff's perverse desires as well as its accompanying mechanisms of repression will allow us to deepen our understanding of Hitchcock's celebrated self-reflection on the spectator's voyeuristic tendencies.[3]

Although Laura Mulvey uses *Rear Window,* as well as *Vertigo,* to critique Hitchcock's "patriarchal" male gaze, Tania Modleski's awareness of the decidedly unheroic, perverse tendencies of the main character ("the film's protagonist is fixated at an infantile level of sexual development") leads her to see in the film's *female* lead a more assertive figure: "In *Rear Window* the woman is constantly shown to be physically superior to the hero, not only in her physical movements but also in her dominance within the frame."[4] As I have noted in the introduction, I believe the truth is somewhere in between these two views. In the case of *Rear*

Window, there is no question but that Jeff is the one gazing, Lisa the one who enjoys being gazed at, although I would agree with Jane Wager's notion, in *Dangerous Dames*, that the so-called "male gaze" is (especially here) an unstable one.[5] Lisa Fremont may indeed be, as Grace Kelly was for Hitchcock, "the perfect woman," but this perfection is less a reality than a function of the same "perverse" imagination that causes the male protagonist to "turn away" from any woman who seeks to become a wife, and thus a mother.

Whereas Modleski sees the Jeff/Lisa story as a corrective to the story of Thorwald and his wife, I would agree with Robin Wood that the latter is better seen as the unconscious reality of the former, for both are part of a world in which "the attitude towards marriage is remarkably bleak and skeptical," and where "we have not seen one image of an enviable marriage."[6] It would be hard to reconcile George Toles's excellent point about Lisa's becoming the ghostly, murdered wife Anna in putting on her wedding ring for Jeff to see with anything positive.[7] Jeff's "castration by the rear window" will thus be seen as a logical consequence of his attempt to escape the Madonna-figure who would become his wife through the darkness of perverse desires that are aroused by the very figure who would deny them. From this psychoanalytical point of view, the debate is less whether Lisa is active (Modleski) or passive (Mulvey) than why, as a projection of Jeff's (and the director's), she is both.

Lisa

As many critics have noted, *Rear Window* is "a compulsively self-reflexive film," a film in which "Hitchcock demonstrates how the movie experience is calculated to persuade viewers (Jeffries's surrogates) that the story belongs to them."[8] The film begins with the three bamboo shades (which later reappear in *Vertigo*) being raised curtain-like onto the courtyard before which, like Jeff, the viewer shall be rendered largely immobile and invisible for the next two hours. The massive telephoto lens which Jeff substitutes for his binoculars in order to better spy on the murderer Thorwald, as well as the flashbulbs that Jeff later uses to defend himself against the same, are other, more conspicuous examples of these "metamoments." However, I would like to argue that these oft-noted self-reflexive moments are less about film in the formal sense than about the *desires* of filming. The flashbulbs and the telephoto lens are used in the film to see what is not normally seen, either because it is too dark or because it is too far away. Hitchcock's film would thus differ from other metafilms (although not unique in this regard) in calling attention, not just to the act of filmmaking, but to the act of filmmaking as the means to gratify abnormal, perverse desires. If, as Mary Ann Doane has claimed in her essay on "Veiling Over Desire," the visual arts—film as well as painting—are about the desire, the "gaze," to see what one can not "normally" see, then Hitchcock's film is also a "metafilm" in being about film as the desire to see what is hidden behind what is looked at, rather than what is looked at itself.[9]

The song "Lisa," which reaches its completion just as the film does, is an example of the way Hitchcock turns *Rear Window* into a commentary not only on the art of filmmaking but also on the desires behind the art of filmmaking. It is the same song we have heard repeatedly throughout the film as it is being composed by the struggling musician occupying one of the apartments Jeff has been observing, but this time the song has lyrics that, like the closing credits, name their object: "Lisa." Lisa is Lisa Carol Fremont (Grace Kelly), the wealthy young socialite whose attempt to get Jeff to settle down with a steady job and her is the second main plot of Hitchcock's film.[10] Like the film's initial shot of the bamboo curtain being raised on a courtyard, which is at once referential and purely cinematic, the song similarly blurs the distinction between the supposedly real, referential object within the film and the usually transparent technical devices (the bulbs and the telephoto) that make that reality possible. This mixing of background into foreground music is heightened when the song is completed just as the film is itself concluding, when the recording of the song is unveiled at a "release party" in the composer's apartment (in which Hitchcock had earlier made his customary cameo). Although Fawell is one of the few critics of the film to discuss this song at length, and to note its connection to the film's self-referencing ("When Lisa hears 'Lisa' coming out of the composer's window and says 'Where is that music coming from?' it is funny because we have the sense, à la Pirandello, of a fictional character commenting on its author's device," *Rear Window,* 126), he does not ask the most obvious but important question of why Hitchcock adds this particularly odd bit of self-referencing. Since *Rear Window* is far from being a musical or even musical-related, why would Hitchcock take his metacinematic concerns so far as to break into a song about the film's main character at the film's end?

Hitchcock would not have allowed his film to break into a song about Jeff or, for that matter, any of the other characters in the film. He does so about Lisa because, in some way yet to be determined, she is a song; in fact, she is the song "Lisa." That is, there is something in her character, or in what she represents as a character, whose being is that of a song. What this is we shall discover only by analyzing Grace Kelly's performance, where the metacinematic song is linked to a character for whom the protagonist L. B. Jeffries's desires are as incompatible as the film *Rear Window* is with the genre of the musical.

Compare the final reference to the completed song "Lisa" with this same character's first entrance in the film. After the famous kiss with which, according to Modleski, our princess magically awakens the sleeping voyeur, Lisa turns on three lamps, announcing with each illumination "Lisa" "Carol" "Freemont." While Modleski sees this important association between Lisa and light as part of her "confident nomination of herself [which] reveals her to be extremely self-possessed" (76), Jeff, who knows who kissed him all too well, asks Lisa: "Who are you?"[11] He would prefer, it seems, not to know her; that is, he would prefer to have with Lisa the same impersonal, voyeuristic relationship he has with all the characters across the courtyard on whom he spends his time spying. And, to support this notion of Jeff's preference for anonymity and darkness, recall that he has made clear in the preceding scene with his nurse Stella that he doesn't really like Lisa, at least not the part of her that, unlike the perverse "rear window" lives of himself and those around him, is "too perfect." So when Lisa desperately tries to distract him from the enticements and attractions of his subjects across the courtyard by twirling around before him in her glamorous thousand-dollar gowns, Jeff has the opposite reaction to this "front window" show that he has to the other "rear window" spectacle behind him. Instead of intrigue there is disgust, and he soon begins bickering with Lisa over her attempts to marry and settle down with him.

"Who are you?" The soporific question Jeff poses to Lisa after he awakens is similar, in tone as well as content, to the question the murderer Thorwald poses later when looming in Jeff's doorway: "What do you want from me?" (One might also note the similarity of the name "Lars" to "Lisa.") In addition to the obvious reference to the blackmail scheme that Jeff had earlier used to lure Thorwald out of his apartment, Thorwald's question suggests a similar annoyance as Jeff's in being disturbed by an outsider who insists on wrenching him out of his perverse, nocturnal desires. As Modleski notes, Lisa's famous kiss is thus not really the romantic moment it is usually taken to be (it "suggests the underlying threat posed by the desirable woman," *Women Who Knew too Much,* 76), and in its eerie silence is also decidedly unlike the romantic song that appears at the film's end. Rather than serving to bring the two lovers together it functions in just the opposite way in pulling Jeff out of his preferred narcissistic immersion and fantasy that, as we shall see, defines his character and the film as a whole.

This conflict between love and narcissism is confirmed by Lisa's insistence on turning Jeff around to look inside the apartment at her instead of outside at the courtyard and in her insistence on turning on the three lamps, which effectively reverse his preferred position of staring at other, lighted apartments while being, himself, suffused in darkness. And whereas Lisa names herself with each flip of a light switch, Jeff significantly knows none of the names of the people he observes with the exception (much later) of Thorwald, preferring names he has coined himself like Miss Lonelyhearts, Miss Torso, etc. His own name is also markedly different from those with which Lisa announces herself. "Jeff" is actually L. B. Jeffries, and we might surmise that, in addition to its denial of the usual ways of naming, the attenuation of Jeff's two first names, and the mutation of his formal surname into an informal Christian name is part of Jeff's general rejection of adulthood and its formalities, a rejection also evident in his rejection of Lisa's perfection and her plans of formalizing their relationship through marriage.

Each light that Lisa Carol Freemont turns on as she announces her three names imposes her objective, dazzling presence on Jeff, in marked contrast to the momentary, ineffective way Jeff will later use his flashbulbs to defend himself against the approaching menacing figure of Thorwald. Naming herself to Jeff while turning on the lights in his room is evidence of a conscious presence to which Jeff's more nocturnal, unconscious, narcissistic perversions are opposed. It is not surprising, then, that Jeff's later use of a similar device to ward off Thorwald should prove so ineffective, since the flashbulbs that are part of Jeff's narcissistic projections lack the steady permanence of Lisa's abiding presence and the formal, adult perfection her presence represents.

The first image of Lisa in *Rear Window,* however, is not this entrance, but the photograph of the fashion model that appears in the opening sequences of images with which Hitchcock introduces us to Jeff and his surroundings. Although the image is not really of Grace Kelly, the chic model featured on the fashion magazine is clearly a stand-in for Lisa (compare, in *Vertigo,* the stand-in for Kim Novak used in the film's title sequence), who not only resembles the model physically but professionally; she later admits to Jeff that she is wearing the latest Parisian gown.[12] The image is particularly interesting because it appears in two forms: the first a rather garish negative which, ironically, is elegantly framed, while the second, "positive" image is seen only on a stack of magazines. Toles mentions this negative as an example of his metatextual thesis that the film is about the "process by which images of the sort we have been looking at are generated" (*House Made of Light,* 175). But why, one must ask, does Jeff frame this negative of Lisa and place it alongside the stack of positive images?

7. The curiously framed negative of a Lisa Fremont (Grace Kelly) look-alike.

We know that Jeff openly disdains the chic lifestyle of Lisa, whose career as a model and fashion consultant he relentlessly ridicules, especially when Lisa suggests that Jeff settle down to a career of making the same kind of photographs as the one in the fashion magazine. The mere fact that the garish image is the only nicely framed photograph, even though he also has other, more spectacular pictures highlighting his career as a risk-taking action photographer (including the photo of the race car accident which resulted in Jeff's broken leg), can only be taken as further evidence of his disdain for such images. It is a cruel joke, meant to mock the glamorous superfemininity of the fashion model with her darker, inner truth (the negative as X-ray).[13] But like most jokes, especially cruel ones, the image also has its serious side. Not unlike the ghastly cadaver of Norman's petrified mother that is revealed at the end of *Psycho,* the negative represents (as we shall see) the repressed, dark side of an unconscious truth that underlies the meaning of this and the other Hitchcock films analyzed in this book. If Toles is right (and I think he is) that the film tries to "clean up" its disturbing references to voyeurism—both the film's and the main "benign" protagonist's—by justifying it in the end (*House Made of Light,* 177–78), then this "negative" might stand as a potent symbol of the film's darker, more perverse meaning.

Jeff's surprising rejection of the seemingly ideal woman who wants desperately to marry him is certainly a key question confronting viewers of Hitchcock's films.[14] Jeff says that his rejection is due to the fact that Lisa is "too perfect," and, as Modleski notes, we should not brush aside his complaint as quickly as does his nurse Stella:

STELLA. What did you do? Have a fight?
JEFF. No.
STELLA. Her father loading up the shotgun?
JEFF. What? Please Stella.
STELLA. It's happened before you know. Some of the world's happiest marriages have started under the gun, as you might say.
JEFF. No, she's just not the girl for me.
STELLA. Yeah, she's only perfect.
JEFF. She's too perfect. She's too talented, she's too beautiful. She's too sophisticated. She's too everything but what I want. . . . Can you imagine her tramping around the world with a camera bum who never has more than a week's salary in the bank? If she was only

ordinary. . . . I need a woman who's willing to go anywhere and do anything and love it. So the honest thing for me to do is just to call the whole thing off and let her find somebody else.

STELLA. Yeah, I can hear you now. Get out of my life. You're a perfectly wonderful woman—you're too good for me.

Modleski rightly asks us not to ignore Jeff's seemingly illogical complaint, because a woman who is too perfect would indeed threaten a man whose sense of identity requires that she lack something which he possesses—i.e., the phallus. In this respect, Jeff's helpless, cast-rated position throughout the film (he also cannot help Lisa in her hour of need) should be seen, in psychological terms, as an effect of his fear of Lisa, his fear of the "perfect woman." Yet, whereas Modleski sees Lisa's perfection as something real, I would argue that the fear is based on the male's projection of a woman who possesses what the male lacks and desires but which is nonetheless denied him by a very powerful taboo. Modleski is right to invoke Freud's theory of castration anxiety, but it is important to go further in explaining why the desire for perfection should be frightening. In Freud's essay on *The Medusa's Head,* one of the places he discusses his theory of castration anxiety, the source of fear is less that of the sight of a castrated being (the woman) who threatens the boy with the loss of his own penis than it is that of the sight of the *mother's* genitals. Castration anxiety, as Freud explains in the essay "is linked to the sight of something," and that something "is linked to" the mother. The source of the anxiety occurs "when a boy, who has hitherto been unwilling to believe the threat of castration, catches sight of the female genitals, probably those of an adult, surrounded by hair, *and essentially those of his mother.*"[15]

Jeff's fear of the "perfect woman" which strikes the film's viewers as so strange and which is linked to his own "cast-ration," is thus fear of a woman who is the original object of desire, and thus "perfection," but whose possession would produce castration, and so must be denied. This denial takes many forms. As Barbara Creed has shown in her recent study of woman in horror films, one of these is the form taken by the Medusa, a figure who was once a beautiful woman but who became a monster because, according to Freud, she possessed the adult female genitalia ("surrounded by hair") of the mother, which thus needed to be shorn or, in her case, severed. (Visual depictions of the Medusa's snaky tresses, such as Caravaggio's famous painting of 1601, can be seen as anamorphs of adult female genitalia.)

The "perfect woman," as well as her counterpart, the "monstrous feminine," is in Freudian terms the mother, the woman whose perfection is also a means of denying the very sensuality that is the basis of the forbidden maternal desire: "The principal means of protection used by men . . . consists in *lowering* the sexual object in their own estimation, while reserving for the incestuous object and for those who represent it the overestimation normally felt for the sexual object."[16] Like the Madonna-figure, reverence for the perfect woman is the result of an initial sexual attraction, which, when denied, returns in the form of a sexless, spiritual attraction. (Note the final shot of the narrative "proper," in which Jeff's head is cradled in Lisa's lap like the *Pietà,* or [according to Fawell] like "a baby in her lap," *Hitchcock's "Rear Window,"* 58). Enter also the "loose woman," the fallen, degraded, but overtly sensual figure who is found as often in Hitchcock films as the sexless, maternal "Madonna-figure." The fallen woman is thus also a maternal figure, but one whose association with forbidden sensuality makes of her a "harlot."

In complaining that Lisa is "too perfect," and rejecting her for this reason, Jeff expresses his fear of the maternal ideal. This terror takes numerous forms in Hitchcock's films, but in terms of Jeff's relationship with Lisa, one would interpret such scenes as her insistence on running his life, even to the point of replacing his beloved old cigarette case, as male paranoia that projects onto the repressed mother figure a kind of rape, the result of the male's own terror of himself having sex with a woman he must not have. The frequent "bossiness" of these women in Hitchcock's films (Mrs. Thorwald, Mrs. Bates, Mrs. Brenner, et al.) is also to be understood as a function of the mother's power over the child, a power which is as desired as it is later feared, and which is, in either case, a phantasm of the infantile imagination as opposed to any sort of reality.

In many of Hitchcock's films one often finds the two women, the "Madonna" and the "whore," split into two distinct figures (cf. Annie and Melanie in *The Birds,* Lil and Marnie in *Marnie,* Judy and Madeleine in *Vertigo,* etc.), but just as often one finds both elements condensed into the same figure, albeit to various degrees. Miss Torso, who bears a striking resemblance to Lisa and is explicitly compared to her by Lisa herself, also presents an interesting contrast to our fashion model. As a dancer she is more physical than her model counterpart, and the fact that she is most often seen from behind, wiggling her bottom, confirms her identification with the darker, sensual side of Jeff's desires. Grace Kelly, it goes without saying, is never shot from this angle. Miss Torso's constant stream of admirers is also telling in this regard, forming as it does a marked contrast with Lisa, who has made it clear that, while she too has had such admirers in the past, she is now interested in Jeff and Jeff only. (This resembles Melanie Daniel's similar admission, in *The Birds,* to a notorious past that she is now ready to leave behind in lieu of marriage.) Miss Torso's bevy of what Freud refers to as "injured third parties" also signals her role as the "loose woman" who is as sexually promiscuous as her more idealized counterpart is faithful.

And yet if Lisa is the spiritual ideal, the Madonna in contrast with Miss Torso's "harlot," what is one to make of the highly overt sexual advances that Lisa makes to Jeff throughout the film? This, I would claim, is the "exception which proves the rule" and thus not really an exception at all, for according to Freud's theory the Madonna-figure should also be capable of manifesting the other, "loose woman" of which the Madonna is merely the repressed counterpart. The "perfect woman" is, after all, really a sexual object the desire for which must be repressed as part of the incest taboo that underlies its "perfection." It is for this reason that Lisa, like other "ideal" women in Hitchcock, is capable of manifesting the other "fallen" side of the same complex that creates her ideal role. For example, she brings her negligee over to Jeff's when his own invitation is not forthcoming and then proceeds to invite herself to spend the night even though Jeff continues to resist Lisa's advances by protesting that he'll have to check with the landlord first! Jeff clearly does not want to have sex with Lisa because, again, he is terrified at the prospect of having sex with the perfect woman. His statement that he would prefer someone more ordinary is also telling in this regard, for it is merely a reference to the "loose woman" type that would prove, if pursued, even more unsatisfactory insofar as she lacks the perfection of the Madonna-figure just as the Madonna-figure lacks the earthy sensuality of her more promiscuous counterpart.

There are negligee scenes in a number of other Hitchcock films of the period studied here, for example, in the famous "honeymoon" sequence in *Marnie* as well as in the *Birds*, when Melanie has to purchase a rather frumpy nightgown in the local hardware store of Bodega Bay. While the scene in *Rear Window* is the most extensive of these, it forms a group with the first two scenes just mentioned, for all involve women who have been recently married or are seeking to be so: Melanie tells Mitch she's no longer interested in playing the field, Marnie is on her honeymoon, and Lisa has made it clear to Jeff that she expects a proposal imminently. The negligee is not, it seems, the accoutrement of the "loose woman" we might assume it to be, which is another indication that in Hitchcock the desired separation of the two types of women—the "Madonna" and the "whore"—has not yet occurred (*Vertigo*, where the two types are indeed the same woman, will prove to be the best example of this). Melanie Daniel's frumpy nightgown, purchased at a Bodega Bay hardware store, is a case in point, as is the monkish robe that Marnie wears on her honeymoon in order to ward off Mark's advances. In *Rear Window* the nightie promises to be more stylish, but significantly it is never completely removed from the tiny "Mark Cross" compact case into which it is stuffed. This negligee is thus, as in the other films, covered up, and the conversation about the negligee in which Lisa asks Jeff if she can trade her female intuition "for a bed for the night" reiterates the covering up of the nightgown, which signals its identification with the maternal woman, and the accompanying terror at the prospect of having sex with her. If the case containing the negligee is, according to Modleski, another of those "vulgar" Freudian symbols that figure in Hitchcock (cf. Marnie's purse), it is significant that, in this case, the "vagina" is seen as more of an object of fear than of desire.[17] It is worth recalling, in this regard, Freud's notion that it is sight of the *mother's* pudenda which turns the boy's desire into terror, and the once beautiful woman into the Medusa.

Jeff's friend Doyle's reaction to the sight of the negligee protruding from the case becomes the source of an interesting exchange of furtive looks and whispered comments between the two men. Doyle's first reaction when he sees the case is to register, with a half-smile, his understanding of the nightgown's significance—he is, after all, a detective whom Jeff has called in to deal with Thorwald's suspected murder of his wife. Significantly, Jeff's inability to convince Doyle about his suspicions regarding Thorwald succeeds only in raising Doyle's suspicions about Lisa's sleeping with Jeff. Throughout the scene, while Doyle steadfastly rejects Jeff's hypotheses about the murder, the detective keeps looking at the nightie suspiciously until Jeff finally addresses Doyle's suspicions by telling him to "Be careful!"—exactly what Doyle is telling Jeff to do with his suspicions about Thorwald. This important exchange thus parallels the larger plot, and reinforces the notion of Wood, Fawell and others that the Thorwald story is meant to parallel—if not symbolically represent—the Jeff/Lisa story. As such the scene turns Jeff's "front-window" relationship with Lisa into a rear-window one, which is confirmed after Doyle leaves when Lisa will ask Jeff if Doyle suspected her of stealing the compact case he kept stealing glances at. The fact that Lisa sees nothing secretive in her staying with Jeff but the two men do is another indication of the arrested, narcissistic relation to sexuality of the male protagonists in Hitchcock's films, which reduces any "normal" sexual relation to its origin in perverse, infantile sexuality.

We can now (finally!) return to the question concerning the song "Lisa" which is being written throughout the film and which is finished, with the new lyrics, when the film itself concludes. Like most of Hitchcock's endings the cheery conclusion masks a far more disturbing, "negative" ending.[18] The end confirms our notion that the film is ultimately about Lisa; or, more specifically, about everything that this "perfect" ideal woman represents for Jeff, as well as the darker elements of perverse, narcissistic desires with which Lisa is competing for Jeff's interest. The perfect woman is thus given a triumphant song as part of the completion (etymologically related to "per-fection") of this perfect (in both senses) movie. But it is also part of Hitchcock's genius to mock such closure as an all-too conscious attempt to deny the deeper, darker, and ultimately more truthful secrets lying beneath the conscious surfaces of things—recall, again, the framed negative of Lisa. The sappy song, which wells up like the typical end of a Disney film of the same period, is as ironical as the notion that Jeff will live happily ever after with Lisa, whose two shapely legs stand in marked contrast to the two fractured limbs of the sleeping narcissistic hero seen at the film's end.

And yet this ending, like all of Hitchcock's dubiously "happy endings," is not without its optimistic critics who, ignoring the scene before them, maintain that "Jeff is healthier for having escaped his passivity and isolation, for having learned to live and love."[19] In their excellent essay on *Rear Window* Stam and Pearson also argue for a development beyond the early immaturity of Jeff to a "rendering possible of mature sexuality with Lisa" which leads to an "indictment" of his earlier voyeurism, and even Robin Wood, who insists elsewhere on the "bleak" nature of even Hitchcock's happy endings, waivers between the idea that "Jeff is ready to accept marriage" at the end and the fact that despite "his overcoming of Thorwald, the victory is equivocal."[20] Modleski, I believe, comes closer to the truth in interpreting the end as demonstrating Lisa's power over the sleeping male, although, "power over a sleeping male," in psychoanalytical terms, is also far more sinister than her thesis of "the women who knew too much" would allow.

JEFF

In his most important essay on art, "The Poet and Daydreaming," Freud goes beyond the notion that art provides us with the return of repressed desires that the real world of civilized behavior deems unacceptable. Freud goes on to explain that such repressed desires are themselves derived from the early stage of "narcissistic omnipotence" from which, both ontogenetically as well as phylogenetically, all conscious thought is later derived:

> The feeling of security with which I follow the hero through his dangerous adventures is the same as that with which a real hero throws himself into the water to save a drowning man, or exposes himself to the fire of the enemy while storming a battery. It is this very feeling of being a hero which one of our best authors has well expressed in the famous phrase, "Es kann dir nicht g'schehen!" It seems to me, however, that this significant mark of invulnerability very clearly betrays His Majesty the Ego, the hero of all day-dreams and novels.[21]

One could argue that Freud's theory of original narcissism is the real "cornerstone of psychoanalysis" and not the later, more object-oriented Oedipal complex that can itself be seen as a function of the former in its fundamental denial of the "law of the Father." Edenic, golden-age scenarios in all their forms, such as our fascination with paranormal "X-files" and other extraterrestrial projections of a universe that continues, even after the "Copernican Revolution," to reflect our subjective fantasies, are clear evidence of the persistent desire to return to a world of our own making, as are all the various forms of artistic re-creation (in all senses of this word).[22] Art does not represent the world but, as Freud teaches us, represents it according to our repressed unconscious desires, all of which stem from an early stage of narcissistic omnipotent nondifferentiation whence we began. Hence the popularity in film of the two great staples, romantic love and transgressive violence, both of which clearly bear the stamp of our narcissistic desire to deny the "reality principle"—to say "no" to "no," as it were.

Freud himself cross-references his essay on "The Poet and Day-dreaming" with his various lectures on dreams, noting that the key to understanding dreams is in their relation to day-*dreams* and vice versa.[23] In both dreams and art one finds the determining presence of "wish fulfillment," which is itself a function of the narcissistic desire to gratify our individual desires without the interference of the real world with its myriad obstacles. Hence the popularity in art of the hero, the perennial figure who triumphs over every obstacle, or at least the important ones blocking our reentry into a quasi-Edenic world of love, wealth, fame, etc. Such projections of our narcissistic fantasies are all too common in popular art of all times, but are also not absent in "high art," although there the fulfillment of our fantasies is sometimes less obvious. A difference in degree exists between the "adult fairy tales" of high art and their more juvenile counterpart, but not a difference in kind.[24]

As we have seen in the preceding chapter on *Shadow of a Doubt,* it is not unusual for Hitchcock to begin his films with characters in bed or even asleep, but it is noteworthy that, in *Rear Window,* the protagonist is sound asleep at both the beginning and at the end of the film. This would suggest that, even more than in his other films, *Rear Window* is about the narcissistic dream state of its protagonist.[25] As Fawell argues, the entire film, in which Jeff is unable to do much of anything by himself and must constantly rely on the help of others (Lisa, Stella, and Doyle), mocks its hero's supposedly active lifestyle.[26] And Modleski rightly invokes Freud's essay in noting how, even at the film's end, men more than women continue to "sleep and dream their dreams of omnipotence" (85). And yet the film's "back-story," Jeff's actual career, which serves as the symbolic backdrop for his period of recuperation in the film, also reflects this unreal persona. For in traveling around the world, leaving at a "moment's notice" to photograph the latest crises and upheavals, Jeff is the very embodiment of the repressed unconscious which is "always elsewhere" because never static or objectifiable. One could also call this narcissistic insofar as Jeff is risking his life not because he is suicidal but, on the contrary, because by surviving he is heroically overcoming the realistic "reality principle" that the world is in fact greater than us. The accident that put him in his current state of disrepair is a case in point, for we are told that he deliberately put himself in harm's way in order to photograph life at its moment of extreme dissolution—a race car crashing—thereby affirming his own transcendence as well as foreshadowing his similar life-threatening involvement in Thorwald's murder of his wife. (In addition to seeing Jeff's current predicament, as Fawell does, as "mocking" Jeff's former life, it also repeats it.) When Jeff's involvement in these life-threatening actions is understood not as the cause but rather as the effect of his narcissism, we can then understand his action in *Rear Window* as merely a variant—although a highly original variant, to be sure—on what Freud sees as the typical "daydream" of art: the hero's narcissistic vanquishing of the reality principle in lieu of his own fantasy. If Jeff, unlike Freud's typical hero, eschews the "prize" of the beautiful woman that awaits him, that is because Lisa is adamantly opposed to the hero's fantasy life in insisting on a "real relationship," which would curtail the protagonist's heroic quests around the world. In Fawell's apt terms, *Rear Window* reflects a typical Hitchcock theme (cf. *Vertigo*) of "a man who rejects a real woman while lost in the dream of an imaginary one" (*Hitchcock's "Rear Window,"* 67). Modleski is certainly correct in noting that "despite Freud's claim that women tend to be more narcissistic than men . . . the film has consistently shown the opposite state of affairs to be the case," but it is important to add that the women in this and other Hitchcock films are functions of that male narcissism rather than being alternatives to it.[27]

Notwithstanding Fassbinder's comment that Hitchcock's *Suspicion* is "the most drastic film against the bourgeois institution of marriage I know," this is in fact a recurrent theme in the director's oeuvre (cf. Hitchcock's only "comedy," *Mr. and Mrs. Smith*).[28] Indeed, I would argue that it is *Rear Window* that contains one of the harshest critiques of marriage in film, up to and including Kubrick's *Eyes Wide Shut.* This might seem to contradict the notion that marriage, in uniting two people as one, seems deeply narcissistic, but it in reality the critique of marriage and defense of voyeurism and narcissism go hand in hand. According to Freud, marriage stands in relation to the "sexual life of human beings" as consciousness stands in relation to the unconscious.[29] That is to say, marriage and its concomitant emphasis on reproduction is a societal convention that is meant to repress our sexual lives in all their perverse splendor just as consciousness is meant to repress the unconscious, notwithstanding the fact that both marriage and consciousness are ultimately motivated by the very pleasure principle they would deny. Narcissism, then, is bound to come into conflict sooner or later with the non-narcissistic, contractual obligation of marriage: sooner in the case of the newlyweds in *Rear Window* whose marriage disintegrates before our eyes within the short span of the film (regarding which Toles notes how "the 'tender trap' of marriage, engineered . . . by females, proves to the man inside it a heartless bondage"), later in the case of Thorwald, who can no longer stand the hen-pecking of his irascible, invalid wife.[30]

If Martin Scorsese, with the famous propensity for brutality in his "gangster" films, could nonetheless call *The Age of Innocence* his most violent film, one might equally contend that the violent arguments between Jeff and Lisa in the first part of the film match the actual physical violence done to Thorwald's wife. Nor is the violence of this scene atypical in Hitchcock, for it is part of a larger pattern of the cruelty of males toward the women with whom they are romantically involved that is seen in films like *Notorious, North by Northwest, Vertigo,* etc. As Lisa presses home her intention to get Jeff to marry her, the tension mounts:

LISA. (*referring to the composer's music.*) It's enchanting. It's almost as if it were being written especially for us.

JEFF. (*referring to the struggle the composer is having with the piece.*) No wonder he's having so much trouble with it.

LISA. At least you can't say the dinner isn't right.

JEFF. (*exasperated.*) Lisa, it's perfect, as always.

LISA. It's ridiculous to say that it [traveling to exotic locales] can only be done by a special, private little group of anointed people.

JEFF. I made a simple statement, a true statement, but I can back it up if you'll just shut up for a minute!
LISA. If your opinion is as rude as your manner, I don't think I care to hear it . . .
JEFF. SHUT UP! Did you ever eat fish heads in rice? . . . Did you ever get shot at? Did you ever get run over? . . .
LISA. You're too stubborn to argue with.
JEFF. I'm not stubborn, I'm just truthful.
LISA. I know, a lesser man would have told me it was one long holiday . . .
JEFF. Oh well now, wait a minute. Now wait a minute. *If you want to get vicious on this, I'll be very happy to accommodate you.*[31]

What are Jeff and Lisa really arguing about? Although one might tend to ignore this sort of violence as incidental to the more overtly violent story of Thorwald and his wife, as well as focusing instead on the couple's better relationship in the film's second half, it is hard to ignore the significance of this fight, whether in psychoanalytical or any other terms. Ostensibly Jeff feels the couple is incompatible due to their different careers, his that of the dangerous traveling photographer, hers that of the sophisticated "Park Avenue" model/fashion writer. But this incompatibility is more the result of their incessant arguing then it is its cause, for their lifestyles are no more incompatible than most, and Lisa's notion that Jeff would have to stay in one place is no more compelling than his notion that she would have to travel to dangerous places in high heels. No, the couple's incompatibility is caused instead by the incompatibility of their two narcissisms, his being the "objective type" of the risk-taking world traveler who desires to immerse himself in the world, and thereby eradicate the subject/object split, hers being the "subjective type" of the alluring fashion model who makes others grovel at her feet in admiration:[32]

JEFF. There's nothing wrong with you Lisa. You've got this town in the palm of your hand.
LISA. Not quite it seems. Goodbye Jeff.

Lisa's "subjective" narcissism is the more usual type, and even her desire for the one man who doesn't desire her can be seen as a way of achieving ultimate desirability.[33] His narcissism, however, is in conflict with hers in being of a much more primitive, infantile type. Rather than being in love with this beautiful, ideal woman, Jeff is threatened by her because she represents the perfection of an objective ego-ideal rather than the more fragmented, "perverse" reality he craves. Indeed, since this conflict is not only characteristic of other couples in this film but in other Hitchcock films as well, one might say that Jeff and Lisa are as compatible and incompatible as the ego (consciousness) is in its relation to the unconscious pleasure principle which both generates and opposes it. Although Hitchcock's only comedy, *Mr. and Mrs. Smith,* offers a rather lighthearted view of a marriage's dissolution, the seriousness of the husband's statement in that film that, if he had it do over, he wouldn't have gotten married (and this to Carole Lombard!) has not been lost on the film's few critics.[34]

Given Jeff's narcissistic lack of interest in Lisa it is important to look at where his interest does lie: namely, in his "rear window" lifestyle and, specifically, in Mrs. Thorwald's murder. As mentioned, Jeff is not particularly interested in gazing at the half-naked woman available to him and, prior to the murder, his most affectionate reaction is to Miss Lonelyhearts, to whom he offers a non-ironic toast when she is having dinner with her imaginary guest. (Most viewers of the film probably find Miss Lonelyheart's imaginary dinner party far less amusing.) Jeff effectively substitutes himself for the person Miss Lonelyhearts thinks is sitting across from her, and this substitution is particularly important given Jeff's own preference for his silent, imaginary world over Lisa's all-too-real, garrulous advances. And the fact that the character Jeff is most interested in has murdered and is in the process of dismembering his nagging wife would lead us to conclude that Jeff is not only interested in spying on people's secret lives but, moreover, that this spying is a function of a deeper interest in denying—even murdering—the real love object, something which is confirmed by Jeff's dislike of Lisa as well as by Hitchcock's own jaundiced view of marriage evident in the dissolution of the newlyweds' relationship during the course of the movie.

"What do you want from me?" This sentence, which leads into the only lines spoken by an otherwise silent Thorwald, could also be asked more generally about what Jeff wants from anyone. George Toles, who applies the three "lenses" of Marxist, deconstructive, and feminist criticism to his analyses of *Rear Window,* would have been able to do more with this question "for which there can be no adequate reply" if he had added a psychoanalytical lens to his camera.[35] Given his voyeuristic tendencies, we might conjecture that one thing he, like Thorwald, wants is *silence*, for most of the characters Jeff spies on are rendered mute by his distant gaze, a technical, cinematic gaze that enhances the visual while diminishing the aural. It would be hard not to imagine that Hitchcock, too, whose formative years were in the silent era of filmmaking, shares Jeff's preference for looking over talking. Moreover, it is significant that the garrulous figures in this film, and in other Hitchcock films, are all women. Recall the scene, quoted earlier, when Jeff has to tell Lisa to "shut up," and when he is similarly annoyed at Stella's harangues (where he is unable to get a word in edgewise), and the long droning speech about brotherhood delivered by the woman whose dog was murdered by Thorwald. Ordinary language, which according to Freud is synonymous with the reality-principle of consciousness, is typified for Jeff and Thorwald in the nagging of a voice that, like language in general, represents the interdiction of original, narcissistic desire.

That Thorwald is stuck with a nagging, invalid woman whom he eventually murders is thus central to Jeff's own desires. Although Modleski argues that this mirroring involves a reversal that is expressed in Thorwald's serving his wife meals whereas Lisa serves Jeff his, I would agree with the majority of critics, including Wood and, more recently, Fawell, that the figures on whom Jeff is spying, especially Lars Thorwald, "are expressions of Jeff's unconscious world" (*Women Who Knew too Much*, 65). Mrs. Thorwald's status, I would argue, is symbolically that of the mother whom Lisa wishes to become in being associated with the home, which in this case she is unwilling or unable to leave. Up until the murder Thorwald sheepishly serves her and tolerates her criticisms, which is also typical of the recurrent "maternal superego" figure in Hitchcock's films (*Notorious, Psycho, The Birds, Marnie, Frenzy,* etc.) where the hypercritical mother is purely a function of an Oedipal desire that must, since it is forbidden, be denied by the desired mother herself. The nagging, and somewhat overbearing mother figure of Stella in *Rear Window* is another such figure.

Thorwald's question, "What do you want from me?" is thus so haunting because he doesn't understand why his "successful" resolution of the Oedipal complex—his murder of the maternal superego whose nagging is but a projection of the need to deny his love—should be a problem for Jeffries, who is like Thorwald in trying to rid himself of the mother figure (here Lisa) who cradles his head in her lap, *Pietà*-like, after Thorwald has defenestrated him. Seen this way, one might also detect here a curious "Catholic" variation on the Oedipal paradigm in which the son returns to the mother having been rejected "from heaven" by the father who has no real need for either the son or the mother. This is why Jeff uses the "jokingly ineffectual" flashbulbs so ineffectively to stop Thorwald as he advances toward him: the infantilized son is always, as in Kafka's *The Judgment*, nightmarishly impotent when faced with the large, looming figure of the father (a symbol for which Raymond Burr's size is particularly apt).[36]

As in the backstory of the film, Jeff again breaks his leg taking pictures which represent his own narcissistic desires. And, also like the earlier "cast-ration," we do not know for certain that there isn't any film in Jeff's camera, film which would return us to the beginning of the movie in producing another award-winning photograph to place alongside his "negative" photo of Lisa. Nonetheless, if Murray Pomerance is correct, the ghost of L. B. Jeffries will indeed return, some five years later, in *Vertigo*, where the "same" figure (James Stewart) is involved in the same impossible search for the original love-object.[37]

4
NTILEVER:
Vertigo

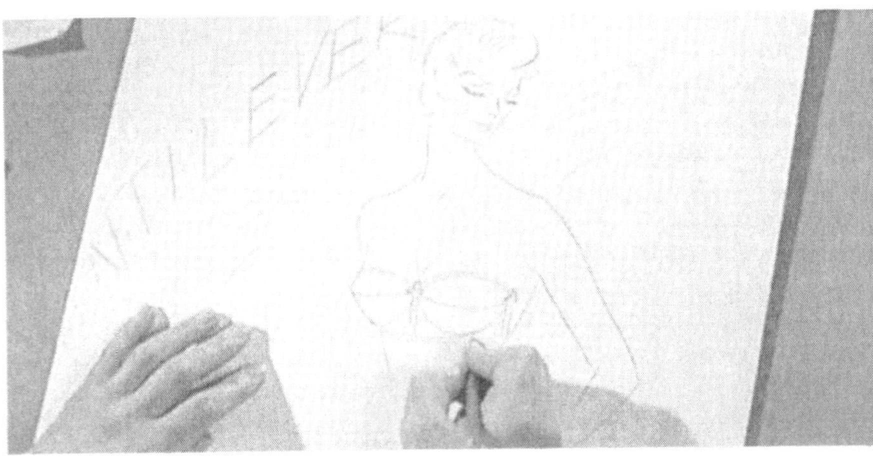

8. Midge's sketch of a bra based on the principle of the cantilever bridge.

> Vertigo is just a movie, but no other movie I know so purely conveys the sealing of a mind within a scorching fantasy.
>
> —Stanley Cavell

> "You're not lost, Mother is here."
>
> —Midge to Scottie

"SCOTTIE," ACCORDING TO LAURA MULVEY'S SHORT BUT HIGHLY influential reading of *Vertigo*, "has freely chosen to be a policeman . . . As a result, he follows, watches and falls in love with a perfect image of female beauty and mystery."[1] The fact that Scottie is no longer a policeman (actually, no longer a detective) when he is hired by his old friend Gavin Elster to follow his wife Madeleine is, perhaps, symptomatic of an influential reading that, as discussed in the introduction, oversteps itself somewhat in decrying the "patriarchal" authority of its rather pathetic male protagonist ("He has all the attributes of the patriarchal superego"). For Mulvey's reading goes on to describe the rest of the film as demonstrating how this "policeman" "breaks her [Judy/Madeleine] down and succeeds in exposing her guilt. His curiousity wins through; she is punished." The problem with this view is that this man, who is not a policeman, does not "break down" Judy, he just happens to discover Madeleine/Carlotta's necklace, and the last shot of Scottie looking down from the top of the tower from which Judy has accidentally fallen is a very equivocal "punishment," and certainly one in which Scottie is himself implicated.

But, of more concern here is the limited and limiting view of the female protagonist of the film as "a perfect image of female beauty and mystery." That is, to paraphrase a famous line from *Silence of the Lambs,* "frankly the sort of thing one would expect a male, patriarchal viewer of the film to say." Or, as D. N. Rodowick says with regard to Mulvey's tendency to reify gender roles and Freud's views of same: "Mulvey must be questioned, as she herself questions Freud, as to whether or not 'anatomy is destiny.'"[2] Madeleine Elster, who thinks she is Carlotta Valdez, but who is really Judy Barton, is in many ways a total mockery of perfection, for she is so hopelessly split between so many different personae that we hardly know the truth about any of them. In her more sympathetic view of the "women who knew too much" in Hitchcock Tania Modleski argues that identifying the "uncanny" Madeleine and her surrogates, as well as the male figure who is, to be sure, responsible for the confused identities of all these women, is anything but clear or certain:

> . . . identification is "disturbed, made problematic" (Wood) at the very outset of Scottie's investigation—just as we saw his identity as a man thrown into doubt with his very first words . . . despite all his attempts to gain control over Madeleine, Scottie will find himself repeatedly thrown back into an identification, a mirroring relationship, with her and her desires, will be unable to master the woman the way Gavin Elster and Carlotta's paramour are able to do.[3]

The identification of Judy/Madeleine/Midge/Carlotta is indeed, as Modleski maintains, very confused, but it is also the case, as

Mulvey claims, that the source of this confusion is Scottie. As I will try to demonstrate in the following analysis, the woman Scottie is looking for is always already someone else, one of Carlotta's many surrogates, because she is the "original object of desire" which is always also denied by the very person who is pursuing her. In trying to recreate the original love object that is lost to him Scottie is doing nothing more, nor less, than acting out the desire which, according to Freud, haunts all humanity, just as, according to the film, it haunts "mad Carlotta": the desire to return to the original mother.[4] (In our interpretation we will argue that Carlotta's search for her child and Scottie's search for his "mother" are the same.) It is for this reason that one rarely encounters the figure of the "femme fatale" in Hitchcock, a figure who Mary Ann Doane has rightly argued is practically synonymous with the rise of modern cinema.[5] None of the aforementioned women of *Vertigo* would qualify, and the reason for this remarkable omission in Hitchcock's oeuvre is, I believe, that the various permutations of the mother figure found in Hitchcock (the Madonna, the harlot, the fallen woman, the nagging wife/mother, etc.) don't allow for women who are as aggressively sexual as the *femme fatale*—women who, like Eve Kendall in *North by Northwest,* can only, at best, pretend to act that way.

The Three Beginnings

In one of his (and Saul Bass's) most impressive title sequences, Hitchcock begins *Vertigo* (1958) with a sort of filmic hieroglyphics which does more than merely provide us with a series of dazzling visual images. The sequence begins with the camera panning in from the right onto a close-up of the bottom half of a woman's face.

Moving in even closer, the camera moves up the face to the eyes, stopping while the woman nervously looks left and right, and then resumes its movement to the left onto the woman's right eye. There, adding a red filter, which colors the previously black and white images, the camera moves in still closer until—as in *Psycho*—the pupil is replaced by a series of kaleidoscopic spirals around their blackened centers (the sort of image which computers and their screensavers have since made commonplace). The close-up of the actual eye, again with the red filter, returns only briefly at the end, when Hitchcock's own credit appears for the second time.

Can these hieroglyphs be deciphered beyond noting, with Barr, that they "announce the themes of vision and subjectivity," or should one pass over them in silence to discuss the "main part" of the film, a practice which is surely counter to what psychoanalysis has taught literary criticism about looking to the apparently insignificant in order to discover the latent, "true" meaning?[6] That Hitchcock uses a woman's face (a Kim Novak stand-in, much as we saw a "stand-in" for Grace Kelly in the opening shot of the magazine cover) for the anonymous close-up is obviously significant, as are the particular camera movements, the darting looks right and left, and the spiraling dissolves into and out of the woman's pupil—spirals which are related to the "spirals" of Madeleine's hair to be discussed later. We are also struck by the similarity of this sequence to *Psycho,* where another blonde woman's nervous glances result, after her murder, in the same spiralings.[7] It would seem unwise, then, to adopt the position that such images are not significant without at least first trying to decipher their meaning.

The furtive glances are one of the sequence's most important features. Such darting glances are often associated with flight from the law, and, together with the spiralings, with the vertiginous loss of grounding that occurs whenever the law is transgressed by the unconscious, which is by definition lacking in definition, in a ground.[8] And it is just such a furtive encounter with a fleeing criminal that will carry forward the title-sequence's important association between a "golden-haired female" (seen in one of Hitchcock's earliest films, *The Lodger),* flight from the law, and the groundlessness of vertigo.

In this second beginning, starting immediately after the title sequence, we see the hands of a criminal grasping onto a ladder as he climbs onto a roof to escape a pursuing policeman and the "hero" of our film, "Scottie" Ferguson (James Stewart). Although one can, theoretically, transgress the law horizontally, that would lead only to another boundary needing to be crossed, whereas a vertical escape, being "above the law," is more symbolic of the criminal's desire to transcend the law altogether. It is for this reason that the omnipotent gods are often placed in some sort of heaven above, rather than merely elsewhere. The rooftop setting for this pursuit is not, then, just a way to set the scene for Scottie's first experience of vertigo, it also explains that vertigo by establishing, as did the title sequence, its proper context without which we would never know why Scottie experiences the vertigo that causes the other policeman's death in the first place.

The policeman has successfully made the leap onto an adjacent pitched roof before he has to turn back to rescue Scottie, who failed at the very same maneuver. The pitched roof serves to emphasize what the abysmal space between the two roofs already established, namely, the idea of a loss of grounding which is symbolic of the unconscious. The criminal and the policeman easily negotiate the jump (indeed, the criminal seems completely at home with these surroundings) because they are both secure, the one in a lack of footing, the other in having "both feet on the ground." Why, then, does Scottie fail to negotiate the jump?

Scottie's failure is, in Freudian terms, a parapraxis, *Fehlleistung,* or "slip." That is, it is an "accident" that is really the sign of a hidden desire whose hiddenness takes the form of its having the status of chance. (In art, as Freud points out, such slips are even less likely than in life to be the result of "pure chance.")[9] I am not suggesting that Scottie wants to fall, but rather that his slip is symptomatic of a conflict in his character that the remaining narrative of the film explains, it being the function of narratives in general to explain the necessarily veiled truth of the unconscious in such a displaced form. For now we can only register our suspicion that Scottie's accidental fall is not the cause but rather the effect of a psychical vertigo which signals an uncertain grasp on reality and a related vulnerability to the inherently groundless unconscious. That Scottie causes the death of a policeman and the escape of a criminal is symbolic of a general ambivalence running through Hitchcock's films that causes the director and his characters to lose their grip on the "normal" world of conscious truth and morality in lieu of a darker world of unconscious desires.

The third and final beginning of *Vertigo* occurs in the aftermath of this scene, when the recovering but still crippled Scottie, seated in his friend Midge's studio, discusses the "illness" that caused him to quit the police force, and the surprising call from Scottie's old college acquaintance Gavin Elster that begins the narrative "proper." The scene begins with a shot of Scottie gleefully balancing on one finger the cane he is forced to use because of his unexplained injury until, because of the corset he is also forced to wear, he loses his balance and the stick falls as Scottie winces in pain. The delight Scottie experiences in balancing the long walking stick on one finger is a familiar one of an almost euphoric sense of weightlessness, a topic that is explicitly addressed in the scene shortly thereafter when Midge explains how the new brassiere she is drawing is based on the principle of the cantilever bridge, with no straps required to hold it up. Modleski notes how different Scottie's attitude toward fashion is from that of the character he plays in *Rear Window*, but this difference is less significant, I think, when one considers how different Lisa is from Midge, who is a designer, not a fashion model.[10] Seemingly insignificant, the discussion of the strapless, "cantilever bra" is the "bridge" connecting the scene with the film's most important concerns: Scottie's vertigo as well as his odd relationship with his "maternal" friend Midge and the other "two" women in the film with whom he will become involved (Madeleine and Judy). The word cantilever itself contains a pun—"Can't I leave her?"—which describes *in nuce* the drama of the abiding mother fixation that underlies the various substitutions in *Vertigo* of an original love object that can never be found, but that can also never be relinquished—a dilemma that constitutes the central theme running throughout many of Hitchcock's films, and certainly of all of the films discussed here.[11]

One could take as the centerpiece of this third beginning the pink brassiere which is displayed conspicuously on the desk between Midge and Scottie. The bra, which is held up by a scaffolding of black metal wires, is conspicuously in view throughout the scene and even, at one point, shot in such a way as to appear monstrously large. The bra is also conspicuous by virtue of being seen in multiple formats, including the sketch Midge is working on as well as being a verbal object when its merits are discussed by the two principal characters. Nor is it coincidental in this regard that the central concern of the film is Scottie's pursuit of Kim Novak, a well-endowed starlet whose uncharacteristic (for Hitchcock) size betokens, as we shall see, the special role that mothering and the maternal breast play within this film.

Although the bra is obviously to be associated with the maternal in general and here, specifically, with the overly and overtly "motherly" Midge ("Don't be so motherly," Scottie tells Midge in this scene), we will first deal with the issue of weightlessness to which the bra is here specifically related.[12] Scottie begins the

9. Brassieres abound in this scene in which Midge (Barbara Bel Geddes) and Scottie (James Stewart) discuss various sorts of weightlessness.

discussion by complaining about the discomfort of his own corset as he hurts himself while gleefully balancing his cane—the cane is, like the corset, another support mechanism that is here being reversed as Scottie supports it rather than the opposite. Scottie then announces to Midge that he will soon regain his "freedom" and be able to do such things as scratch himself (recall the similar statement by Jeff—also played by Jimmy Stewart—in *Rear Window* of 1954) when the restriction is removed the following day. Midge, not surprisingly, is unsympathetic to this announcement as she continues sketching the bra without responding to Scottie's statement, for her support, unlike Scottie's, cannot be removed so easily. The entire scene, and even the entire movie, turns on this question of freedom—sexual and otherwise—and the uncomfortable restrictions that society, consciousness and the ego impose upon desire, especially the desire for the maternal, and the breast. The ever-astute Robin Wood approaches this idea when he notes that "the desire to fall and the dread of falling" is "worth keeping in mind in relation to the whole film," but he does not consider, as we shall attempt to do here, why this is worth "keeping in mind."[13]

Hence the importance of the "strapless" bra and the walking stick that becomes the source of great bliss when it ceases to be a means of support. In light of these attempts to deny gravity we might say that what causes Scottie to faint and fall into Midge's arms when he stands on a chair and looks down at the streets below is less important than what causes Scottie to attempt to defy gravity in the first place by rising above it. As Freud points out, the breast, the penis, and other erogenous organs are symbolically represented in dreams through flying because they all associate sexual arousal with an engorgement and/or erection that causes them to seem to defy gravity.[14] This, I would argue, is key to understanding Scottie's vertigo, a condition that the film itself never explains; we don't know how Scottie acquired the condition, nor do we know why he overcame it. The goal behind balancing the cane on his finger, himself on the chair, and the breast without apparent support is to achieve a heightened state of desire in defying gravity, in all senses of the word. Scottie suffers from vertigo and falls because he desires something unconsciously that his conscious mind, literally and figuratively, cannot support. The film, too, cannot support these unconscious desires, but nonetheless provides the answer to this question in displaced narrative form—not unlike the principle of the cantilever ("can't-I-leave-her") bridge—through a series of different women who, as we shall see, are all the same woman. Indeed, if there were ever a film that is most explicit about such displacements of the original object of desire, the maternal which "can-never-be-left," it is *Vertigo*.[15]

There is another pun contained within the discussion of the cantilever bridge that is both verbal and visual in that it is revealed by a camera shot of the sketch pad on which Midge is drawing the bra in question. When extracting stills from Hitchcock's films they seem to function as balanced compositions, almost as paintings. (This is, of course, no accident, but a result of Hitchcock's meticulous control of every shot.) The shot is particularly interesting because only part of the word "cantilever" is written on the pad: NTILEVER—"UNTIL EVER" (see image at the beginning of this chapter).[16] In a film which, as we have begun to demonstrate, is about an unconscious desire for the maternal—the original love object—which is displaced onto three different women (Carlotta/Madeleine/Judy) who are desired and denied as the original love object always must be after the infantile stage of attachment, the phrase "until ever" takes on special significance. For "until ever" is the way Freud consistently describes the time—or rather the timelessness—of the unconscious: "The processes of the system Ucs. are timeless (*zeitlos*); i.e. they are not ordered temporally, are not altered by the passage of time; they have no reference to time at all. Reference to time is bound up, once again, with the work of the system Cs."[17]

Since repression, displacement, sublimation, and other manifestations of the conscious never completely suffice to eliminate the desires, such as that for the Mother, of the unconscious, these original desires therefore persist "until ever." If Hitchcock's *Vertigo* strikes a particularly powerful chord among film critics in general as well as Hitchcock's admirers (the author of a recent BFI study notes how the film "engaged Hitchcock in an especially profound way; and it has exerted a comparable fascination on many of its viewers"), I don't believe it is because, as Pomerance suggests, that we sympathize or "share" the feelings of Scottie, Midge, Madeleine, and others in the film; Hitchcock's characters, in general, are never really sympathetic in that way.[18] It is because Scottie's predicament, his unwillingness to accept a substitute for an original object of desire that he can never regain, is, like the predicaments of Oedipus, Phaedra, Hamlet, and Charles Foster Kane, less his own aberrant pathology than our own universal human condition.[19]

The Trial

Not infrequently in Hitchcock there are scenes in which the "reality principle" seems to completely break down and is replaced by an absurd but psychologically compelling expression of the film's deeper, analytic truth. In my chapter on *North by Northwest* I discuss (as does Robin Wood) the elevator scene in which Thornhill's mother, and everyone else, starts laughing oddly and inappropriately at her son's very real and very dangerous predicament. The inquest scene in *Vertigo,* where Scottie is "tried" for his role in Madeleine's death, is another such scene, which plays more like a Kafkaesque fantasy than it does as a real inquiry into Scottie's role in Madeleine's murder. (The influence of Kafka on Hitchcock, here and elsewhere [e.g., *The Wrong Man*], is worth more attention than it has received thus far in Hitchcock criticism.) Silent throughout, Scottie listens as the judge subjects him to an unrealistically humiliating speech about the cowardice that he sees as having caused not only Madeleine's death, but that of the policeman shown in the opening scene as well, when he "allowed a police colleague to fall to his death": Scottie "would have seemed the proper choice . . . but as you have learned it was an unfortunate choice. *However I think you'll all agree that no blame can be attached to the husband.* Mr. Ferguson's weakness, his fear of heights, would make him powerless when most needed . . . he could not face the tragic results of his weakness, and ran away" (italics mine).

The judge's surreal harangue is as absurd in terms of normal judicial practice as it is understandable in terms of Scottie's psychological condition and, in particular, his vertigo. Indeed, so surreal is the courtroom scene that Hitchcock faced trouble with the studio's censors, who feared a lawsuit because the speech "could not properly be made by the man presiding at the inquest. It is not judicial in tone or concept."[20] But to say that the courtroom scene is a variation on the vertigo-theme is also to say that we should examine the scene for information in understanding why Scottie suffers from vertigo—something that (again) the film never explains. The courtroom is filled almost exclusively with men, many of whom bear a striking resemblance to Gavin Elster.

As the dialogue just quoted reveals, Elster, who is the truly guilty party, is himself expressly exonerated by the judge from

10. The jury of Gavin Elster look-alikes listens to the evidence of Scottie's cowardice.

any blame in Madeleine's murder and is even praised for his actions in hiring Scottie, thus forming an antithetical relation between Elster and Scottie in which the latter is blamed for everything because of his "powerlessness"—synonymous with "impotence." And yet, one important element of abuse is left out amid the litany of Scottie's failures that the judge enumerates which the rest of the film also leaves out, but which will provide us with another important clue in understanding Scottie's condition.

Strangely missing from the long litany of Scottie's failings is any suggestion of the fact that he was having an adulterous affair with the wife of his old college friend, the man who hired him to protect his wife. This, together with the strong Oedipal implications underlying the seduction of a woman who "belongs to" another, is the real reason for all the guilt imposed upon Scottie in the courtroom, and also why the jury of Gavin Elster look-alikes declare him not guilty of charges unrelated to this after the judge, who does not resemble Gavin, has clearly convicted him.[21] If the reason for this plainly surreal scene is to put Scottie in the position of a little boy who has been condemned by the father for the illicit mother fixation we have already noted, and will continue to see elsewhere in the film, then Scottie's real crime is not in fact known to the jury, even though it is the unconscious truth behind the judge's irrational harangue. Modleski is right in arguing that "Madeleine's" madness is really a projection of his own, for the courtroom scene acts out the unconscious Oedipal paradigm that is the root of Scottie's neurosis by having the father figures, the Elster look-alikes, rightly exonerate Scottie for the crime for which he is officially charged (sc. not having saved the suicidal Madeleine), all the while accusing him of a moral weakness whose real cause—the adulterous affair—is completely ignored.[22] It is for this reason that the stony silence that Scottie maintains throughout this scene is carried over into the aphasic state that continues for months after the trial, and from which Scottie only fully recovers when he rediscovers his original love object in the form of Judy Barton. Scottie is silent because the truth of his condition, an attachment to the original love object, the mother, cannot be spoken, but can only generate substitutions such as, here, a narrative that is itself about such substitutions.

There is much that we can learn about Gavin Elster in light of Scottie's Oedipal fixation.[23] Among all the other things *Rear*

Window and *Vertigo* have in common is their similar focus on a husband's murder of a wife in which both Jimmy Stewart's characters are curiously implicated. Also in both films both "sons'" are marked by handicaps that render their attempts to save the women in question and to apprehend the husband/murderers impotent. In *Rear Window,* Jeff can only defend himself from Thorwald by the highly questionable tactic of shooting off flashbulbs in his eyes before the murderer can be apprehended by Lisa, Doyle, and the police—and not until after Thorwald has succeeded in throwing Jeff out the "rear window" he had been spying from. As in *Rear Window,* the wife's murder in both films is a projection of their protagonists' pathological conditions and/or "handicaps" (voyeurism brought on by a broken leg and vertigo, respectively) that are themselves the result of illicit sexual desires for a forbidden maternal figure.

Gavin Elster's murder of his wife, for which the film also offers no explanation, is thus more than indirectly related to the pathological condition, the vertigo, of the film's main character. If, as we shall continue to demonstrate in the remaining parts of this analysis, Scottie suffers from a mother complex that causes his futile search for the "original love object" (a search that, I would claim, runs through the various substitutions of the entire Hitchcock oeuvre), then Elster's murder of the same original love object is the logical result of the son's loss of the mother to the father. In classic Oedipal terms, Elster's murder of his wife is simply a function of the son's loss of the mother to the law of the father, an interpretation that fits perfectly with Pomerance's point about how "Elster is to Scottie's eyes everything Scottie is not, happy, married, well-off, socially engaged, and in control" (*Eye for Hitchcock,* 228). It is for this reason, then, that the judge in the inquest scene completely and illogically vindicates the husband while just as completely and illogically implicating Scottie.

The Lost Love-Object

In "Alfred Hitchcock and Therapeutic Culture in America" Jonathan Freedman notes the double structure of *Vertigo* in offering a murder-mystery that is solved and a therapeutic, psychoanalytical mystery which is not.[23] The "therapeutic" story of Madeleine Elster's "illness" turns, of course, into the "murder-mystery" when it is revealed that the story was used, and the illness feigned, in order to lure Scottie into the plot to kill Elster's wife. There is much more, though, to the strange story of Carlotta Valdez that Gavin Elster uses to lure Scottie into the trap of following Madeleine. If, as Modleski argues, "Scottie will find himself repeatedly thrown back into an identification, a mirroring relationship with her [Madeleine] and her desires" (*Women Who Knew Too Much*, 92), then the "therapeutic" story of Madeleine, which is the story of Carlotta, is also his story, just as the story of Madeleine's madness is also the story of his madness.

Carlotta Valdez had been the mistress of a wealthy San Franciscan who heartlessly abandoned her but kept the child they had together. Carlotta then became "mad Corlotta," a sad, pathetic woman known for wandering the streets of San Francisco looking for the lost child that had been taken from her. The story captivates Scottie when told it by the owner of a local bookstore to the point of Scottie's comically abandoning Midge in the store immediately after hearing it because, I would argue, it is a disguised version of his own story. Modleski comes very close to the reading offered here—both in this chapter as well as in this book —when, in commenting on the story she says

> Carlotta becomes on her death a figure of terror and omnipotence. *In contradistinction to the Lacanian scenario, according to which the dead father is endowed with an omnipotence that "real" fathers lack, Hitchcock presents us (not for the first or the last time), with the imago of a mother who assumes unlimited power in death . . .* thereby avenging her losses on patriarchy (italics mine).[24]

The last phrase is one of the many examples of Modleski's attempt to distance her reading of Hitchcock from Mulvey. Her own counterthesis argues for the independent importance of the "women who knew too much" in Hitchcock, but that thesis causes Modleski to avoid taking the final step and seeing Carlotta's story of "a mother who assumes unlimited power in death" as the story, not of Madeleine, but of Scottie. It is Scottie who repeats the action of the story in wandering through the streets of San Francisco, and in following a woman whom he falls hopelessly—madly—in love with. *The story of "mad Carlotta" searching desperately for the child who has been taken from her by the father is also the story of the child who has been separated from the mother by the father.* Specifically, it is the other half of the story which we have postulated as a story of the loss of the original love object—the mother—at the hands of the father. Scottie is not, then, just pursuing Madeleine but also—literally and figuratively—the Carlotta-figure who is searching for her child just as he is searching for his mother; in both cases, the "enemy" is the father who, like Elster, seeks to replace the child's relationship to the original mother.[25] In Winnicottian terms, there is thus no "good enough mother" for Scottie, nor for Hitchcock's protagonists in general. They are all, as reflected in this story, mothers who have been lost to the child before any such transitional figure has been found. The mother here is, in the terms of André Green, "the dead mother," a figure whom Green associates, not insignificantly, with high artistic achievement.[26]

Midge

As one of the film's four "versions of Carlotta" (with Carlotta, Madeleine, and Judy), Midge attempts to conjure up these echoes of the past—also reflected in the eerie scene among the ancient Redwood trees of Golden Gate Park, when Madeleine, pointing to the trees' "rings of time," says "Here I was born, here I died,"—when she paints herself into the museum's portrait of Carlotta holding the spiral nosegay. The scene reminds us of another story of substitution involving flowers: the shocking story Mark Rutland tells, in *Marnie,* of just such a lovely bouquet of flowers which is actually made up of camouflaged insects—a perfect symbol of the negative, unconscious "underbelly" of romance conjured up in many Hitchcock's films (one thinks of the framed "negative" of the fashion model in *Rear Window*) and, here, of the horrible story of abandonment and murder that lies underneath the portrait, and in Midge's own disasterous attempt to paint herself into this portrait of necessarily displaced, missing mother figures. That Midge is the most maternal figure in the film is evident not only from Scottie's own reference to her "mothering" mentioned in the earlier scene when they discussed the brassiere she was designing but, more importantly, to Midge's own strange comment when she is nursing Scottie back to health after the death of Madeleine: "You're not lost, Mother is here." This comment, which is so odd that it is rarely mentioned even by the film's best critics, is crucial for a film which is "all about my mother," all about the impossibility of replacing a mother once she is lost, as well as the impossibility of replacing the loss of a replacement.[27]

Summoned to Midge's studio Scottie wonders what is so important that Midge had to see him right away. Midge denies any urgency, but this denial reflects the status of the scene itself, which is of paramount importance in the film as a whole but not at all to the plot as such. Since *Vertigo* is a film about substitutions, this scene in which Midge substitutes herself for Carlotta, who is herself substituted for by Madeleine, who is herself substituted for by Judy, both of whom are substituted for the original Madeleine Elster, is more important than its seeming irrelevance to the plot would suggest.

Midge is chuckling to herself as she contemplates the surprise she is preparing for Scottie, although the joke will, by the scene's end, be on her. For when Scottie finally looks at the new portrait he sees it as a grotesque parody of the original painting, and of the love he now has for the woman whom he believes believes herself to be the original. When Scottie walks out on her in disgust Midge realizes her mistake in forcing Scottie to acknowledge what he will only, in another fit of rage, understand at the film's end: that the closer one comes to the original mother the greater the certainty that one will only discover a deceptive substitute. This is what causes Midge to tear her hair in despair at the scene's end, for Midge is herself such a substitute, and so, in ridiculing Scottie's belief in the substitution process the joke, as they say, is on her. Finally, it is also significant that, in despair over her bad joke, Midge twice pulls her hair back as she mutters "Stupid, stupid." Hair that is pulled back and/or in a bun in Hitchcock is always important (note the final transformation in this film of Judy back into Madeleine, which requires just such a change) because it is ultimately symbolic of the nonsensual, maternal ideal who stands in repressive opposition to the loose, dark-haired sensual woman who threatens to violate the incest taboo. Midge's hysterically pulling her hair up, in this respect, is symbolic of her impossible desire to forego her maternal role in order to become Scottie's lover. Pomerance is right when he says, commenting on Midge's resemblance to Madeleine when she pulls up her hair, that "Midge is Madeleine waiting to emerge—a woman falling into, and also out of the past" (*Eye for Hitchcock*, 245). But Midge's attempt to become Madeleine is doomed

11. As one of the film's interchangeable mother figures, Midge (Barbara Bel Geddes) paints herself into the image of Carlotta Valdez.

by a maternal nature that, ironically, brought her closer to the real Scottie than Madeleine ever was.

MADELEINE/JUDY

Madeleine Elster is supposedly a virtuous, married woman. She is blonde, rich, sophisticated, and always wears her hair up in the (according to Walker) "vaginal," spiraling bun which, like Carlotta's similar hairstyle, are "like golden whirlpools that suck at our attention and threaten to pull us under."[28] Judy Barton, on the other hand, is a single, dark-haired, lower-class woman of questionable repute who always wears her hair down. According to Freud and, as it turns out, according to the film as well, these two types of women are actually the same woman (hence the spiral as combination of both types), the "original mother" to whom the primary erotic attachment must be repressed and thereby splits into a desire for both the virtuous married woman whose sensuality is denied (the so-called "Madonna-type") and the sensual woman who is "fallen" because she manifests the very earthy sexuality which must be denied.[29]

> The second condition of love, that of the "loose" character of the object chosen, seems on the other hand to stand in sharp opposition

> to a derivation from the mother complex. The grown man's conscious mind likes to regard the mother as a personification of impeccable moral purity, and few suggestions from without are so insulting, or from within so painful, as those which cast doubt on the mother's character in this respect. This very relation, however, of sharpest possible contrast between the "mother" and the "harlot," would prompt us to study the developmental history of the two complexes and unconscious relation between them, since we long ago discovered that a thing which in consciousness makes its appearance as two contraries is often in the unconscious a united whole.[30]

Paula Cohen notes that "the true Judy behind the role is only another facsimile of our own desire," and her deft reading of Scottie's (and the viewer's) ambivalence about the transformation of Judy into Madeleine is compatible with the explanation of a "Madonna/Whore complex" offered here.[31] This pattern is common in Hitchcock's films where, moreover, the repressive mother figure usually prevails, leaving the son in a blind, impotent rage over his inability to possess the mother or to be satisfied with her readily available promiscuous counterpart (Lil in *Marnie*, Annie in *The Birds*, Marion in *Psycho*, et al.). Yet, nowhere is the pattern more evident than in *Vertigo*, where the two types of women destroy, as they must, the possibility of each other, leaving only the third maternal figure, the impossibly frustrated Midge, as another sign of Hitchcock's unrelentingly pessimistic vision of our impossible human condition. In his recent book on *Vertigo* Charles Barr also notes that

> The opposition between the remote romantic female image (Madeleine) and the more earthy and available one (Judy) becomes part of his [Scottie's] own scenario, expressive of a classic Madonna/whore dichotomy. Each time he gets close to reconciling the two figures, and relating genuinely to the "real" woman, he finds himself compelled to relinquish her immediately.[32]

The "Madonna/whore" complex to which the author here refers is more important to the entire Hitchcock oeuvre than the author's passing reference, which makes no mention of Freud or of his theory of the mother complex which is the basis for this dichotomy, would allow. There is, in fact, no "real woman" here, but Barr is certainly correct in noting that, in *Vertigo*, there is also no way of reconciling the two sides of the dichotomy, no way to fulfill Hitchcock's own dream, as stated to Truffaut, of turning the sophisticated blonde into a "whore in the bedroom."[33]

The supposed Madeleine's supposed obsession, in which she goes into a trance-like state and becomes the tragic Carlotta, is part, I have argued, of Scottie's own obsession. Indeed, the entire film should be viewed as nothing more (although that is a lot) than a projection of Scottie's own pathological condition. As mentioned earlier, Carlotta Valdez is herself a fallen woman, a mistress who has reverted to the role of the Madonna in wandering the streets of San Francisco looking for her child. Her tragic story is thus a "nachträgliche" foreshadowing of Scottie's own tragic attempt to merge the two types of women, to have sexually a maternal figure that is unavailable to him as such. Uncle Charlie in *Shadow of a Doubt* reveals the terrible consequences of actually acquiring the mother surrogate, a pattern of serial murders which is related to the end of *Vertigo*, when Scottie too tries to kill the acquired "mother."[34] Scottie's pursuit of Madeleine follows Carlotta's labyrinthine wanderings as she enters flower shops from hidden alleyways and disappears mysteriously from the boarding house into which Scottie has followed her. Such elaborate intrigue, particularly the latter disappearance, is markedly unnecessary to the stated plot of luring Scottie into Elster's trap, but it is important as representing, as we have argued, the importance for the son of the persistent desire for the forbidden original love object. Madeleine's wardrobe, which is limited to the grey suit which Hitchcock insisted was "very important and represented the character's view of herself in the first half of the film" and which Scottie later forces Judy to copy when he is making her over into the now-deceased love object, is also telling in this regard.[35] Like her hair, which is always kept pinned up in the aforementioned bun, Madeleine's suit marks her as the virtuous mother image—the Madonna—as well as the woman whose marital status is being jeopardized by Scottie's secretive pursuit of her as she wanders the streets of San Francisco.

The actual relationship (if it is even possible to use that word when discussing *Vertigo*) between Scottie and Madeleine begins when Madeleine appears to attempt suicide by jumping into San Francisco Bay. Interestingly, Freud himself writes specifically about saving a woman from drowning as symbolic of a boy's incestuous relationship with his mother:

> The various significations of "saving" in dreams and phantasies are especially clearly recognizable when they occur in some connection with water. When in a dream a man rescues a woman from the water, it means that he makes her a mother, which in view of the considerations discussed above means that he makes her his own mother. When a woman rescues someone else (a child) out of the water, she represents herself as the mother who bore him, like Pharaoh's daughter in the Moses legend.[36]

When Madeleine later awakes in Scottie's bed after he has fished her out of the bay, there is a delicate exchange between the two on the subject of his having undressed her. Like similar relationships between other virtuous maternal figures in Hitchcock's films, here too the seduction is disguised, veiled under the pretense of something less overt (such as Mitch and Melanie's discussion of lovebirds in the petshop, Mark's concern with Marnie's kleptomania, etc.), often involving a rescue. Saving is more of an issue in all these cases than seduction because, as with the "saving grace" of the Madonna herself, the underlying erotic desire must be sublimated into some higher form of activity that nonetheless preserves the special bond that existed and continues to exist between the mother and her child.

Scottie's relationship with both types of women climaxes in two scenes where the love-interest falls from the same bell tower of the same old Spanish mission. The mission into which Madeleine flees is itself architecturally significant, with numerous arches and cupolas symbolic of the maternal body. The tower itself, however, is decidedly phallic, and the entire scene plays as a symbolic representation of Scottie's forbidden desire for the mother. Earlier, Scottie experienced vertigo in attempting to reach Madeleine because he knew that rescuing Madeleine would result in the consummation of an incestuous relationship with another man's wife. The fact that it is the real Madeleine whom Gavin Elster throws from the tower in that first bell-tower scene is also significant, for it too represents the father's position atop the phallic tower, denying the son the original object of desire.

Why, then, does Scottie not experience vertigo when he returns to the tower, dragging Judy to the top in order to relive the earlier scene? Again, the film is surprisingly silent in not providing an answer to this crucial question. Robin Wood believes that Scottie's vertigo is cured because he knows the truth, but he does not explain what that truth is; if it is simply the truth that he has been "had," this does not explain why that truth would cure him of his vertigo.[37] Pomerance's notion that Scottie's vertigo is related to the way "a recurring theme in *Vertigo* is recurring themes" (*Eye for Hitchcock*, 245) is certainly correct, but doesn't explain the vertigo of those recurring themes. Our analysis of the unconscious desires underlying the film's manifest content helps us to understand this and other confusing aspects of the film's controversial ending.

For example, Marian Keane has written: "Her leap from the bell tower is both her declaration that she refuses the violations of Stewart/Scottie's vision, and it is her final and decisive proof to him that she is not a ghost but a living being."[38] Yet Judy falls, startled by the nun, and does not leap, and her inability to convince Scottie that she is a "living being" and not a "ghost" continues to the end. If Scottie is, as Keane states (in direct opposition to Mulvey) "condemned" at the end, it is because of an Oedipal guilt from which he will never escape. Because of Judy's "slip" in keeping Carlotta's necklace for herself Scottie realizes that the virtuous mother figure he was in love with is in fact one and the same as the fallen, sensual woman whose virtue is always suspect because of her overt association with an illicit sexuality which must be denied.[39] Scottie's rage is palpable as he drags this sinful creature up the tower to "strangle Judy, to break her neck, to throw her off the tower," ignoring her pleas for understanding and tender protestations of love.[40] It is this decision to murder the mother figure he has been in love with throughout the film that cures him, for the moment; of his incestuous, vertiginous desires. For some other director reconciliation of the two types of women might be possible, but not for Hitchcock, who is relentlessly faithful to the impossibility of mediating the virtuous conscious with the illicit, incestuous unconscious. It thus matters little whether Scottie pushes Judy off the tower or whether, as happens here, a nun (herself the ultimate symbol of a sexless "mother" figure) punishes the transgressive sinner. For, in either case, the dream-like ending fulfills its goal of denying the mother figure whose tender protestations of love, horribly and ironically, seal her doom.[41] I would disagree, then, with Tania Modleski's assertion that Scottie is angry with Judy because she is not Madeleine: "At this moment Scottie's sadism reaches its peak, for it becomes clear to him that he never was in possession of the woman, that she has always eluded his grasp" (97). Scottie is furious because he now knows that the woman he is in love with *is* Madeleine, is the original object of desire and not another substitute for an original who is always desired, but can never be acknowledged as such.

5
ROT in *North by Northwest*

12. The ultimate "super egos," Roger Thornhill's "founding fathers," form the symbolic climax of *North by Northwest*.

CRITICISM OF *NORTH BY NORTHWEST* HAS BEEN SOMEWHAT BLINDED by the irresistible beauty of this most lavishly Technicolor of films (it was also the first MGM VistaVision production), and by the irresistible charm and comic brilliance of its leading man. This was not, of course, Cary Grant's first film for Hitchcock, but while *Suspicion* belongs, according to Rothman, to that group of important but somewhat tentative first American films of the 1940s,[1] and Cary Grant's role in another black-and-white masterpiece of the 1940s, *Notorious*, is also decidedly less charming, no one has ever doubted that *North by Northwest* belongs with both Hitchcock's and Grant's greatest achievements. And yet, it is important to recall that Hitchcock followed *North by North-*

west with a grisly black-and-white thriller which is, as we shall maintain, more related, and relatable, to *North by Northwest* than one might think. Indeed, as we shall argue in this and in the subsequent chapter, *Psycho* stands in relation to *North by Northwest* as its ghostly cadaver, just as the mother's body of the later film was once living, breathing, and probably even beautiful.[2] One might even be tempted to compare the dissolve shown above of Grant's face into those on Mt. Rushmore to the famous shot of Norman's face morphing into that of Mother at the end of *Psycho;* in both cases, the dissolves may be seen in psychoanalytical terms as the underlying, unsettling unconscious truth which belies even the most comforting, stable of appearances.

Many critics of *North by Northwest* have seen it as a film in which the certainty of identity is precarious, and where the sense, often referred to explicitly in the film, of staginess and "playing a role" is taken to an extreme. After Thornhill refers to a date he has to attend the theater with his mother (more of which later), not only is the protagonist mistaken for someone else, but the someone else he is mistaken for does not even exist, leading one to ask: if one is mistaken for someone who doesn't exist, might one not, in a sense, be that person? Eve Kendall, the other major figure in the film, is also not who she pretends to be, and when we find out who she really is (a counter spy who is really working for the government and sleeping with the enemy, as in *Notorious*), we are still not completely sure about her, nor are we sure about the government that seems coldly indifferent to killing off the two characters we care about most.

Arguing along these lines, Murray Pomerance has argued that *North by Northwest* is a film which leads us to ask "If we are not who we seem to be, if our genuine essence is inner and unknown; if others, indeed, cannot quite understand us, do we at least know ourselves?"[3] Pomerance ultimately answers this question in the affirmative, arguing that, in the end, "*North by Northwest* can therefore be seen to be a journey in which, by stages, the central figure becomes a person capable of direct and complex experience."[4] Although I will disagree with Pomerance's and others' interpretation of the end of the film as the successful reintegration of personhood, I certainly agree with Pomerance and other critics who rightly perceive *North by Northwest* as preeminently concerned with the problem of identity. But underlying and, I shall argue, motivating this film about unstable identities is a mother figure who is of paramount importance in the film. The protagonist's mother is, after all, the reason that Roger Thornhill is mistaken for George Kaplan in the first place, and her role in the first part of the film is important in other ways as well. And when, in the second part of the film, Roger Thornhill, or George Kaplan, or whoever he is, begins his "affair" with Eve Kendall, whoever *she* is, we will argue that her unstable identity is also the result of a "dissolve" into the unconscious that is the result of the earlier mother complex demonstrated in the first part of the film.

"ROT"

Despite the fact that much Hitchcock criticism would agree with the claim of William Rothman that "In Hitchcock's films the camera performs gestures that have the force of claims, demonstrations, and arguments," it is rare that these "claims" and "arguments" are considered in anything other than a formalistic way.[5] The question I would like to consider here and that I believe leads to one of the essential "arguments" on which Hitchcock's film is based refers to a scene where Roger Thornhill and Eve Kendall are conversing aboard a train, and Mr. Thornhill offers Ms. Kendall a light from his monogrammed matchbox.

What, one might ask, does the suave, debonaire Roger Thornhill have to do with the notion of decomposition (emphasized by the unusual coffin-shaped "O") implied in the acronym formed by his initials?[6] Or, to phrase the question in a slightly different way, which may or may not lead us to the same answer, what does it mean for the charming Mr. Thornhill to carry a monogrammed matchbook that bears such a decidedly unflattering designation? According to Dan Williams "commentators on the film have noted, Thornhill's initials, R.O.T. . . . suggest, albeit in a light-hearted way, his lack of true heroic status"—this despite Rothman's insistence that Thornhill is "a true American hero."[7] Stanley Cavell relates the monogrammed matchbox, and particularly Thornhill's reply to Eve that the "O" of ROT stands for "nothing," to the lack of identity of Thornhill as both an advertising man and as someone whose own identity is questioned throughout the film.[8] Following Cavell, Murray Pomerance, too, sees Thornhill as an identity-less advertising man in a con-

13. The matchbox spelling out the protagonist's name: ROT.

sumerist society who, for all intents and purposes, *is* George Kaplan, the spy he is mistaken for.[9] Likewise, Modleski refers to "the nothingness which is at the heart of Roger O Thornhill."[10] However, there is more to the monogram than just the "O," and the nothingness to which Thornhill explicitly says it refers; not to mention the fact that what a character in Hitchcock says is often far removed from the "truth" of the film in which the dialogue occurs. To stay with the context of Cavell's brilliant reading of the film's relation to Hamlet, "there is something *rot*-ten in *North by Northwest*" that also needs to be explained.

In *Psycho* (1960), which was released just one year after *North by Northwest*, we find the most famous example of such decomposition in Hitchcock's work, where the cadaver of Mrs. Bates is kept "alive" by her son Norman in the family house in which they continue to live together. Indeed, the stark contrast between these two adjacent films, the one in stunning Technicolor the other in a decidedly garish black and white, might be understood in terms of the difference between a neurotic gentleman who merely carries the name ROT in his breast pocket and between a psychotic young man who carries the whole rotting corpse of his neurotic mother around with him. But, if the difference is one of degree rather than one of kind, one might well ask to what extent Hitchcock's earlier film is merely a more glamorous version of the film he was to make just one year later. Does the "O" really stand for nothing, or does his whole monogram suggest a connection to his counterpart in *Psycho,* and Norman's "rotting' mother?

Towns-End

Richard Millington has referred to the importance of names such as "Townsend" and "Thornhill" in terms of the many spatial references contained within "*North by Northwest.*"[11] Space, and spatial references, are indeed of pivotal importance in the film, but I would like to suggest that the most important meaning of the spatialization in Hitchcock's most spatial film, a film whose trajectory moves, as with many of Hitchcock's American films, from East to West, involves the problematic separation from the protagonist's home. That this place of origin, of one's identity, is in both *North by Northwest* and *Psycho* a place of decomposition ("ROT" is Thornhill's "*family* name") would suggest that the movement away from the home is potentially liberating, but the fact that this movement eventually leads, in both these films, back to the home would imply that the decomposition associated with the protagonist is due to the inability to leave, and the necessity of returning to, the place of one's origin after one has supposedly "grown up" and replaced the older mother with a younger wife. The spatial reference in the name "town's end" would thus suggest, not only a movement away from civilization but, as spoken by the drunken prophet of Bodega Bay in *The Birds* (another marginalized locale, like that of the Bates Motel in *Psycho*), "the *end* of the world."

One might, as indeed many critics of the film have, object that the end of *North by Northwest* provides just this sort of successful resolution, with Eve Kendall's having successfully replaced "mother" as the object of Thornhill's affection. The aforementioned essay by Cavell also sees the end of the film as moving toward a positive resolution whereby Thornhill "is finally getting a message through to a woman" (Cavell, "*North by Northwest,*" 261), as does the reading of Murray Pomerance mentioned in which "the central figure becomes a person capable of direct and complex experience."[12] Or, one might interpret the end of the film (as we shall attempt to do later in this chapter) and its return back East in less up-beat terms which are more in line with the ironic endings of all the films discussed in this book—such as the celebration of Santa Rosa's "favorite son" (in reality a serial murderer) at the end of *Shadow of a Doubt*, or *Marnie*'s final statement: "Oh Mark, I don't want to go to jail, I'd rather go with you."

The notion that the journey to or away from home that one frequently encounters in Hitchcock is involved or even implied in this film needs to be explained, for it might seem that there is no actual sight or reference in *North by Northwest* to Roger Thornhill's home. But this, I would argue, is precisely why the two nightmarish scenes at the Townsend home where, as Robin Wood notes, "all [Thornhill's] proofs of identity are disdainfully refused," loom so very large in establishing the basis for the rest of the film.[13] The two scenes at the Townsend home, I would argue, are so powerful precisely because the Townsend home *is* Thornhill's home insofar as it is the place where he encounters the "father" and the two "mothers" who determine his fate throughout the rest of the film.

As we saw in the discussion of the courtroom scene in *Vertigo*, there is a decidedly Kafkaesque quality to certain scenes in many of Hitchcock's films which is evident in *North by Northwest* in the way Thornhill is unexpectedly picked up by Vandamm's two henchmen in the middle of his "martini lunch" and whisked away to the Townsend mansion without any explanation of the crime that he has committed and/or is being perpetrated upon him. Less like Kafka, however, is the curious "parabastic" quality of the scene as it unfolds in the Townsend mansion, where Thornhill is told by Vandamm (ironically, since he is posing as Townsend) to cease the playacting of insisting on his real identity and to admit that he is indeed one George Kaplan. As with the overarching question of identity posed by the film discussed earlier, the importance of this and numerous other "metatheatrical" references in this film which call into question the supposedly reality of what is going on before us must be understood in more than merely formal terms.

That the first, explicit encounter with this major motif occurs in the film's only home is not coincidental, particularly not when we consider the fact that Thornhill will later bring his own mother back to the house in order to prove, unsuccessfully, that he isn't lying about what went on there. Just as the film as a whole, as

Robin Wood rightly contends, is about much more than the specious spy story of its MacGuffinesque plot, this scene is about much more than an encounter between Vandamm and the spy he has supposedly captured.[14] Indeed, the scene doesn't even make sense in this regard, for Vandamm doesn't really seem that interested in getting information from "Kaplan" or in checking out Thornhill's story. One might also question the whole elaborate set up of using the real Townsend's home to carry out this encounter —if there is some reason for this elaborate charade, it is never explained.

On the other hand, in terms of the film's underlying, unconscious truth, the use of the Townsend home makes a great deal of sense indeed. In being brought to the home of the representative to the United Nations Roger Thornhill is in effect being hauled before a court of the highest authority (the "supreme symbol of potential world order"), and the scene plays itself out as an interrogation in which the suspected criminal is brought into a "study" in order to be studied.[15] Thornhill protests his innocence (part of the "wrong man" theme in Hitchcock that needs to be reconsidered when viewed in psychoanalytic terms), and the suave, utterly unflappable Vandamm can only smile at Thornhill's feeble efforts to deny the truth.[16] The fact that it is Vandamm who is really the criminal, and Thornhill who is really innocent, does not change the nature of this "interrogation scene"; in fact, this reversal is perfectly understandable in terms of the scene's underlying psychoanalytical reality. The "truth" of the scene is that the main character is brought before the authority Townsend to confess his guilt, and the fact that, to invoke Winnicott's terminology, one "good" authority figure has been replaced by a "bad" one does not contradict this, but rather points to the fact that Vandamm is simply the alter ego of Townsend, the other side of an Oedipal desire to prove one's claim to authority over that of the father. As his Luciferean name would suggest, the evil Van-damm is simply the displaced projection of Thornhill's own desire to possess the mother, a desire that turns Thornhill's guilt into a false identity imposed upon him by a father who must, at the same time, be deemed evil. And yet I would agree with Michael Walker, who notes that the Townsend house, despite Vandamm's dominance, is actually, like most houses and mansions in Hitchcock, dominated by mother: "Mansions without mothers or mother figures are also uncommon. . . . Townsend's mansion in *North by Northwest* is protected from exposure as a spy hideout by a highly plausible performance by a fake Mrs Townsend."[17]

Mother

In order to prove his innocence Thornhill brings not only the police and his lawyer back to the house where he was interrogated, but also his mother. But before discussing this scene it is important to remind the reader of the mother's role leading up to this point in the film. Although the role of the mother in *North by Northwest* might be easily overlooked (Dan Williams does not even mention her in an overview of characters which includes Leonard and the Professor) Thornhill's mother, one will recall, is the origin of the film, for Thornhill is first mistaken for the spy George Kaplan when he raises his hand at the aforementioned business lunch to beckon a waiter so that he can send a telegram to his mother at the same time as Kaplan is being paged.[18] Symbolically, one could interpret the fact that Thornhill is mistaken for someone else because he feels the need to contact his mother about their dinner plans as meaning that Thornhill's unhealthy attachment to his mother has resulted in his being whisked away by two strangers in order to appear at "home" before a father figure whose lack of real authority is to be understood as merely a projection of Thornhill's own desire to escape the "law of the father."

After Thornhill has succeeded in escaping from Vandamm's henchmen by getting himself arrested, his usual "one phone call" is made to mother:

> Hello Mother? Hello Mother, this is your son, Roger Thornhill. I'm in the Glen Cove police station. . . . These two men, they poured a whole bottle of bourbon into me; *no, they didn't give me a chaser.* You get my lawyer right away and come and bail me out . . . no wait, tomorrow morning he says . . . she wants to know who says? Sergeant Emil Clinger. Emil? Sergeant Emil Clinger; *I didn't believe it either.* (italics mine)

The lighthearted tone of this scene must be explained as due to more than just Thornhill's drunkenness, for that would merely "beg the question" in leaving unanswered the question of why

Hitchcock decided to play this scene, as well as all the scenes between Thornhill and his mother, for laughs. The reason for all this comedy, I would suggest, is that without it the relationship between Thornhill and his mother would be too uncomfortable for the viewer to bear. As is often the case, humor alleviates the very discomfort that provokes it, and the fact that bantering such as that just quoted is much more appropriate to an adult couple (in, say, a "screwball comedy") is also indicative of the fact that what we have here is an inappropriate relationship between a boy and his mother that is not just the effect of his being placed in jail, it is also the *cause* of his being placed in jail.[19] Hitchcock's use of an actress (Jesse Royce Landis) who was actually younger than her "son" (this by a director who is often celebrated for his attention to details) is compatible with, and perhaps even to be explained by, this Oedipal attraction, as is this same actress's appearance as Grace Kelly's flirtatious mother in *To Catch a Thief.*

When Thornhill is finally brought before the judge his mother who is sitting behind him continues the pattern of comic, inappropriate behavior by disdainfully laughing at Thornhill's attempts to assert his innocence:

> JUDGE. (*To Thornhill's lawyer.*) You know him to be a reasonable man?
> LAWYER. Absolutely.
> MOTHER. (*To herself but so that all can hear.*) Ha!

The mother's behavior here is surprising, but it allies her with Vandamm who, in the earlier scene discussed, also contemptuously discounted Thornhill's assertions of innocence. If Vandamm, as I suggested, is acting out the role of the father in denying Thornhill's attempt to assert his identity, then the mother's role here is similar in her refusal to support her son's innocence as he stands before the law. Behind the apparent absurdity of such scenes is a repressed truth through which the latent meaning of the film is expressed—specifically, that of Thornhill's Oedipal desire for his mother which is expressed in the disguised form of his claim to be innocent while his mother laughs at him.

In another equally surreal scene involving Thornhill's mother (not, however, the last such scene we will analyze) Thornhill, his mother, the judge and lawyers all return to Townsend's house in order to confirm Thornhill's version of what happened there. Everything has been rearranged to remove any evidence corrob-

14. Attempting to prove his innocence, Roger Thornhill is mocked by his real mother (Jesse Royce Landis) and a woman who looks, and acts, very much like her.

orating Thornhill's account—everything, that is, except for the woman who pretended to be Mrs. Townsend. As Robin Wood has noted, the woman pretending to be Mrs. Townsend bears a remarkably close resemblance to Thornhill's mother, and also acts in a manner that is "effusive, *motherly*, yet equally [to his mother's] cynical treatment of Thornhill."[20]

Throughout this scene Mrs. Townsend, as well as Thornhill's mother, treats him in a decidedly condescending, infantilizing manner, playfully reproaching him for his bad behavior the night before. Both women—both mothers, that is—insist that Thornhill accept his guilt, something that the son is unwilling to do, not just because it is untrue, but because the two mothers who are demanding it represent another identity which it is Thornhill's purpose throughout the film to deny. Again, Thornhill's mother's role (as well as Mrs. Townsend's) here is key, because in strangely mocking and disbelieving him she is revealing herself to be on the opposite end of her son's attempts to prove his innocence.

In the final scene between Thornhill and his mother which concludes what Wood refers to as the first half of the film, Thornhill brings his mother back to the hotel from which he was abducted in order to search for the real George Kaplan. This is strange enough, but even stranger is the little scene in which Thornhill has to bribe his mother with increasing amounts of money in order for her to agree to get the key to Kaplan's room. Both the bribery as well as the suggestion of a sexual relationship between Thornhill's mother and Kaplan (who is really Thornhill!) raise the question of the mother-as-harlot, a relationship explained in psychoanalysis as the result of a repressed desire for the mother which makes her into a harlot as a way of resolving the illicit nature of such affection.[21] This notion is realized more fully in what is doubtless the strangest, most dreamlike scene in the film which occurs next when, standing in a crowded elevator after they have left Kaplan's room, Thornhill finds himself again cornered by Vandamm's two henchmen.

Robin Wood correctly notes the truth of this bizarre scene when he describes it as "one of the film's funniest and most uncomfortable moments."[22] Although the scene makes little sense at the manifest level, it is all the more important in expressing the latent significance of the film. Again, as in the earlier courtroom scene, rather than expressing concern for her son's well-being when she realizes the cause of her son's anxiety, Thornhill's mother instead laughs at him, and is moreover joined in her laugh-

15. Roger's mother (Jesse Royce Landis) laughs at the prospect of her son being murcered by the two henchmen on Cary Grant's left.

ter by everyone in the elevator—everyone, that is, except Thornhill himself. As absurd as the mother's behavior here is, it makes perfect sense in terms of the psychoanalytic truth of the film. The mother laughs at the notion that "these are the men who are trying to kill my son" because, as the primary object of her son's infantile desire, she represents not only an indifference to the law and its punitive forces, but also an indifference to death as the appropriate form of punishment for such an offense. No wonder, then, that at the end of this scene Thornhill goes running from the elevator to begin the long journey from home that constitutes the second half of the film. For if, as in the case of *Hamlet,* there is something rotten here, it is the R.O.T. of Thornhill's own attraction to the most interdicted love object, the "abject" (in Kristevan terms) mother.[23] The infantile attempt to flee from the mother's laughter and indifference suggests that, also like Hamlet, Thornhill's attempt to overcome this desire may ultimately prove unsuccessful. Although he scarcely discusses Roger's mother in his chapter on *North by Northwest,* Murray Pomerance does suggest that, at the end of the elevator scene, "It is not just the antipathy of Licht and Valerian that Roger escapes as he runs across the lobby, but also the old lady's (*sic*) reach."[24]

Eve

Eve. "Maybe you're planning to murder me tonite."
Roger. "Shall I?"
Eve. "Please do."

The only way to make sense of the strange relationship between Eve Kendall and Roger Thornhill, a relationship that begins with a delightfully shocking scene in which Eva Marie Saint boldly and explicitly propositions a dumbfounded Cary Grant, is to realize, as the film explains much later, that Eve is only pretending to be the sort of woman who would be so forward as to offer herself to a stranger on a train and, moreover, to be willing to go to bed with someone she knows is being sought by the police for murder. However, there are a number of reasons for discounting, or at least bracketing, this explanation of Eve Kendall's "slight hint of nymphomania."[25] First, Eve's aggressively seductive character is significant in and of itself, playacting or not; for if Hitchcock had wanted the seduction could easily have occurred in a more traditional, and less "nymphomaniacal" way. Second, since the viewer of the film experiences the seductive role Eve is playing long before the truth behind her actions is revealed, the affective power of these earlier scenes is felt in and of themselves. Third, even after one does learn that Eve is really a double agent working for both Vandamm and the CIA this does not really do much to change the viewer's (or Thornhill's) opinion of her character as manifested in these earlier scenes. The fact that she is "in bed" with both these other men, in one case literally, does little to contradict the way Eve is acting in the earlier scenes in which she first makes her appearance in the film.

What, then, does the sadomasochistic, nymphomaniacal behavior of Eve Kendall mean? In terms of Hitchcock's other films, it is noteworthy that Eve's character contains two different roles which are usually divided among separate characters: that of the overtly sexual, even promiscuous woman (Marion in *Psycho,* Annie in *The Birds,* Lil in *Marnie*), and that of her more virtuous —less sexual—counterpart (Mother in *Psycho,* Melanie Daniels in *The Birds,* Marnie in *Marnie*). In *Psycho* we find an example of how these two types can be condensed into the same woman when Marion tells Sam they must stop meeting clandestinely and get married, and when she decides to return the money she has stolen, but a better example of the sort of condensation we find in *North by Northwest* is in *Vertigo,* where the virtuous Madeleine Elster turns out to be the "fallen" woman Judy Barton, both of whom are themselves condensed in the once virtuous and then fallen mythical figure of Carlotta Valdez. Seen as part of this pattern, Eve's promiscuous advances can be understood as part of a "Madonna-whore" complex in which the male is caught between his lustful desire for the mother and his denial of that same desire.[26] Dan Williams touches on this important aspect of Eve's character when he writes "It can be argued that through the character of Eve the film combines the fantasy of the *femme fatale* with the fantasy of the morally pure woman.... The viewer is allowed to decide how far Eve's early actions constitute a charade. By leaving her role slightly open-ended the film makes her transition from spy to Mrs. Thornhill more ambiguous."[27]

Eve's completely uninhibited, aggressively sexual demeanor represents the male fantasy of a totally sexual, i.e., promiscuous woman, which is the result of a fantasy of a mother who, in being sexually available, would be denying one of the most fundamental laws of repression. In this respect, the fact that it is Eve, and not Roger Thornhill, who takes the lead in carrying out the seduction on board the train is also significant, for, while the mother may take the lead in violating the incest taboo, the child, who is much more of an object of the law and so much weaker in the face of it, would be much less likely to violate the law him- or herself. And since, as we saw, Thornhill's mother's own lack of scruples and playful demeanor in the first part of the film closely resembles Eve's similar behavior in the second part, both may be viewed as the result of Thornhill's fantasy of a sexually available mother who does not "play by the rules."

Confirmation of Eve's role as a displaced mother figure is found throughout the rest of the film. *Indeed, I would maintain that this "love affair," and the mother complex on which it is based, is the real meaning of Hitchcock's film relative to which the entire espionage story serves only as a more manifest, MacGuffinesque "screen" memory.* All of the major incidents that occur in the second part of the film as Roger Thornhill moves "north by northwest" across America in the subsequent scenes will be shown to involve Eve Kendall in a fundamental way, and so it will thus be possible to view Thornhill's adoption of the identity of the no longer nonexistent George Kaplan (whom he thus does become) as symbolically representative of his attempt to win the equally identity-challenged Eve. That the truth of these characters is paradoxically revealed through their role-playing reminds us of the opening scene of the *The Birds*, where Mitch Brenner and Melanie Daniels also first become involved by pretending to be other people. In both cases, we can interpret such role-playing psychoanalytically as a necessary result of the displaced, Oedipal desires, which are at work in many of Hitchcock's films and which cause characters to reveal their true selves only when their "normal" identities are called into question.

Romantically inclined viewers of Hitchcock's film often ignore the fact that the famous "crop-dusting" scene at Prairie Station in which someone tries to murder Roger Thornhill by attempting to machine-gun him from a plane is the direct result of Eve's duplicity in having sent him there for what was supposed to be a meeting with the real Kaplan. Moreover, keeping in mind a certain cynicism toward romantic love which is everywhere apparent in Hitchcock, one will note that there is nothing in the film to suggest that Eve is not in on the attempt on Thornhill's life; in fact, when Thornhill returns unexpectedly to confront Eve after his escape she is clearly surprised to see him and, for his part, Thornhill is clearly convinced that she has set him up to be killed. As Wood notes about Eve: "we are made to remember that (whatever her motives) she did in fact connive at the attempt on his life."[28] Curiously, the earlier scene in which the two lovers joked about murdering each other has now been realized, thus reminding us, again, that such play-acting always has a way of revealing the truth of Hitchcock's films. Nor does the fact that Eve turns out later to be a double agent change matters; in fact, it makes her part in setting up the murder at Prairie Station all the more disconcerting when one realizes that she is not, in fact, loyal to Vandamm. With regard to the connection between Eve's seduction of Thornhill and subsequent involvement in the attempted murder at Prairie Station, Cavell notes that "Something cataclysmic happened to Thornhill and Eve the night before [sc. the attempted murder], and I understand the attack the next day to be simultaneously a punishment for the night and a gaudy visual equivalent of it."[29] I would only add that the "gaudy visual equivalent" of the previous night's bold sexual encounter is part and parcel of the illicit nature of the romance between Thornhill and Eve, and of the mother complex that necessarily leads to its potentially castrating punishment.

That Eve and the head of the CIA were both involved in the attempts to have Roger Thornhill killed (the CIA, earlier, had also declared him expendable) is not an exception to the romantic plot of the film; it is, I would argue, the essence of the romantic plot of the film, provided that one understands, as Brill has argued, the true nature of this unbelievable "romance."[30] For Roger Thornhill has already fallen for a woman who offered herself to a suspected murderer within minutes of meeting him. As we saw, that fantasy-seduction can be understood as a forbidden, Oedipal desire for the "fallen woman" in which the seduction is also, as the crop-dusting sequence shows, murderous. The fact that this same woman, in the next scene, sends Thornhill off to be murdered at the behest of her two "husbands" is not an exception to the romance or a problem in the film; it *is* the film. This is also why the romance between Roger Thornhill and Eve not only does not cease at this point, it actually thrives as Thornhill becomes jealous of Vandamm and accuses Eve of being a "whore" who will sleep with anybody ("Isn't everybody in her room?" he asks, recalling his similar indictment of Alicia Huberman in *Notorious*).[31] For Roger Thornhill, like many of the protagonists of Hitchcock's films, is fixated on a mother or a mother-surrogate whose "looseness" or "fallenness" is essential to her nature in "always already" belonging to another man, and/or in being an illegitimate object of desire by the son.

What, then, of the more virtuous Eve whom Roger Thornhill tries, in the last part of the film, to save from both of her "husbands"—the Professor who is using her as bait and almost gets her killed and Vandamm who also tries to kill her? It is, I would suggest, no coincidence that in attempting to save Eve from both "fathers" Roger Thornhill and Eve both end up, in the magnificent climax of the film, clinging to the faces of the "fathers of our country": There is probably no more powerful example—in America, at least—of the Freudian concept of the "superego" than that of the gigantic faces of the founding fathers carved into the top of Mt. Rushmore. To understand this justly famous scene it is helpful, if not imperative, to look at certain relevant scenes preceding this "cliffhanger," as well as at the epilogue into which this scene dissolves.

"Big Face, Small Razor"

After the scene on the train between Thornhill and Eve described earlier there is a moment of comic relief in which Thornhill stands in front of a mirror shaving with a tiny razor he borrowed from Eve. The sight of Thornhill trying to shave with this small razor, and the quizzical look he gets from another man in the lavatory, is significant beyond its apparent levity. For the scene, and the comment made to Eve moments later to explain his delay ("Big face, small razor") "precalls" the scene on Mt. Rushmore in which the relatively miniature Roger Thornhill is walking on the faces of the founding fathers in order to escape Vandamm and his henchmen. The significance of this first scene follows from this comparison, for in both cases the protagonist is emasculated, rendered impotent in the face (or faces) of a superior masculine figure of authority. In the shaving scene this is perhaps not as obvious because the large face is Roger Thornhill's, but this is

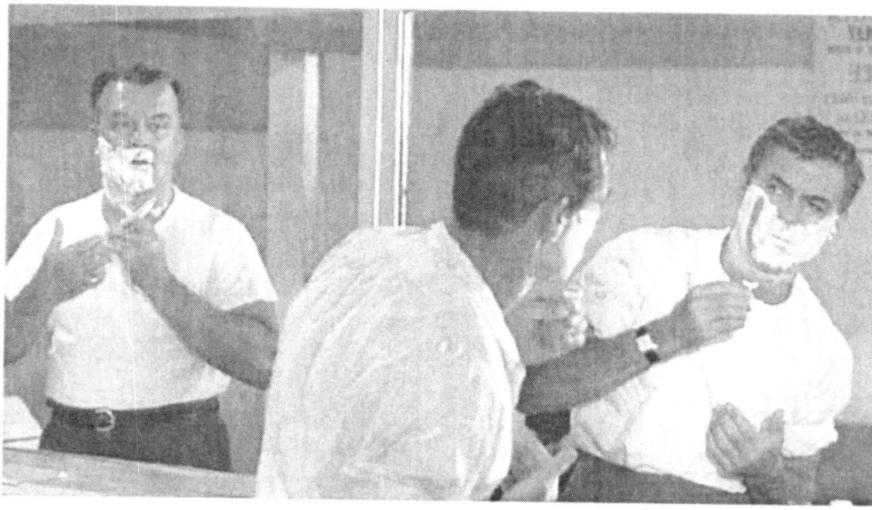

16. Roger (Cary Grant) is looked at askance by another man as he attempts to shave with Eve Kendall's (Eva Marie Saint's) tiny razor.

quickly explained by the fact that in wielding the ridiculously small, inadequate razor and attempting the difficult task of shaving with a razor which, moreover, belongs to a woman, Thornhill is himself emasculated, and his large face in this scene, unlike those of the founding fathers on Mt. Rushmore, is contradicted by the tiny razor that the owner of that face must use to shave it.

This emasculation/castration of the male protagonist is typical of the Hitchcock corpus, where there is a conspicuous absence of heroes in the traditional sense. As such, this pattern is crucial not only to our Freudian interpretation of this film but to our understanding of the director overall. It is a mark of Hitchcock's genius that he so thoroughly eschews the typical male-hero figure which was such a staple in Hollywood at the time and which has continued largely unabated to the present. But one wonders, if Lesley Brill is correct (as I believe he is) that Hitchcock's films are more about fantasy and romance than they are about their supposedly "reality," why there exists this steadfast refusal to believe in the victorious power of the male (or, for that matter, female) hero.[32] Even someone like Camus couldn't resist, as Sartre rightly argued, redeeming his otherwise absurd heroes in novels like *The Stranger*. The answer lies, I believe, in the fact that if the hero were to assert his authority rather than, as in *North by Northwest,* dangling helplessly from one of its essential symbols, this would mean that he would cease to maintain the mother as a love object, and cease to be the son who is helplessly small when compared to the father. Paradoxically, Hitchcock's films gain their power by the impotence of their male "heroes" (Jeff in *Rear Window,* Scottie in *Vertigo,* Mitch in *The Birds,* Blaney in *Frenzy,* et al.), infantilized men who can only thus gain access to the original mother. If, as Maurice Yacowar has written, "a Hitchcock hero never enjoys a simple success. . . . Hitchcock's heroes are of at best a dappled virtue, and his villains of civilized elegance," this should be in turn be understood as a function of their infantile neuroses and the "mother fixations" that also dominate these films.[33] Even in *The Birds* the supposed hero Mitch Brenner never does anything heroic and, moreover, almost gets his sister and his lover killed when he attempts to act heroically by throwing a rock at the birds, which Melanie has to stop him from doing, and thereby saves all their lives.

Insofar as it sets up the climactic scene on Mt. Rushmore it is also important to note the CIA's surprising insistence on forcing Eve back to Vandamm, thereby effectively sealing her doom. Indeed, Thornhill has to be knocked unconscious by one of the Professor's henchmen to stop him from interfering with this plan. As unbelievable as all this is at the manifest level, it makes perfect sense when we recall how, earlier in the film, the Professor had condemned Roger Thornhill to death in a similar manner:

What are we going to do?
PROFESSOR. Do?
About Mr. Thornhill.
PROFESSOR. We do nothing.
Nothing?
PROFESSOR. That's right, nothing. . . .
How long do you think he'll stay alive?
PROFESSOR. That's his problem.

The fact that he is doing the same thing again, this time to Eve, is important in demonstrating the real significance of the government's—and particularly the *head* of the CIA's—role in the film in relation to the two characters whom they are so willing to write off. The head of the CIA, or "the Professor," is himself merely a front for a much more important role that Leo J. Carroll is playing, namely, that of the father to whom Eve is effectively married "till death do them part," and with whom she has a bond of responsibility that preexists and also conflicts with that of her newfound love object Thornhill.

In explaining herself to Thornhill Eve points to a seemingly sordid past from which first Vandamm and later the Professor rescued her.

> EVE. Eventually the Professor and his colleagues approached me with a few sordid details about Philip [Vandamm].
> ROGER. So you became a girl scout?
> EVE. Maybe it was the first time anybody ever asked me to do anything worthwhile.
> ROGER. Has life been like that? How come?
> EVE. Men like you.
> ROGER. What's wrong with men like me?
> EVE. They don't believe in marriage.

Eve thus fits perfectly the aforementioned "Madonna-whore complex" in embodying both the "loose woman" as well as its more virtuous counterpart, the virtuous woman who consciously rejects that role (Melanie Daniels, Marion Crane, Judy Barton and others undergo similar transformation). The fact that Eve does this twice, first with Vandamm and then with the professor, cautions us against seeing her as either the "loose woman" or the "Madonna." She is both, and understanding this will help to understand the real significance of her new relationship with Thornhill.

The fact that Eve is sent back to the malevolent Vandamm by the supposedly benevolent Professor and must then be rescued by the overtly apolitical Thornhill from both these "husbands" is crucial to understanding the scene on Mt. Rushmore. To the extent to which, as we have argued, Eve is a mother figure she must be taken away, not just from another man, but from a paternal order that holds authority over her and, especially, over the son who would usurp the father's role. In the film's most memorable scene Roger Thornhill and Eve Kendall are both hanging from the face of one of the country's patriarch's, suspended over the abyss far below. In Freudian terms, the explanation of this crucial scene must begin with the obvious fact of hanging from the face of the "super ego," the agency of "higher truth" and moral consciousness for which there is perhaps no better symbol than these monumental faces on Mt. Rushmore. By definition the superego is larger than the individual, and particularly so when dealing with the individual's attempts to transgress the law. In acknowledging the helplessness of Thornhill and Eve as they cling to the face of the father before being rescued by another patriarch, the head of the CIA, one must conclude that while it is not the son who prevails in the face of his unconscious desires but the "law of the father," it is also the case that such vertiginous, unconscious desires do prevail in the mind of the director —a figure whose resemblance to "the Professor" ultimately embodies both the unconscious as well as the super-ego which would deny it.

This is why the end of the film, which magically dissolves from the scene on Mt. Rushmore into Roger Thornhill lifting the new "Mrs. Thornhill" up into their sleeping compartment on board a train similar to the one on which they first met, is not as upbeat as might appear. Richard Millington, for example, argues that the film finally reveals how the "American character [Roger and Eve] might be rescued from the constraints the film so richly describes," while Cavell, like Rothman, optimistically notes how Thornhill is able to resolve his earlier difficulty in getting a message through to his mother by "finally getting a message through to a woman."[34] Yet, if it is only by becoming "Mrs. Thornhill" that Eve can be raised up from the abyss of the unconscious in which all sexual perversions reside (and into which the "perverse" homosexual Leonard has just appropriately fallen), one must question whether adherence to the law through the marriage-contract will really succeed, or whether it is going to produce the same result as Thornhill's previous marriages. One must contemplate the same question that appears of the end of *Rear Window*, another film about murder, infidelity, and perversion that ends with a similar and rather unbelievable nod to a future life of marriage and normalcy. In both cases, the fact that perversion and the unconscious are the reality of these films while normalcy only begins when the film ends cannot but call such normalcy into question. If, as Stanley Cavell has argued, the microfilm that is taken out of the cracked figurine at the end of the film is *North by Northwest* itself, then we should assume that, rather than progressing forward, the film can only repeat itself, à la Beckett, with a story which ends with the beginning of a story which ends with its beginning.[35] (Note our similar interpretation of the possibility of film being in Jeff's camera at the end of *Rear Window.*) Regarding the broken female statuette out of which the "micro-film" appears at the end, Brigitte Peucker has added that "the fate of this statue demonstrates that the female body [sc. Eve's] must be shattered, fragmented, in order to produce it [the film]," another point which belies the notion of the sort of "perfectly happy ending" which Hitchcock so typically eschews, and which the broken, fragmented but endlessly abiding figure of the Mother so thoroughly denies.[36]

6
Disrepectful Respectabilties: *Psycho*

"You make respectability sound . . . disrespectful."
—Marion to Sam

IN WILLIAM ROTHMAN'S CLASSIC READING OF HITCHCOCK'S *PSYCHO*, the author perceives a certain air of death and nihilism that hangs over the entire film, a sentiment that is shared by George Toles, who interprets Norman's gaze at the film's end as signaling "an incurable appetite for nothingness," and Raymond Bellour, who contrasts *Psycho* with *The Wrong Man* in noting how "the role of shadows grows incessantly . . . from its beginning to its end":[1]

> Marion Crane's dead eye and Norman/mother's final grin prophesy the end of the era of film whose achievement *Psycho* also sums up, and the death of the Hitchcock film. In *Psycho*, Hitchcock's camera singles out a human subject as if for the last time, then presides over her murder. Marion Crane's death in the shower, mythically, is also our death—the death of the movie viewer—and Hitchcock's death. . . . Yet perhaps this art may be reborn out of its own ashes.[2]

What Rothman means by the morbid atmosphere that pervades *Psycho* is, among other things, the way everything and everyone is already marked for death. This would distinguish the world of *Psycho* from other films, such as *Shadow of a Doubt*, where the "rosy" world of Santa Rosa will finally awaken from the nightmare of Uncle Charlie's visit, and *North by Northwest*, where the "wrong man" will finally escape from the vicious circle of pursuing those who are pursuing him. And yet I think Rothman would agree that the difference he rightly detects between *Psycho* and Hitchcock's other films is one of degree rather than one of kind. The look on young Charlie's face in the final shots of *Shadow of a Doubt* suggests strongly that she does not share Detective Graham's or the town's optimism about the future; nor, as we have suggested in the previous chapter, is the "ROT" of Roger O. Thornhill's own life—and name—only a matter of mistaken identity. This is because, as I will attempt to demonstrate here, the smell of death that pervades *Psycho* emanates, primarily, from the "dead mother" who may be alive in Hitchcock's other films, but is only different from her terrifying cadaverous counterpart in degree, not in kind.[3]

The mother complex underlying Uncle Charlie's courtship murders of widows in *Shadow of a Doubt* (chapter 1) continues to underlie the films from Hitchcock's so-called golden era of the 1950s (*Rear Window, Vertigo, North by Northwest*) and early 1960s (*Psycho, The Birds, Marnie*); indeed, as I argue in my afterword, central mother figures are rarely absent anywhere in the Hitchcock oeuvre from *The Lodger* on. Although the mother is not always actually present in these films, the symbolic role of "absent" mothers such as those of the nameless young woman in *Rebecca* (Mrs. Van Hopper, Mrs. Danvers, and Rebecca herself), or Norman in *Psycho,* is all the more powerful as a continued reminder of the maternal dominance of the adult's infantile unconscious. Whereas, in *North by Northwest* and *The Birds* the mother's actual presence serves to limit her omnipotence to some degree (both Roger Thornhill and Mitch Brenner, respectively, are at least involved in transferring their maternal desires elsewhere), in *Psycho* Hitchcock has crossed the fragile line dividing neurosis from psychosis to reveal the protagonist's utter dominance by the hallucinated phantasm of the Oedipal mother.[4] In this sense, Rothman is certainly right in declaring *Psycho* the very death (i.e., the ultimate end) of Hitchcock's films, for the struggle against the mother complex that ends in failure in all his other films is here finally resolved, although it is hardly the successful resolution that civilization, unlike art, demands.

MARION CRANE

Much has been made of Hitchcock's startling formal innovation in dividing the story of *Psycho* in two (roughly speaking) by first focusing on and then killing off the "leading lady" in the first part of the film. And yet, despite the tendency to view Hitchcock and his work in formalist and technical terms, Hitchcock's genius as an artist should serve as a reminder not to overemphasize form at the expense of content: "It is similarly wrong to consider Hitchcock a craftsman first and only secondarily an artist . . . only because form is content can Hitchcock say 'I am interested not so much in the stories I tell as the means of telling them.' "[5] Focusing on the victim of one of Hollywood's first serial killers was, first of all, a highly effective way to present the horror of a murderer and his previously unknown victim. But the "double plots" are related in many ways that belie Barbara Klinger's notion that "The Marion-centered narrative is not merely replaced by that concerned with Norman, it is forcibly rejected from representation and rearticulated in terms of a 'new' story," and Bellour's statement that "the end, apparently, in no way replies to the beginning: the psychiatrist's commentary on the case of Norman Bates has little to do with the love scene between Marion and Sam."[6] As Barbara Creed notes in her study of *The Monstrous Feminine,* "both stories [Mrs. Bates' and Marion's] are related intimately with the son's story and his problem with the body of woman."[7] As I shall argue here, the story of Marion Crane and her perverse quest for respectability helps us to understand important thematic connections not only between the two parts of this film but, analogously, between this film and other Hitchcock films as well. Moreover, the relation between the apparently disconnected two parts of the film can itself be seen as the relation between the conscious mind and the unconscious desires to which it is only apparently unrelated, with the story of Marion as the "respectable" part of a film that is ultimately revealed as the repression of its own disrespectability.[8]

One might begin the analysis of Marion Crane by considering the meaning of her flight from Phoenix in the context of the other "fugue states" that run throughout Hitchcock's films. Uncle Charlie moves westward, in *Shadow of a Doubt,* from Philadelphia to his family's home in Santa Rosa. Roger Thornhill moves "north by northwest" not only, as I have argued elsewhere in this volume, because he is mistaken for a spy but because of an unusual relationship with his mother that was both literally and figuratively the cause of his escape. Melanie Daniels follows Mitch Brenner from San Francisco north to his family home in Bodega Bay, and Marnie regularly leaves and returns to her mother's home in Baltimore. In all these cases, the origin and/or destination is *home* and, even more specifically, a family house which is supposed to represent respectability but where a beloved but aggressive mother figure is waiting to undermine the characters' futile attempts at independence from a deep-seated fixation from which these protagonists can only vainly hope to escape.[9]

Comparison of Marion's flight from Phoenix to California to these other "fugue states" will help us to unify the two parts of *Psycho* as well as the film's relation to the other films just mentioned. Paradoxical as it may seem, Marion is actually trying to attain respectability by stealing forty thousand dollars from her office in Phoenix and fleeing to California. For, in an earlier discussion in their hotel room with her boyfriend Sam that she has after one of their afternoon trysts, Marion declares that she "hates having to meet like this." She insists on meeting "respectably" in the future, at family dinners, etc. In order to achieve this, Marion is on the way to join Sam when she flees with the $40,000 she has stolen in order to remove the one obstacle to their marriage, his lack of money. Marion is thus attempting to escape her illicit affair and to move from a sordid hotel room to a respectable home with Sam in California when she stops to spend the night at the Bates Motel. "Marion's sexuality," writes Barbara Klinger, "is seen as overtly problematic to the family . . . and is subsequently effectively 'regulated' by the family which it threatens."[10]

Indeed, the family home Marion discovers will fulfill the other characteristic we have just mentioned of the "return home" in Hitchcock: the discovery of an aggressive mother who represents the same pattern of "disrespectful respectability" demonstrated in the crime that brought Marion to Norman's home in the first place, and which is also represented in the motel/house opposition that is repeated in Marion's futile attempt to move from one to the other. For while Norman's mother persecutes him with constant reproaches for his "disgusting" thoughts, by murdering the objects of Norman's desires she, like Marion herself, acts "disrespectfully" in the name of respectability. And it is not insignificant that the place where this pattern of "respectable disrespectability" is revealed is the house where the very model for this pattern first occurred, namely, Norman's murder of his mother in order to attain the respectability of no longer desiring her. If, as Freud maintained, incest is the "crime of crimes" such that, relative to it, other crimes are not even crimes at all, then we are in a better position to understand this pattern in Hitchcock's films where the incestuous origin of criminality is finally revealed when the criminal "returns home" to escape his or her crimes only to discover one that is far more horrific.[11] (Sophocles was the first to utilize this pattern in having his protagonist finally discover a crime far worse than the terrible one—regicide—he thinks he has committed.)

This notion of a "disrespectful respectability," which has its origin in the uncanniness of the home ("uncanniness" is "*das Un-heimliche,*" "that which is (not) of the house"), the paradoxical place where what is "of the house"—the incestuous love between child and parent—is denied to the point of "not being of the house," is as key to understanding Marion Crane's actions and subsequent fate in the first part of Hitchcock's film as it will be to understanding Norman's actions in the second.[12] In both her interactions with her boyfriend Sam, where she insists on their ending their affair in lieu of a more respectable relationship, and with the drunken businessman who propositions her before Marion steals his money, Marion reveals the same "elision" of respectability into disrespectability. Marion rejects both men's sexual advances but then, as a direct result of her feeling offended, steals the businessman's money in order to marry Sam. This odd pattern is also "preminiscent" of *Marnie,* where we will encounter a similarly strange mixture of criminality and virtue wherein Marnie maintains her virtue by stealing from wealthy businessman who are sexually attracted to her.

As strangely contradictory as Marion's behavior may seem it is not at all unusual among Hitchcock's characters, or from a psychoanalytical perspective in general. Indeed, in Hitchcock's films it is far more the rule than the exception to expose characters like Uncle Charlie who epitomize respectability as murderers and their like; in *Shadow of a Doubt* Hitchcock even takes this further by having Uncle Charlie's respectability reemerge again at the end of the film during his public burial as a local hero. And it is far more the rule than the exception, in psychoanalytical terms, for respectability to be unmasked this way as merely the repression of contradictory desires. Although it is Marion who accuses her boyfriend Sam of "making respectability sound . . . disrespectful" when he gently mocks her dreams of Sunday dinners with the family, it is actually Marion who better fits her own criticism by stealing money from a very disrespectful businessman and using her ill-gotten gains to attain the desired respectability with her future husband. Hitchcock's films consistently demonstrate that the desire for respectability, which in Freudian terms is modeled on the incest-taboo, that has its symbolic origins in the uncanny (*unheimliche*) house, is nothing other than the repression of the contradictory, illicit desire which is its truth. And, if most forms of civilized behavior are not as criminal as Marion's and Norman's, that is because Hitchcock's characters are caught in an attempt to recover the "original love object" that "normal people" have replaced with more acceptably mediated, i.e. compromised, objects of desire. This is why, in Hitchcock's films in general, and certainly in all the films discussed in this book, "the attitude towards marriage is remarkably bleak and skeptical. This may account for the perfunctory nature of so many Hitchcock happy endings . . . without much evidence of enjoyment or conviction."[13] Even Hitchcock's sole comedy, the wonderful and underrated *Mr. and Mrs. Smith* (1940), gives ample evidence of this sense of the hypocrisy of the marriage contract and all the violence and repressed desire that underlies it. (The recent *Mr. and Mrs. Smith* [2005], featuring Brad Pitt and Angelina Jolie, is thus by no means as unrelated to its earlier namesake as the first wave of criticism would indicate.)

It is not surprising, then, that even before Marion replaces the light of Phoenix for the rainy darkness of the Bates Motel she gives us ample evidence of the shift between light and dark in her own character. The long scene in which Marion exchanges her car for a new one seems more significant in terms of its color symbolism (a black for a white car) than as a way of eluding authorities, who are watching her as she makes the change. The same shift, albeit in the opposite direction, occurs in her lingerie, which changes from white in the opening scene to black after the robbery. The point of these dramatic changes is to show that Marion is incapable of respectability, of controlling her libido or, for that matter, of giving into it either. The fact that her life will end while she is ecstatically showering in a bright white bathroom is also significant in this respect, for the strong pulse of water showering down upon her is similar to as well as different from the knife that is about to "rain blows" down upon her naked flesh. That cleansing should motivate both "showerings" (both Norman and his mother are obsessed with removing dirt) is another powerful example of the perverse elision of light and dark in *Psycho*, of respectability made disrespectful. For this reason, I would object to Rothman's rather harsh indictment of Marion in describing her murder as "just comeuppance": "In her hubris, Marion has denied the world in the person of Norman Bates, denied Hitchcock, and denied us."[14] Although, as their similar names would suggest, "Marion" and "Norman" are both implicated in the same pattern of "disrespectful respectability," Marion is ultimately as different from Norman as, say, the "wrong man" Blaney is from the murderer Rusk in *Frenzy*.[15]

In contrast to the hollowed out eyes of Norman's mother, Marion's eyes are often conspicuously wide open.[16] Indeed, in certain scenes, such as the one with the police officer, we almost never see Marion blink. Marion's "wide-eyed innocence" can in turn be placed in the context of the castration complex whose most blatant symbol is the beak-like knife that Norman's mother uses to cut off his desires: "It is above all the sudden high-pitched shriek of violins, so compellingly suggestive of an attacking bird-like creature, that creates the shock that constitutes *Psycho*'s best-known effect."[17] In *The Birds*, this connection between the attacking birds and open eyes is made explicit on a number of occasions: "Cover your eyes!" The opposite of Marion's gaze is evident when the State Trooper questions her, his eyes blackened by sunglasses while hers are wide open.

This contrast between the fleeing criminal and the policeman reveals that "eyes wide open" symbolize, for Hitchcock as for Kubrick, forbidden sexual desire, while eyes shut or covered symbolize the law's repression of the sort of dilation that occurs whenever one sees something forbidden. The famous "exquisitely slow dissolve" (Rothman) from the shower drain to Marion's open eyes after she is murdered is also to be contrasted with the empty eye sockets of the castrating mother seen at the film's end: as in the confrontation with the policeman, the one is the epitome of the object of sexual desire while the other is the origin of the taboo against that same desire. I would disagree slightly, then, with Barbara Creed's notion that "The cellar scene, perhaps

17. The state trooper interrogates the fleeing criminal.

even more than the shower scene, emphasizes the all-pervasive presence and indestructible power of the mother as the controlling castrating parent," for it is really the son's desire which turns the mother into the agent of castration.[18] And, just as the mother in *Psycho* is actually a symbol of both original desire and its nec-

18. Eyes wide open, Marion (Janet Leigh) confronts the invulnerable eyes of the law (see previous image).

essary denial, so too Marion, as a young woman and potential mother, symbolizes both in the larcenous and lascivious desires that lead her to try and attain respectability before being hacked to death by the very mother she would like to become. In this sense it is fair to say, in answer to the question that Barbara Creed and others have posed about who Norman's "real" mother was: she is clearly none other than Marion Crane herself, the bird who, like Mother, also remains to be "stuffed," if only in a trunk.[19]

ANL 709

We begin this discussion of "anal-compulsive behavior" in *Psycho* with a discussion of Marion, whose car bears the "vanity plate" of our subtitle, and use this important topic to begin our *anal*-ysis of the second part of the film—the "Norman-story."[20] Although Marion Crane is the typological "loose woman" who functions as a part of the mother complex that runs through many Hitchcock's films she is also, à la Marnie, obsessed with attaining the very respectability that her criminal action undermines. This, as we shall now see, is not essentially different from the same contradictory "anal-compulsive" behavior that Norman manifests, and will serve to link the two apparently unrelated parts of the film—to clean up, as it were, the sort of messiness that Hitchcock's famous obsession with total directorial planning and control would never tolerate.[21] In this regard it is worth recalling the comment by Hitchcock's wife Alma that "He is the tidiest man on God's earth. I've never known him to leave a toothbrush or a tube of shaving cream out of place, or ever to walk out of a lavatory without making sure that the washbowl was immaculate."[22]

Both Marion's and Norman's (again, the anagrammatic names themselves suggest the two characters' similar identities) odd ways of trying to attain respectability fit Freud's theory of an "anal-compulsive" obsession with order that is based on the repression of an anal-eroticism that is, at bottom, a desire for the very filth that repression would condemn. In other words, Marion's desire for respectability is not really the contradiction of her stealing but, according to Freud, is rather to be seen as the same as her stealing just as, for the child, the intense satisfaction derived from controlling its bowel movements, and then from control in general, is the same as the desire for a release from such control. For Norman or, more specifically, for his maternal superego, such anality manifests itself in his desire to get rid of a "disgusting" Marion—in the shower, in the bathroom—as a way of mastering his own illicit desire. As Barbara Creed states in her excellent study of the female monster in film, "Mrs. Bates is, in a sense, still toilet training her son, that is, still teaching him about the clean and unclean areas of body and mind."[23] Creed's references to "toilet training" in *Psycho* are, I shall argue here, even more significant than her brief study suggests.

Less obvious but equally relevant to Freud's theory of anal-eroticism is the emphasis in Hitchcock's film on money, gifts, and wrapping: "It is possible that the contrast between the most precious substance known to man [gold] and the most worthless, which he rejects as 'something thrown out' has contributed to this identification of gold and feces."[24] To understand Freud's identification here of gold and feces one must keep in mind that, from his earliest essays through his most explicit statement of the idea (the essay on "The Antithetical Sense of Primary Words,") Freud saw the unconscious as a force which undermines the repression of antithetical meanings.[25] Thus, gold and feces are united in the unconscious with the worthlessness of excrement being the repression of its value as a source of pleasure to the child, and conversely, with gold as that pleasurable substance that one hoards, retains, and doesn't give up. (The fact that, as the saying goes, 'money has no odor" is simply further evidence that gold is the "antithetical sense" of feces.)

This antithetical identification of the most precious substance with the most worthless also explains, psychoanalytically, the *gift*, the *giving up* of what is most precious to another. If feces is, before repression, a precious substance, retaining it is evidence for Freud of a narcissistic attitude while the relinquishing of that object is evidence for Freud of a "transformation" in which the precious substance is turned into a gift, something that is mine but that is objectified insofar as it is given to the other: "the process of defecation affords the first occasion when the child must decide between a narcissistic and an object-loving attitude."[26] It may seem far-fetched to identify, as Freud does, gift-giving and the wrapping-up without which it is not complete with excrement, yet our repugnance over the notion is perhaps its own evidence of an unconscious antithetical identification.

We can find further evidence of the psychoanalytic significance of gift-giving and anal-compulsive behavior in the characters and actions of *Psycho*'s two main characters.

The wad of cash which Marion stole from her boss is highly significant in this regard. The large roll of tightly wrapped bills is suggestive of both the "fecal stick" that Freud speaks of in its identification with the phallus as well as of the process of retaining that is continued in the insistence on wrapping-up as part of anal eroticism. The emphasis on wrapping up this already wrapped up wad of bills will be even more evident when Norman obtains the money, but this was already an issue with Marion. Her wrapping up the money tightly, folding (or attempting to fold) the large wad of bills in half, stuffing it first into an envelope and then into her suitcase, is indicative of Freud's identification of money with feces as its original meaning. The "wad" speaks for itself, but the wrapping and folding of this money that proves at once so difficult and yet also so significant in this film is also indicative, for both characters, of their obsession with bulging, illicit objects of desire that must be concealed, hidden, or wrapped up.

The mere fact that Marion steals the forty thousand dollars in order to attain respectability is understandable in terms of Freud's theory of anal-eroticism, for Marion's perpetrating, simultaneously, the most disrespectful act in order to attain respectability fits Freud's pattern of anal-erotic behavior as the desire for the very filth that produces its denial. As the embodiment of the classic type of anal-compulsive behavior Marion's tidiness, her otherwise prim and proper behavior, are indicative of something very different that lies beneath, something much more loathsome that, at the end of the film, is rendered as human feces, the rotting cadaver of Norman's mother. It may seem shocking to suggest, as we have once already, that the beautiful Janet Leigh, with her eyes wide open, of the first part of the film is synonymous with the rotting corpse of the mother—also with eyes wide open—in the second half of the film, but given the fact that both are the objects of Norman's anal-eroticism the identification between the beautiful object and its abject opposite (also made by Poe) is important.[27]

The lecherous older man who serves as the impetus for Marion's crime by propositioning Marion before she steals his money functions as another abject (in the Kristevan sense) object of desire similar to Norman's mother, and as such is another important indication of Marion's anal-compulsive behavior. Cassidy's offensive manner and remarks, which include not only a vulgar proposition but also his drunkenness and an incestuous comment or two in which he compares Marion to his daughter, is in marked contrast to Marion's attitude toward him, which is very high-minded, upright, and polite (more so than the other office worker Caroline, played by Hitchcock's daughter Pat, who is hurt that it was Marion and not she who was propositioned). Similarly, Norman is also deeply offended by his mother's bad behavior. Both characters exhibit similar high-minded, "officious" behavior that then turns into its opposite when they steal and murder, behavior that reminds us, again, of the child who protects his hidden pleasure from an ogrish parent who is merely the reflection of a desire that is illicit, and even immoral. In desiring and denying her desire for both the older man and his money, in remaining prim and proper in the midst of the most sordid behavior, Marion is not so different from Norman after all.

Another example of Marion's anal-compulsive desires occurs when she leaves the large wad of bills in view of the state trooper who stops to question her. There are no parapraxes, no *Fehlleistungen,* within the artwork; such "accidents" are always more, not less significant because of their "arbitrary" status.[28] The wad of bills that Marion hides from the policeman can be seen, for a number of reasons, as her own fecal deposit. First, because she is embarrassed by it and is very anxious to cover it up, to "flush it away." Second, because the covered eyes of the trooper peering into the car—"blind justice"—represent precisely the sort of superego that is in charge of civilization's "toilet training" in enforcing the law of what *must* not, not just what *should* not, be done. And, lastly, money and/or gold, as we have learned, is synonymous in Freud's view with excrement (he adduces many examples from fairy tales as additional support of this identification) as a wad, or pile, which we like to fondle as a reminder of the pleasures associated with defecation, long since repressed. Seen this way, Marion's "accidently" leaving the wad of money in full view of the trooper is hardly unintentional, and resembles the strange "gift" that criminals habitually leave at the scene of their crimes. And, lest this comparison seem far-fetched, we should recall that the line leading from Marion to the serial murderer Norman is very short and, as their similar names would suggest, inevitable.

While Marion's theft of the forty thousand dollars is motivated by the desire to give this money to Sam so that he will be free to marry her, this is hardly a logical reason for the theft. The lack of practicality and even logic in giving the stolen money to Sam (not to mention the fact that this will surely destroy the very relationship it is meant to save) underscores its significance as a "gift" in Freud's sense of the term. For, as nonsensical as the gift of forty thousand dollars to Sam is, in psychological terms it makes perfect sense, because the stolen money which is meant to assure Marion's respectability through her marriage to Sam closely resembles what Freud describes as the child's giving up of his feces as something precious, which, for example, he or she proudly shows his parents. The fact that this is a gift and, as such, involves a partial relinquishing of Marion's narcissistic desire is, unfortunately, no more an indication of surpassing her infantile behavior than is Norman's doomed attempt at establishing a real relationship with Marion right before he murders her.

Indeed, Norman's own telling version of the gift-giving sequence occurs when he offers to share his dinner with Marion. A number of things stand out in this scene that cause it to fit Freud's pattern of anal-compulsive behavior. Norman is clearly desperate to have Marion's company, so much so that he fails to realize that he has neither the food nor drink to provide her with a real dinner. Like Marion's own desperate behavior, Norman's behavior signals a childish state of excitement, even glee, rather than a "real" assignation. This infantile state of gift-giving, like Marion's to Sam, is also revealed in the particularly childish selection of food and drink that Norman offers—milk and peanut-butter and jelly sandwiches—that is destined to have the opposite effect from the one that is desired.

Norman's own anal-compulsive behavior is best seen, however, in the way he compulsively cleans and wraps up the items in Marion's room after he kills her. We have already mentioned the involution of killing Marion *in* the bathroom *in* the shower. This pattern of containment continues when Norman wraps Marion's body up in the shower curtain, which he then places inside the trunk of her car before he then places the car itself within the neighboring swamp. Similarly, the forty-thousand dollars which is wrapped within a newspaper is also wrapped within the trunk within the car which is, then, itself wrapped up inside the swamp. Although he does not mention *Psycho,* Murray Pomerance notes how, in *Marnie,* there is a similar pattern of involution that occurs when, preparing for her latest robbery, Marnie "places herself silently in one of the [bathroom!] stalls, she is a pouch inside a pouch inside a pouch."[29]

The wrapping up process that is a prominent feature of anal-compulsive behavior must be understood, from a psychoanalytic perspective, as antithetically related to the "disgusting" substance that is being contained and retained within: "I refuse to think of disgusting things because they disgust me," complains Norman's mother. As this quote reveals, Norman is caught (as he himself says) within "his own private trap" of denying, wrapping up, something that asserts itself through its own denial. The intensity with which Norman cleans and wraps up the mess left after the killing is ultimately no different from the intensity with which he kills his victim, ripping into her naked flesh repeatedly with a kitchen knife, for that too is a form of wrapping up, of containing and hiding his desire for Marion's naked flesh. Indeed, Norman has even already begun the process of cleaning up his messy desires by neatly murdering the object of his desire in the shower.

When Norman is showing Marion her motel room he reaches a point when he can only gesture and stammer: "And the . . . over there." Marion, with a smile, provides the missing words: "the bathroom." Norman is clearly a very respectable, tidy young man, so what is it, exactly, which blocks Norman from using the word "bathroom" here? The most likely answer would also have to be the most obvious: Norman hesitates precisely because the bathroom is the place where such neatness and efficiency, despite our best efforts, is most effectively denied. More private, in many ways, than even the bedroom, the bathroom is the place of excretory functions where what is most disgusting merges most effectively with what is most clean (the euphemistic "lavatory"). Norman refuses to say the word "bathroom" because the disgusting things that occur there need to be covered up, cleaned up, washed down the drain, buried in a swamp, etc., much as the euphemistic word "bathroom" itself attempts to clean up what really happens there.

"Respectability," then, is even more of a force in Norman's life than it is in Marion's. As is sadly the case with many violent offenders and, in particular, sex criminals, Norman is not a murderer because of his sexual attraction to Marion but, rather, because of a need for respectability that is fueled, as was the case for Marion, by his own forbidden, infantile desires. Norman's voyeuristic peeping at Marion is thus less the result of sexual desire (she had earlier invited him to her room, to which he declined) than it is the result of an anal-compulsive need to repress his sexual desires. When Norman returns, moments after this scene, dressed as his mother to kill Marion in the shower we observe the logical fulfillment of his earlier inability to utter the word "bathroom," for we are witness here to the murderous sort of "toilet training" noted earlier by Barbara Creed in which the mother is violently repressing her son's "filthy" desires.

The attraction for Norman is not, then, as much for Marion Crane as it is desire for the mother who represses desire for the "loose woman" who is, herself, a displaced version of the "Madonna" figure. There is a wonderful, oft-commented-upon moment in the film after the murder when Norman is standing at the edge of the suck swamp waiting for Marion's car, and the dead body he has stuffed inside, to sink below the surface and thus wrap itself up. Norman, who seems positively giddy at the prospect of flushing one more thing down the toilet, suddenly grows apprehensive when the car momentarily stops sinking. His glee is even greater, however, when the "toilet is flushed" and the gurgling resumes as the car is finally pulled under the surface. Norman's smile here is important, not just because it reveals the viewer's own sympathy with his character, but because it reveals the full, pathological extent to which his pleasure has been transformed back into his anal-compulsive desire to conceal his desire, as desire for the mother always must be concealed.

The importance of anal-eroticism in *Psycho* is, finally, also evident in the fact that the crucial clue that leads to Norman's apprehension is literally found in the toilet, where Lila finds a very tiny slip of the paper on which Marion had written her calculations for returning what was left of the forty thousand dollars she had stolen. The slip of paper, it seems, had not been flushed down the toilet with the other pieces of evidence Norman had disposed of in cleaning up the room after Marion's murder. In arguing for the importance of this small detail it should be recalled that the bit of evidence, and it's curious placement, is of pivotal importance in the film, and that Hitchcock himself, in

19. Norman's (Anthony Perkins) famous smile after the swamp engulfs Marion's car.

one of the typically humorous trailers he filmed publicizing the film, walks over to the toilet, lifts up the lid, and points into it as the place where a crucial bit of evidence in solving a gruesome murder was found.

The piece of paper that is not flushed down the toilet resembles the car that Norman is attempting to dispose of by rolling it into a suck swamp before it stops momentarily, causing Norman considerable anxiety before it is finally swallowed up. Taken together, the two scenes reveal the inability of repression to hide, conceal, or cover up the repressed object of desire. In this respect, the slip of paper represents, *in nuce,* the meaning of *Psycho.* For the bathroom is also the place where Marion was murdered, her blood literally flushed down the drain, as another example of the attraction-repulsion for what is most desired, and therefore most repressed and so only revealed when, as here, there is a Freudian "slip."

The Birds

One of the few liberties that Gus Van Sant allowed himself in his "literal" remake of *Psycho* was to call more explicit attention to the symbolic presence of the birds in Hitchcock's original, even adding them in scenes (such as the final scene in the fruit cellar) where they had not been seen before. However, given their already powerful presence in *Psycho,* and Hitchcock's own continued exploration of "the birds" in his subsequent feature film of the same name, one must question the necessity of Van Sant's added emphasis.[30] It is, however, useful to draw on Hitchcock's own further elaboration of the theme in the second film as a way of understanding their powerful but more muted presence in the first.

In the 1960s, during the period in which both these films were made, it was not unusual to use "bird" to refer to a woman. This association is of course not arbitrary, and Hitchcock could as easily have been drawing on the original subconconscious connections that generated the English and then American slang expression in the first place as he was referring to the linguistic usage of the time. Either way, the connection between birds and women in Hitchcock's two films is obvious even at the most superficial level. Marion is Marion *Crane;* Norman likens her to a bird because of the way she eats; Norman stuffs birds *and* stuffs his mother's corpse; and, finally, when Norman kills it is as a woman holding a beak-like butcher knife with which she repeatedly stabs her victim. In Hitchcock's next film the connection between women and birds is even more explicit: Melanie is associated with birds from the outset of the film ("Back in your cage, Melanie Daniels"), and the birds' attacks are linked explicitly to her presence in Bodega Bay as well as implicitly to the mother's (Lydia's) aggression.

If we start, then, with the identification of birds with women we will then be able to understand their role in *Psycho:* why Norman stuffs them, why they loom over the scenes in the office of the Bates Motel, why there are pictures of birds in the room where Marion Crane is killed and, finally, why these women/birds are themselves capable of being homicidal creatures in both films. Barbara Creed agrees with my identification of Hitchcock's birds with the castrating woman, and specifically the castrating mother: "Insofar as Norman associates his mother/other women with his stuffed birds and their devouring beaks, the birds should also be seen as a sign of the castrating mother" (144). But birds are not just associated with women in the two Hitchcock films just mentioned; they are symbols, to be more precise, of the maternal breast. Soft, with a (more or less) prominently swollen breast, the bird is a natural symbol of that part of the female/feminine anatomy. But it is also the case that in reaching out to touch the breast or breast-like bird one is likely to encounter either a pecking beak, a slap or some other violent rebuke. This rebuke begins with weaning, the crucial stage in human development (both psychoanalytically and otherwise) when the first "No!" enters the child's previously unrepressed, narcissistic existence.[31] It should not surprise us, then, if the birds in these two films come armed with a violently penetrating knife or beak, because the nipple of the maternal breast, the "first love object," has been denied the child and thus turned into a potentially "castrating" weapon against the one who desires it.[32]

In *The Birds* this "phallic breast" is generated, exactly as in *Psycho,* by a son's continued entrapment in his mother's house, and by the mother's double denial of both the son's love for her as well as his transference of that love onto another women—even one who resembles Lydia Brenner as much as Melanie Daniels does.[33] But in *Psycho* the living birds, and living mother, of the next film appear only in the form of the inanimate—stuffed or painted—birds and the stuffed corpse of Norman's own making. This corresponds to another significant difference between the two films, namely, that the blonde "loose woman" (Melanie Daniels) is courted in *The Birds* by the son rather than, as in *Psycho,* killed by him. But the difference between the two films is only one of degree, and the equivalent of the famous shower scene in *Psycho* occurs in *The Birds* when Melanie is similarly hacked nearly to death at the end of the film after she wanders into a room (a room, like that of Norman's mother, at the top of the stairs) of the family house.

Rather than being attacked by the "phallic breast," as Mitch Brenner is in *The Birds,* Norman attacks, kills and retains the maternal breast himself. But, again, the difference is only one of degree; by killing and then stuffing the maternal breast Norman is able to possess the original love object that, otherwise, would have to attack him (as happens in *The Birds*), since his inability to transfer his affection elsewhere means that the first love object and its primordial "No!" will have to deny his attempt to attain it. We can thus understand why Marion *Crane,* a bird herself, must nonetheless be killed, for Norman has already killed the mother whose bird-like presence in turn kills Marion. The murder simply reenacts the scene in which Norman's forbidden love for his mother forced him to kill her to attain it. He in turn murders Marion, rather than have sex with her (recall her offer of same), because his incestuous love for the maternal breast can only be attained by its killing or by it killing. This also explains why it is Norman's mother and not Norman who kills Marion: it is a matter of the maternal phallic breast denying itself but also (as in *The Birds*) denying its transference elsewhere.

The satisfaction Norman feels at killing and then stuffing his birds is a reenactment of his having killed the maternal breast in order to attain it. That both his birds and his mother are preserved in the same way is due to the fact that they both represent the same forbidden love object—the breast—whose traumatic denial in the original weaning process can only be overcome by an equally traumatic denial of the original denial in which the breast is regained by an act of psychic violence as necessary as the fundamental law—the original No—it would oppose. Finally, it is interesting in this regard that Norman stops, after the murder, to replace the print of a bird which has fallen off the wall in Marion's room. Hitchcock took the time to include this seemingly irrelevant action (another "Freudian slip") because it is in fact highly significant. For, recalling our earlier discussion of Norman's "anal-compulsive" behavior, the act of neatly replacing the fallen bird is exactly what Norman does through his taxidermy, through his murder of Miss "Crane," and through his replacing the denied maternal breast with both the stuffed corpse of his mother and his impersonations of her. And it is what Hitchcock himself will do when he replaces the "picture of the birds," and the maternal figure they represent, with his very next picture.

"A Boy's Best Friend is His Mother"

This statement, which Norman makes to Marion Crane, is all the more important because it is incorrect. The correct saying, which is even quoted in one of Hitchcock's own films of this same period, is that "a *girl's* best friend is her mother."[34] The mistake is significant and even a little poignant, for it reveals how Norman has inserted himself (literally) into his mother's life in ways that not only violate normative behavior, but also violate the propriety of the literal—something that his stuttering over words like "fallacy"/"phallus" ("It's a fal-fal-falsity") also demonstrates. But the statement is also incorrect in another, more significant way. Norman may wish to be his mother's best friend but the feeling is certainly not returned. Norman's mother or, to be more precise as well as more fair to Mrs. Bates, the phantasm in Norman's mind of his mother, is a shrewish figure who continues to persecute her son mercilessly and who, shades of *Hamlet,* took a second lover after her husband, Norman's father, died.[35]

It is not unusual for a child to be all the more devoted to a mother who denies him or her its affection. In *Marnie* we see just such a relationship in which Mrs. Edgar's inability to demonstrate any affection for her daughter causes Marnie to steal her affection, literally. Indeed, the similarities between Norman's mother and Mrs. Edgar (and between them and mothers in many other films, such as *Rebecca, Notorious, Shadow of a Doubt, North by Northwest, The Birds, Frenzy,* etc.) are so numerous that we have posited a typological mother figure who reappears in many if not all of Hitchcock's films. An analysis of Norman's mother will perhaps shed the most light on this figure, since *Psycho* clearly shows us the "worst case scenario" of a child's dysfunctional dependence on its mother's love. Perhaps this is why so many of Hitchcock's major critics declare, with Rothman, *Psycho* the director's ultimate masterpiece.

Fathers are almost as absent in Hitchcock's films as mothers are present, and *Psycho* gives us perhaps the clearest explanation as to why this should be the case.[36] Norman's father, we are told, died when the boy was still young, and so his death allowed Norman to live out the Oedipal fantasy of having his mother to himself, an attachment that lead to his intense jealousy when Norman's mother took another lover. But as Norman's mangled statement about "a boy's best friend" reveals, his relationship to his mother is based as much on wish-fulfillment as reality. To understand Norman it is essential to understand that his closeness to his mother is less the product of any real affection—or abuse—on her part than it is the result of his own pathological need (like Marnie's) for a love that neither was nor ever could be there.[37] And this is not, I have argued, so much a real need of a real person than a phantasmatic need expressed through works of art. As such, it is right to suggest, as I have already done, that the real "mother" in *Psycho* is not the shrewish figure of Norman's imagination but, rather, the young, desired figure of Marion Crane herself.

In her analysis of *Psycho* Barbara Creed seems to accept the idea that Norman's mother might have really been the threatening figure whose voice we hear throughout the second part of the film ("Mrs. Bates is a harsh moralist, a castrating maternal figure"), while I would emphasize the notion of the mother in Hitchcock as a pure phantasm of the son's repressed sexuality.[38] Norman's real mother was probably not as abusive as the figure we hear and hear about in the film, because the hallucinated voice we hear spitting out orders and insults is just as likely to be a phantasm of the rejection of Norman's desires as she is to be his real mother. Norman is trapped, just as Marnie is trapped, by a need for the mother's love that is so great that the love he imagines is matched by an equally fantastic persecuting "bad mother" who is merely the necessary repression of his unrealistic desires. This would lead us to the conclusion that, like Norman's mother, the mothers in films such as *Marnie* and *The Birds* are actually nightmarish projections of continued, unfulfilled desires. As in *Psycho,* the mothers in those films (Mrs. Edgar and Lydia Brenner, respectively) are not real figures but rather the hallucinated projections of their children and, since these children are the films' protagonists, of Hitchcock himself. Finally, we can now understand why Norman becomes so angry when Marion tries to take Norman's side in suggesting that he free himself from the shrewish figure and put her in a home. "If you love someone," Norman answers, "you can't do that." For if the persecuting shrew is just the voice of a son's forbidden love for his mother, warning him away, then the idea of freeing oneself from such persecution is almost as abhorrent as tolerating it. As Kaja Silverman notes in her brilliant study of the female voice in cinema: "The female voice figures centrally within these fantasies, often functioning as a lure drawing the male subject to destruction, or as a black hole where meaning drains out of the system."[39]

The Uncanny Mother

The word for the uncanny in Freud's famous essay—*das Unheimliche,* "(not) of the house,"—contains a reference to the "home" that is lost in the word's standard English translation.[40] And, although Freud mentions various species of that very particular sort of fear that accompanies the uncanny (severed limbs; déjà vu; mechanical dolls; the Doppelgänger; criminality; insanity, etc.) the house, and not just the haunted house, is the privileged site for that ambivalent joy/dread that is produced by the return of infantile thoughts and desires. If a talking doll is frightening to so many because it reminds us of a time in our childhood—a time spent in the home—when such projections were not repressed, then the house, the place where the child's infantile, narcissistic consciousness was first surpressed, is bound to be capable of eliciting uncanniness itself (the "haunted house") as well as lending its name to all other species of the same.[41]

It is significant that most of the action of the film that takes place in Norman's house takes place either in the bedrooms upstairs, in the basement "fruit cellar," or on the two intervening sets of stairs where, first, Arbogast is murdered by the mother who comes rushing out of her room and where, at the film's climax, a frenzied mother/Norman suddenly appears on the stairs leading down to the fruit cellar, the butcher knife waving madly above his head. Little occurs, then, on the main floor of the Bates family home, the place where, normally, the family meets together or with others outside the family (the "living room"). It is thus the "ungrounded" parts of the house that are important, the private places that are kept separate or even hidden from interpersonal or public view. The violence that occurs on the stairs leading to these spaces (as we have seen, a common pattern in Hitchcock's films) against those outsiders who are attempting to learn the hidden secrets of the house is further evidence that the house holds certain secrets that must be kept from public view. Finally, the fact that the house is on a rather steep hill overlooking the completely horizontal motel and its "officious" office is another indication of this same separation between the house and the outside world, for the house in toto contains "stairs" leading up to it that are then repeated within the house as well.

Lila's investigation of the two bedrooms upstairs, like Melanie Daniels's similarly useless investigation in *The Birds*, is all the more revealing because it yields practically nothing.[42] The only action that occurs turns out to be uneventful: Lila is startled by what turns out to be her own reflection in the mirror in Norman's mother's room. Even the sculpture of the "severed" hands

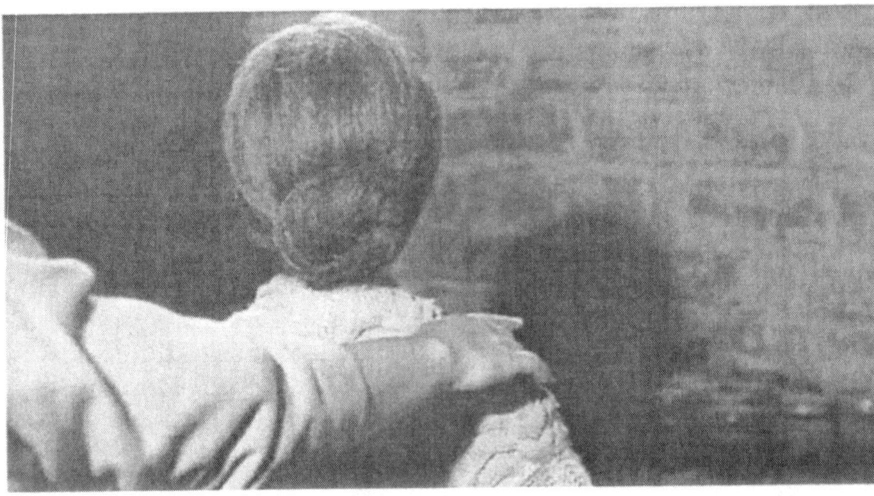

20. Lila (Vera Miles) about to face Norman's uncanny mother.

in Mrs. Bates's room, a potential source of uncanniness explicitly mentioned in Freud's essay on the same, is simply one more object in a typical parental bedroom. And yet, it is precisely the normalcy of the two bedrooms that makes the scene so effective. It is not what is contained in the bedrooms that is important but rather that, as bedrooms, they represent private, forbidden spaces that are not supposed to be entered. The bedrooms, like "haunted houses" in general, are only scary because they can be associated with the forbidden sexual acts, such as incest, which it is their duty to oppose.

The scene following this is as overtly horrifying as the former is not, but it is important to keep both scenes in mind when analyzing the scene in the fruit cellar. Indeed, we realize after seeing the terrifying corpse of Norman's mother smiling at us from its rocking chair that it is this horrifying cadaver that made the imprint in the mother's bedroom upstairs. But it is not the cadaver that Norman loves. The imprint suggests that the horrifying face was turned away from view as it is in the basement, and Norman's own impersonations of his mother mean that the cadaver is merely one device among others that he uses to keep his mother alive. In other words, Norman does not see the horrifying visage either, and he is probably just as terrified as Lila at the sight of his mother's corpse. The uncanniness here, like other species of the same, occurs when something which is most familiar—"of the house"—such as the mother herself or the human face in general (the latter doubtless having its basis in the former)—loses its familiarity and thus becomes especially frightening.

In the story *The Sandman,* which Freud uses to demonstrate the presence of the uncanny in art, the terrifying figure of Coppola/Coppelius is a "bad father" who kills Nathaniel's especially kind father and threatens to remove the boy's eyes because he has spied on the parent's nocturnal activities.[43] Norman, we recall, is also guilty of such voyeuristic spying, and this is also punished by a "bad mother" who likewise continually "castrates" her son by calling his manhood into question and generally browbeating him. This persecution, which, as we discussed earlier, only reflects Norman's Oedipal attraction, led to his first murdering and then becoming the mother as a way of regaining the affection he had been denied. The most prominent feature of the corpse's grotesque visage, the two empty eye sockets, is thus uncanny in the same way that the eye-taking Coppelius figure is uncanny: both represent the taboo against forbidden incestuous desire, sexuality "in the house," whose violation leads to the ultimate insanity of both Nathaniel and Norman.[44] If Norman lapses into psychosis and becomes his mother after looking into the eyeless eyes of her corpse it is because, in desiring his mother, he has seen what cannot be seen and so must, like Oedipus, go blind—if not literally, then figuratively through madness.

In the final scene of the film, just before the psychiatrist launches into his jargon ridden explanation of Norman's personality, the sheriff asks Lila a seemingly insignificant question (indeed, Lila herself looks at him as if to question why he asks this) that is as odd as it is fleeting: "Are you warm enough Miss?" The question only makes sense in relation to the request, received after the psychiatrist's explanation, by Norman (or rather, Norman's mother) for a blanket because (s)he is cold. The odd question creates a parallel between the only two women present: Lila Crane, Marion's sister, and Norman's mother. As such, we are reminded of the way this film, and indeed so many of Hitchcock's films, is dominated by one woman, the phantasm of a "clinging, demanding woman" who castrates her son or daughter and makes him (or her) all the more dependent on her affection. The horrifying uncanniness of this figure in *Psycho,* which returns in the fleeting glimpse of a death's head at the film's end, reminds us that what is most "of the house" is also "not of the house" because it is part of an infantile origin that is contained within each of us and is only as horrifying as it is repressed.[45]

21. "Norman's" mental dissolution into his mother is confirmed by this brief dissolve.

7
The End of the World: *The Birds*

22. The birds have the "last word" in Hitchcock's apocalyptic masterpiece.

> Ein Käfig ging ein Vogeln suchen.
>
> [A cage went looking for a bird.]
>
> —Kafka

IT IS A CURIOUS FACT OF CINEMA HISTORY THAT ALFRED HITCHcock's *The Birds* (1963) inaugurated the immensely popular subgenre of films in which a relatively benign force of nature turns against humanity in an unprecedented and even supernatural way. Spiders, bees, worms, wolves, and the much maligned shark have all taken their turn stalking an anxiety-ridden populace after Hitchcock released hoards of birds upon the sleepy little hamlet of Bodega Bay. This subgenre of the "science-fiction film," which might be compared to the earlier, more majestic forms of sublime erasures of the human beginning in the eighteenth century, is nonetheless markedly different in that *The Birds* is more about a human, family drama than it is about its sensational demonic presences.[1] It is interesting to compare *The Birds* to, say, *Jaws,* in order to see the obvious difference between the two films in this regard. (There is another odd connection to *Jaws:* the proprietor of the hardware store in the fishing village/resort town of Bodega Bay speaks with a distinctly New England accent!) It is also worth noting that all the characters of *The Birds,* and their drama, are original to Hitchcock's film and nonexistent in the du Maurier story which forms its basis. (However, as Ken Mogg has recently discovered, Hitchcock and the screenwriter Evan Hunter were in all likelihood also influenced by a novel by Frank Baker, *The Birds* [1936], in which "apart from the bird attacks themselves, both Baker's and Hitchcock's stories revolve around a grown-up man's relation to his widowed mother at a time of crisis, including the fact that he has just met a woman whom he may eventually marry.")[2] Indeed, it would not be far-fetched to invoke the oft-mentioned "MacGuffin" in considering the supernatural birds of *The Birds* as merely a means to accomplish the real subject of Hitchcock's romantic thriller, which is a son's difficulty in establishing a romantic relationship when he is unable to extricate himself from his mother and their family home in Bodega Bay, where the bird attacks take place. Perhaps it is this confusion regarding Hitchcock's true motive that has kept *The Birds* from assuming the position Hitchcock himself predicted it would hold as the apocalyptic masterpiece of the director's most creative period. Although preferences for particular films or for particular periods of Hitchcock's long and distinguished career are always precarious propositions, we have Hitchcock's own statement, which he made to Evan Hunter while planning *The Birds,* that he felt that "he was entering the golden age of his creativity and that *The Birds* would be his greatest achievement," a prediction with which the author of the present volume would happily concur.[3]

The Birds is essentially a psychological study of its main characters: the Brenner family and its eldest son Mitch's (Rod Taylor) affair with a young woman from San Francisco (Melanie Daniels, played exquisitely by the then unknown Tippi Hedren) who pursues Mitch to his family home in Bodega Bay. There waiting to confront Mitch's new love interest are his mother Lydia (Jessica Tandy) and the mistress he abandoned because of Lydia, Annie

Hayworth (Suzanne Pleshette). In fact, the birds follow Melanie Daniels in her pursuit of Mitch Brenner from San Francisco to Bodega Bay, and the first attack is directed only against her when she is about to meet her lover at the town's dock. Despite the marked tendency among critics of the film to deny any explanation to the birds' attacks, these attacks will be interpreted here as displaced symbols of the characters' unconscious motivations; in particular, they symbolize desires involving the hysterical mother Lydia and her displeasure with Mitch's new lover. Despite Žižek's ingenious "Lacanian" notion that the birds are not a symbol of the mother but a symbol of the symbol of the mother, Barbara Creed has recently written that

> Another fearful image of the monstrous-feminine in classical mythology is that of the harpy, a bird of prey with a woman's head and breasts, a large beak, hooked nails, a vile odour and and an insatiable appetite. Harpies abducted children and carried them into the underworld. The term is still in current usage. *Hitchcock draws connections between women and birds in a later film, The Birds, in which the birds may also be understood as fetish-objects, not of the castrated/phallic, but of the castrating mother.*[4] (italics mine)

The unreality of the birds' attacks is the reality of a Freudian unconscious that, paradoxically, can only represent itself through such species of the unreal. Although Malcom Turvey has recently argued that the psychoanalytical notion of responding to such repressed content is illogical, i.e., we are supposedly thinking about or feeling something we are not thinking about or feeling, this is not only a commonly accepted notion of psychoanalysis but, as Kant argued in his theory of the beautiful and the sublime (the latter is particularly important for any discussion of the horror genre), of aesthetics in general.[5]

Lee Edelman agrees with Robin Wood's assertion that "the film itself is quite insistent that either the birds can't be explained or that the explanation is unknown," although he seems undecided about such undecidability: "in so doing [denying the birds' meaning] it refuses as well to localize the contexts with which this very refusal of meaning takes place."[6] Likewise, Cameron and Jeffery agree with Penelope Houston, who "pointed out gleefully that almost any interpretation would fit *The Birds*."[7] Between the notions that there is no explanation for the birds' attacks, and that any explanation will do, there is a hermeneutical "middle ground" in which the unreality of the birds can be explained as manifestations of an unconscious that expresses itself indifferently with regard to any laws of objective reality. I agree with Margaret Horwitz's contention that "*The Birds* cannot be fully explained at a manifest level. . . . For this reason a psychoanalytic model is most appropriate," although, as I will explain later, I disagree with some of the particulars of her analysis, particularly her contention that the essential conflict in the film is between Melanie and Lydia.[8] We both agree, however, that those critics who fail to acknowledge the interpretability of the birds do so because they do not even try to see a relation between the "real" and "unreal" parts of the film that Hitchcock himself was careful to include, i.e., between the story of a dysfunctional family, replete with the stock Hitchcockian figure of the "nightmarish mother figure" (Rothman), and the birds that follow Melanie Daniels back to this same dysfunctional family's home.[9]

"Back in your gilded cage, Melanie Daniels"

In *The Dark Side of Genius* Donald Spoto recounts how Hitchcock discovered Tippi Hedren when he saw a television commercial in which "an attractive, elegant blond . . . passed across the screen and smiled, turning amiably in response to a little boy's wolf whistle."[10] Edelman, however, adds significantly to the information provided in Spoto's work by noting that the young boy who whistles in the commercial that caught Hitchcock's eye turns out to be the attractive blonde's son.[11] This (supposedly) lighthearted commercial, which is in a sense the beginning of *The Birds*, is included at the very beginning of the film. After a dapper Hitchcock is seen leaving the shop with two small white terriers on a leash (as if to emphasize the sort of chthonic control that the uncontrollable, unconscious forces of the film will gradually overwhelm), Melanie is whistled at by the young boy, at whom she first smiles before casting a worried look at the sky as a large, noisy flock of gulls passes overhead. Lee Edelman sees this brief encounter as "the egg from which the film emerges," and, in hermeneutic as well as psychoanalytic terms, this fleeting moment is all the more important because it is so seemingly insignificant.[12] Melanie, rather than looking annoyed at the young person's advances, is instead amused, and perhaps even

23. In a reprise of the television commercial in which Hitchcock discovered Tippi Hedren the actress is whistled at by a young boy.

flattered; but then, immediately after smiling at the boy, her troubled eyes turn upward to the film's first indication of the bird attacks to follow.

The boy's whistle is itself a "bird call," and so more than coincidentally related to the storm-driven gulls that divert Melanie's attention away from the boy, who had himself diverted her attention away from the shop. For through this fleeting moment—this cinematic parapraxis, if you will—we are already attuned to what our further analysis of the rest of the film will later confirm: attraction to the mother and the resultant repression of that attraction in the form of attacking birds. The film is indeed, as the drunken prophet of Bodega Bay declares, about "the end of the world," although this phrase should be heard in psychoanalytic rather than apocalyptic terms. For the incestuous desire of the boy for his mother, as Freud explains, is the crime that makes all other crimes noncrimes in relation to its constitutive force both for society at large as well as for the individual who recapitulates it.[13]

Once inside the store Melanie Daniels climbs the central staircase to the upper-level, where the aviary portion of the pet shop is located. The staircase foreshadows the end of the film, when Melanie climbs the stairs in the Brenner house only to find herself trapped in an upstairs room filled with birds, where the film's most ferocious attack occurs. So many of Hitchcock's films utilize staircases in this way (most memorably, the crane shot used to film Arbogast's murder in *Psycho*) that their symbolism must be questioned. As was discussed in the preceding chapter on *Psycho,* staircases commonly evoke a strong sense of danger for Hitchcock because they lead to a place where a terrible secret, terrible enough to be protected with violence, is preserved. Since it is always the family bedrooms that are contained at the top of the stairs, we have speculated that the staircases refer back to the "primal scene" of parental and/or incestuous sexuality, of sexuality that must be repressed at any cost. This is why the price to be paid for climbing such staircases in Hitchcock's work is always very high; as Michael Walker notes in his recent study of motifs in Hitchcock: "The sense that the source of the malevolence associated with the upper-level is so often a parent figure emphasizes that this is, at root, a childhood construction, often Oedipal in its overtones."[14]

What, then, happens when the staircase is here joined to an aviary where the first meeting between the two adult "love interests" of *The Birds* is about to take place?

Rather than the usual "courtship" or "mating ritual" in which lovers meet we are treated to a highly attenuated form of double deception in which, first, Melanie pretends to be a salesperson and, second, Mitch pretends not to know that she is pretending even though he recognized her almost immediately. Although both parties are involved in the game, it is important to note that it is Melanie who initiates the deception by first pretending to be the salesperson Mitch first mistakes her to be. This playfulness on her part is hardly an isolated incident. We hear throughout the film of numerous similar but more scandalous episodes in Melanie's past as well as ourselves witnessing Melanie's sneaking into the Brenner house in Bodega Bay, and her then lying to Mitch about visiting her "old friend" Annie Hayworth. Moreover, she is here in the pet shop to purchase a mynah bird that she plans to teach to swear in order to scandalize her Aunt! In a word, Melanie is a lawbreaker in much the same way that Eve Kendall, Marnie, and Marion are all lawbreakers: alluring women whose sexuality is associated with deceptive and illegal acts before being "tamed" (to use Mark Rutland's term in *Marnie*), although the end result of all these films suggest that such domestication is doomed to failure.

Melanie is not just pretending to be a salesperson, she is pretending to be a salesperson as a way of flirting with the handsome gentleman asking her for assistance. For Melanie, like her typological counterparts, sexuality is immediately placed into the context of illicit activity, the implications of which for this and the other films belie the seeming innocence of this scene. For *The Birds* is a film about the transference of illicit sexual desire into the nightmarish, castrating form of thousands of vengeful birds intent on plucking the eyes out of their victims,. The fact that Melanie Daniels's flirtatious deception quickly turns into a rather ugly, angry exchange between the two future lovers is also important, for it is a tamer part of a larger world of psychosexual violence from which our two "lovebirds" are certainly not immune.

It is hardly a hermeneutical "stretch" to claim that the birds in this film are primarily associated with women, and with Melanie Daniels in particular. "Birds," in the 1960s Anglo-American parlance with which Hitchcock was no doubt familiar, referred exclusively to sexy young women. The very first shot of Melanie Daniels crossing the San Francisco street into the pet shop emphasizes the sort of extremely high heels that make their wearer considerably less "earth-bound." Melanie's hair, whose tightly wrapped bun is a typological feature in Hitchcock's films, is decidedly crest-like, and its color resembles that of the canary to which Mitch explicitly likens her: "Back into your cage, Melanie Daniels." In the sequence in which this canary escapes Melanie and the shopkeeper react hysterically to the escaped bird, but it is important to keep in mind that, according to Mitch, the escaped bird is Melanie herself. The pet shop scene, then, in which the bird-like Miss Daniels demonstrates her own deceptive sexual desires, and in which she escapes from "her" cage, is less a foreshadowing of the rest of the film than the rest of the film is a muted "postshadowing" of the deceptive and sexually aggressive interplay between the film's two "lovebirds," and of the larger violence that underlies this charming but disturbing scene.

The caged lovebirds that Melanie purchases to take to Mitch are present throughout *The Birds*, culminating in the odd moment at the end of the film when the little girl Cathy asks that she be allowed to bring the lovebirds with the family since "they haven't harmed anyone." Indeed, in their caged condition, which, according to Melanie, is necessary to "protect the species," they couldn't. One recalls here Freud's discussion of "copulation for the purposes of reproduction" as a means of controlling the numerous forms of "perverse," aggressive sexuality that are magnified forms of an omnipresent, polymorphous infantile sexuality, including the child's continued desire for the mother.[15] The caged lovebirds, then, are just that: the repressed form of sexuality typified by the adult marriage "contract" that is vastly outnumbered by our wilder, more perverse unconscious desires that dominate both the family and these lovebirds, which are last seen caged in Melanie's tiny sports car.

The end of the film is a neat inversion of the opening pet shop scene, for now the lovers and the caged lovebirds are themselves caged while the sea of birds are staring in at them threateningly from outside. This ending, like many of the other decidedly un-"happy endings" in Hitchcock's films discussed throughout this book, demonstrates Hitchcock's (and Freud's) view of marriage as at best a troubled repression of the unconscious and its infantile desires. Melanie Daniels—and everyone else, for that matter—may indeed be placed "back in her cage" at the end of the film, but the ominous cackling of the thousands of uncaged birds with which she is associated suggests otherwise. Camille Paglia is right that *The Birds* is about "a war between nature and culture, with the irrational and primitive vanquishing human illusions," but the irrational is not nature, it is civilization's own "discontents."[16] Ken Mogg is also correct in referring to the force behind *The Birds* and other Hitchcock films as the Schopenhauerian "Will," but, as Mogg himself admits, that notion is highly compatible with what I am analyzing here in more specific terms as the Freudian unconscious.[17]

Annie Hayworth

Annie Hayworth (Suzanne Pleshette) is a very different sort of woman from Melanie Daniels both visually as well as temperamentally, but the difference is one of a related opposition that signals a fundamental unity.[18] As is the case for Judy Barton in *Vertigo,* and Lil (Diane Baker) in *Marnie,* Annie is a love interest scorned by the male protagonist of the film who continues to offer herself despite the male's clear preference for the other, fair-haired woman he is eagerly pursuing. Whereas Melanie, in her first meeting with Annie, is neatly dressed in a long fur coat with her hair tied up and tightly bound in the familiar Hitchcockian manner, and wearing the aforementioned high heels, Annie Hayworth, whose dark hair is always hanging loose, is casually dressed. When we first see her Annie is wearing jeans and a sweater and is somewhat "soiled" from working in her garden (note, also, Marnie's elevated position in this still). The contrast with the more elegantly dressed and refined Melanie couldn't be clearer, and as their relationship develops the interactions between the two continue to demonstrate Annie's "earthier" personality: she smokes and drinks a great deal and, most importantly, is very frank and open in discussing her earlier affair with Mitch and her continued interest in him, and in demonstrating her jealousy toward Melanie. Like Marnie's relationship to Lil, Melanie, on the other hand, is utterly indifferent to her dark-haired rival, and is as reluctant to speak openly as Annie is candid to the point of being blunt.

In his essay on "A Special Type of Object-Choice Made by Men" Freud discusses what would later be called the "Madonna-Whore Complex":

> The second condition of love, that of the "loose" character of the object chosen, seems on the other hand to stand in sharp opposition to a derivation from the mother complex. The grown man's conscious

24. The "Harlot" Annie (Suzanne Pleshette) and the "Madonna" Melanie (Tippi Hedren) meet.

> mind likes to regard the mother as a personification of impeccable moral purity, and few suggestions from without are so insulting, or from within so painful, as those which cast doubt on the mother's character in this respect. This very relation, however, of sharpest possible contrast between the "mother" and the "harlot," would prompt us to study the developmental history of the two complexes and unconscious relation between them, since we long ago discovered that a thing which in consciousness makes its appearance as two contraries is often in the unconscious a united whole.[19]

While Michael Walker's excellent recent study notes the persistence of certain types of women in Hitchcock, as well as the pattern of their hairstyles and colors, it is through Freud's brilliant and groundbreaking analysis of this syndrome that we can understand the prevalence of a certain "object choice" made by the film's male protagonists.[20] In Freud's analysis, the opposition between the two types of women and the particular choice made of the fair-haired female must be understood in terms of a continued mother complex. *The Birds* confirms Freud's theory by not only including the mother figure herself as a strong presence in the film but in having both women demonstrate, very explicitly, the continued importance of Lydia in Mitch's life. Annie Hayworth clearly states, in an otherwise highly equivocal conversation with Melanie, that Lydia was behind the breakup with her son. Melanie herself later states that her success with Mitch depends on Lydia, a view that is confirmed in the film's finale when the badly wounded Melanie is comforted and held in the backseat of her sports car by a still-dominant Lydia. (As I discuss later, Žižek argues for a successful resolution of the conflict with this "Oedipal mother" that is, I believe, belied by the end and the other events of the film.)

Freud helps us to understand why Mitch's mother complex causes him to reject the sensual dark-haired Annie and to pursue the more elegant fair-haired Melanie. For if Mitch is still ultimately under the sway of his mother (he returns weekly to Bodega Bay to spend time with her), he must court a "loose woman" whose overt sensuality distinguishes her from the idealized mother but whose very "looseness" will result in her rejection as a scorned woman who proves unacceptable. Melanie, on the other hand, whose repressed elegance makes her a more acceptable figure to Lydia, reveals Mitch's need to reject Annie and retain the idealized, fair-haired maternal imago. However this preference, caught as it is between the maternal and the sensual, is hardly a solution to Mitch's problems at Bodega Bay, as the birds' attacks that follow Melanie there quickly confirm. And, when the family and the bloodied Melanie leave the Brenner home at the ending of the film it is hardly a victory over Mitch's continuing incestuous need for a mother figure, or for an antimother figure who is thus still a mother figure. As such, the film joins a host of other Hitchcock films whose endings clearly—or cleverly—belie Hollywood's insistence on the typical "happy ending" in lieu of Hitchcock's deeper fascination with the persistence of an incestuous unconscious that can not be resolved.

Also left behind after the family's departure is the dead body of Annie, sprawled in front of her home in an unseemly manner after having heroically rescued Mitch's sister Cathy from the birds' attack. That Annie is dead, and Melanie badly maimed, attests to the fact that both desired objects of the "Madonna-whore complex" must be repressed by the "incest-taboo" that creates and continues to surround them. Moreover, Annie's role as a schoolteacher who died saving one of her "children" is particularly telling in this regard. As a schoolteacher she represents a surrogate mother for Cathy and the other children, not to mention the fact that she became a schoolteacher in Bodega Bay because of her desire to become a mother to Cathy and a wife to Mitch. Her death, then, is the logical culmination of her role as the "loose woman" who must be killed despite any act of repentance for her "loose" behavior—just as Marion *Crane* must be killed in *Psycho* despite her decision to return the stolen forty-thousand dollars, and Judy Barton must be killed despite her protestations of love for Scottie in *Vertigo.* While Edelman argues for the importance of the birds' attacks on children in the film ("they seem to display a strong predilection for children"), I would maintain that children in Hitchcock's films are only significant as the representations of the origin of the complexes and neuroses of the adult characters and their attachment to or representation of the mother figures in the films.[21]

MITCH

Perhaps the most noticeable but also easily overlooked part of Mitch Brenner's character (or, rather, "character type") is the aggression he displays in the first half of the film toward Melanie

Daniels as part of their courtship. We have already noted how, in the first scene, Mitch not only deceives Melanie into thinking he doesn't know who she really is but he then goes on to insult her as a criminal who should be behind bars. In an even more aggressive exchange that occurs at the conclusion of the family dinner that he insisted she attend he not only cross-examines her about her past but also refuses to believe her explanations about the various scandalous incidents he recounts. The violence of these scenes, which should be compared to the hostile conversations between the two lovers at the beginning of *Rear Window*, goes far beyond the playful bantering that often occurs as part of flirting, and so can be interpreted in the light of other aspects of Mitch's character and behavior in the rest of the film.

Mitch, we are told, spends every weekend at his family home in Bodega Bay with his mother and a sister (Veronica Cartwright) who is young enough to be his daughter. As we mentioned, he abandoned Annie Hayworth, the only woman we know he was involved with because his mother disapproved: "Maybe there's never been anything between Mitch and any girl." Now we find Mitch with a new girlfriend who closely, very closely in fact, resembles his mother, all of which helps us to understand the violence of Mitch's assaults upon Melanie as the result of an attraction to a mother figure that must also be repressed. Mitch denigrates Melanie because his feelings for her are based on a mother complex that results in his oscillation between moments of overt hostility in which she is condemned and moments of extreme tenderness (note the phone call to Melanie at Annie's immediately after his fight) in which his repressed affection is allowed to return.

Hitchcock is not much interested, here or elsewhere, in perpetuating the popular Hollywood stereotype of the strong male hero. One cannot readily ignore the fact that in *Marnie*, for example, Sean Connery first assaults and later rapes a nearly catatonic Marnie. Here Rod Taylor, whose close physical resemblance to Connery suggests a typological connection that is confirmed by a comparison of the two films, demonstrates the same sort of hostility and less than heroic stature. In a very telling scene Mitch picks up a rock to throw at the birds that have just pecked his former girlfriend, Annie Hayworth, to death. Melanie has to stop him, knowing that the heroic gesture would not only prove futile but probably also get them all—Mitch, Melanie, and Cathy

—killed. If anyone is the hero in this scene it is Melanie, who saves them all by stopping Mitch from his false heroics. All the male figures in Hitchcock's films are incapable of such heroics because heroics depend, as Freud explains in "The Poet and Daydreaming," on the successful resolution of the Oedipal complex that ends in a "happy marriage," something that Hitchcock's films either overtly deny or, at the least, ironically subvert.[22]

Lydia

As mentioned earlier, there is an extraordinary physical resemblance between Lydia (played by Jessica Tandy) and Melanie, which Hitchcock makes even more apparent by frequently framing the two in shots which emphasize their symmetry.[23]

Margaret Horwitz is one of the few to discuss this resemblance at any length, although she interprets the resemblance in terms of a "rivalry" between mother and daughter rather than considering, as the too-close physical resemblance would suggest, how the two figures are really one projection by the son who, as the below still reveals, stands before them both.[24] (Modleski, like Horwitz, considers the resemblance as leading to "the suspicion that the mother/daughter relationship is actually what is being

25. One of many images demonstrating the close physical resemblance between the mother (Jessica Tandy) and the rival (Tippi Hedren) for her son's (Rod Taylor) affection.

evoked.")[25] Not only does Lydia wear her hair up in the same style as Melanie, but the viewer is also struck by their similar facial features and body types; indeed, Lydia could easily *be* Melanie thirty years later. Seemingly contradicting the resemblance between the two women is Lydia's instant dislike of Mitch's new love interest. However, because of the mother complex that we have seen running throughout Hitchcock's films, it is not difficult to resolve the contradiction between Lydia's resemblance to and antipathy for Melanie Daniels. If, as we suggested earlier, Mitch chooses Melanie over Annie because she is closer to the more idealized (and repressed) image of his mother, this means that Lydia must recognize in Melanie a figure who both resembles her as well as being meant to replace her. The resemblance, unlike other "normal" replacements of the mother, is so close that the substitution cannot but anger the woman who is clearly the real object of Mitch's affection. This contradiction also explains why the figure of the "loose woman" should reappear in Melanie, despite her opposition to the less ambiguously "loose woman" of the film, Annie. Mitch's interest in the notoriously "loose woman" whom the newspapers reported as having swum naked in a fountain in Rome is caused by his own transgressive interest in his mother. However, the fact that Melanie takes great pains to refute, at every opportunity, such scandals as the Rome incident or the one that landed her in court when Mitch was there means that she, unlike Annie, is capable of synthesizing both poles of the aforementioned "Madonna/harlot complex," which is why her name contains both "Annie's" as well as the typical "M-" found in many of Hitchcock's "leading ladies."

If, as Freud maintained, the unconscious is essentially bisexual, this may explain why Hitchcock slips so easily between male and female protagonists in his films' explorations of unconscious reality.[26] Overt concerns with "female sexuality" in films such as *Marnie* (as well as in his use of du Maurier's work) are not, pace Modleski, indications of any feminist inclinations on Hitchcock's part but rather representative of an androgynous or, to use Samuels's recent work, "bitextual" unconscious reality which it is the goal of Hitchcock's genius to explore.[27] A conversation with Mitch, for example, takes on odd turn when Melanie talks about her own mother. Odd because we witness Melanie break down crying, uncharacteristically and with no seeming relevance to the film's plot, when she tells Mitch that her own mother abandoned her and her father when she was young, and continues to refuse to see her. In an effort to compose herself Melanie asks Mitch if he knows what a mother's love is, to which Mitch replies yes, he does. As we shall see, the same mother complex that determines Mitch's incestuous object choices is also manifested in Melanie's own need for maternal love from Lydia. One might also note that the dialogue for this entire scene in which Melanie talks, for the only time, about her lost mother was hastily written by Hitchcock himself.[28]

Mitch's brief comment to Melanie about the importance of a mother's love, although far less dramatic than Melanie's previous tirade, is equally important. It confirms our suspicions that his weekly trips to his home in Bodega Bay are more than filial piety, but rather part of his continued reliance on and concern for Lydia (note Annie's comment to Melanie: "Maybe there's never been anything between Mitch and any girl"). The story of Melanie's abandonment is just the other side of the coin, for it reveals the traumatic effects of losing a mother, which Mitch is trying to avoid: Mitch+Lydia=Melanie-(her own)Mother. Analysis of the scene in which Melanie serves Lydia tea will confirm our sense of Lydia's importance as the focus of the film, and as the very figure responsible for the attacks on Mitch, Melanie, Annie, Cathy, and the other children and citizenry of Bodega Bay.

Lydia makes a number of confessions to Melanie in this scene, while the latter functions almost as an analyst in adding little to the conversation and saying nothing about herself. Indeed, the patient/analyst scenario is further evident in the way Lydia is lying on her bed, with Melanie standing or sitting beside her. First, Lydia admits to not knowing if she likes Melanie. Melanie responds by again asking if this is really so important, but we know from another comment she made to Annie that Melanie does think it important, both for her relationship with Mitch but, more importantly, for her own feelings of abandonment by her mother. The fact that Lydia refers frequently in this scene to her own fears of abandonment, coupled with Mitch's weekly visits to Bodega Bay in order to assuage such fears, helps us to realize that *The Birds* is essentially a film about abandonment. Or, more precisely, about unfulfilled desire for a mother's love that can only return here in the form of phallic, castrating birds/breasts that both represent and deny the "lost love object": "the birds may also be understood as fetish objects, not of the castrated/phallic, but of the castrating mother."[29] Lydia frequently interrupts her conversation with Melanie with concern for Cathy, who is at school; is she safe? will the birds attack her there? won't Melanie go and get her? Although these fears are later confirmed, they seem oddly unwarranted coming as they do abruptly in the midst of her own discussion of her fears of abandonment. But we now realize that, if Lydia's maternal fears of abandonment, and Melanie's own continued trauma over her actual abandonment, and Mitch's desire to maintain his relationship with his mother, are all being enacted through the attack of the phallic/castrating breast/birds, then Lydia's non sequiturs are in fact causally, and not just casually, linked to her fears for Cathy's safety.

Lydia also confesses, in her conversation with Melanie, that she cannot really relate to children on their level, something which, according to Lydia, her deceased husband did easily. Lydia cannot relate to Cathy as a mother at all, a position that is quickly filled by Melanie, who both embraces and is embraced by the child who really should be her daughter given both her relationship with Mitch as well as the obvious fact that Lydia looks and acts much more like a grandmother than a mother for Cathy. What Lydia's comment, and the rest of the film, really means is that Lydia is not, and never has been, a mother for her children. (Note, however, the point made numerous times in this volume that such figures are phantasms of the "original mother" and so not to be taken literally.) The birds' attack is an attack by the mother who abandoned Melanie, by Lydia, and by all the mothers in Hitchcock's films who represent the desire for a mother's love that, when denied, turns into a violent attack by the very object of one's desires.

Finally, although we began our discussion of this "tea ceremony" by noting the resemblance to the patient/analyst relationship, we must now place this scene in its more fitting context: that of the child who serves its mother food in an effort to obtain the mother's lost affection. *Marnie* presents numerous instances of this, as do other Hitchcock's films, such as *Rear Window,* where Thorwald is seen serving his nagging, invalid wife in bed, *Psycho,* and *Frenzy.* Typically it is the mother who nurtures and attends to its beloved offspring, but, in Hitchcock's films, this reversal is more common, and is evidence of a traumatic "weaning" whose loss has never been overcome, and which continues to haunt its victims and the violent acts of retribution that are the focal point of all these films.

MELANIE

We have already noted how Mel-anie contains within her both the "looseness" associated with Annie (and with the "harlot" half of the "Madonna/whore" complex) as well as her resemblance to the repressed, idealized mother Lydia. Since both halves of this complex are determined by each other, neither is true, and the supposed sexlessness of the mother is, in reality, merely the result of the need to repress one's incestuous desires. Similarly, the looseness of the "harlot" is merely the "repression of the repression" of the mother's idealized purity. There are numerous instances of this complex in other Hitchcock films, such as *Psycho,* where Marion Crane insists on the respectability of marriage to Sam Loomis while continuing to meet him in cheap hotel rooms during lunch and then stealing forty thousand dollars in order to attain the desired respectability with Sam. This contradiction is apparent here in the way Melanie Daniels insists upon having a respectable relationship with Mitch despite her scandalous, criminal past but, all the while, pursuing Mitch to Bodega Bay, breaking into his house, lying about knowing Annie, etc. "That may have been good enough then, but it's not good enough now" she explains to Mitch in language that distinctly echoes that of Marion in *Psycho.* This combination of criminality and respectability is the result of the mother complex that dominates these films, that is, the forbidden/repressed attraction to the mother that splits into the desire for a "loose woman" whose criminality represents the transgressive, incestuous desire for the mother and for a respectable woman who rejects/represses, even violently, such illicit activity.

In a now legendary scene that occurs at the end of the film (legendary because, among other things, of the considerable abuse inflicted upon Tippi Hedren during its filming) Melanie, awakened by a sound upstairs, climbs the staircase of the Brenner to enter an attic room where she is brutally attacked by a hoard of waiting birds.[30] The scene has a very dream-like, Pandora-esque quality, for the rest of the family is sleeping while Melanie is awaked and drawn, as if by some irresistible impulse, to explore the noise upstairs. Adding to the dream-like, irrational quality of the scene is the fact that, if Melanie really did believe the birds had entered the house, investigating the noise alone would be the last thing she would do given all the attacks that have occurred before.

We have already had occasion, in discussing the opening scene in the pet shop, to mention the importance of staircases in Hitchcock's films (*Notorious, Shadow of a Doubt, Vertigo, Marnie,* to mention a few) as topographical symbols of the violent penetration into repressed, forbidden "primal" spaces.[31] Since Melanie is driven more by curiosity than anything else in going upstairs, and since this curiosity is illogical in terms of the manifest content of the film, we can understand her actions as a sort of "primal scene" in which the child opens the forbidden door of its parents' bedroom. (As was mentioned in our discussion of *Psycho,* there is a similar scene in E. T. A. Hoffmann's *The Sandman,* where Nathaniel first confronts the horrifying figure of the Sandman when spying on his father.) In this case, Melanie's childlike curiosity is compounded by her need to regain the lost affection of her mother. In either case, the breast-like birds, which are now armed with phallic beaks signaling the repression of the incest taboo and of any such return to the mother, are waiting to confirm the repression/hostility of the mother that has been evident throughout the film.

In the final scene of the film the bloody, wounded and hysterically speechless Melanie is cradled in the arms of Lydia as the family slowly drives away from the sea of birds that have engulfed their family home. As I argued in the introduction and throughout this book, one should resist the temptation to interpret the endings of Hitchcock's films as other than ironically optimistic. "So almost all Hitchcock's films end on an uncertain image, from the new lovers in *The Pleasure Garden* to the mass of abiding doom at the end of *The Birds.*"[32] McElhaney, too, supports Yacowar's notion regarding the ambiguous lack of resolution with *The Birds,* while George Toles finds some hope in the mother/daughter embrace: "At the end of *The Birds,* a somehow suspect, becalmed mother and traumatized "almost" daughter effect a dazed, reconciling embrace as the vehicle which contains them slowly moves through a bird-covered, spectral landscape."[33]

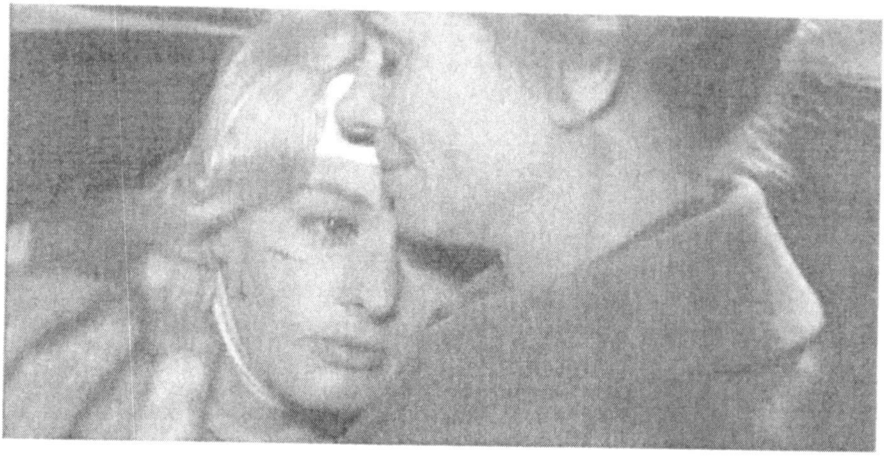

26. The mother's (Jessica Tandy) triumphant embrace of her wounded rival (Tippi Hedren).

Among many examples contradicting the notion of a "happy ending," and Žižek's assertion that "at the very end of the film, Mitch's mother 'accepts' Melanie as her son's wife, gives her consent, and abandons her super-ego role (as indicated by the fleeting smile she and Melanie exchange in the car)" is the fact that, just before entering the car it was Lydia who questioned Mitch's demand that Melanie be taken immediately to the hospital.[34] Far from upbeat, one should interpret Lydia's smile as she cradles the bloodied Melanie in her lap as part and parcel of the cackling crows and other birds that have proven victorious in the end. Like them, and like Norman's mother in *Psycho,* Lydia too has succeeded in thwarting her son's attempt to replace the mother that he will never have. In this sense I agree with Margaret Horwitz, who argues that as always happens, more or less literally, in Hitchcock the rivalry between the mother and the love interest has been decisively won by the former.[35] For the nurturing maternal breast, the "original love object," has become the omnipresent castrating bird that excludes all from the very object, the original archetype, of one's desires. In the words of the drunken prophet of Bodega Bay, the birds' attack is indeed "the end of a world" whose beginning is always sought, but necessarily lost forever.

8
A Mother's Love: *Marnie*

"You don't know the whole story; and nobody knows but me."

—Marnie's mother, Mrs. Edgar

In her essay on "Early Stages of the Oedipus Conflict" (1928), the Freudian psychoanalyst Melanie Klein considered one of the female equivalents of castration anxiety as "the girl's fear of having the inside of her body robbed and destroyed," a fear that is itself based on the desire to rob the mother of the objects contained within her body.[1] The very first word spoken in Hitchcock's *Marnie,* "Robbed!, refers to the most recent in a series of thefts from male businessmen, like Strutt and Rutland (their similar names betray other resemblances which will be analyzed later), by a frigid young woman whose main purpose in stealing money is less to acquire wealth herself than to win her mother's love. A propos Klein's comment, it is also worth noting that, in both thefts just mentioned, the money is taken from large, human-sized safes.

The following Freudian analysis will argue that the "whole story" of *Marnie* is revealed, *in nuce,* in those crucial moments of the film in which Marnie repeatedly kneels alongside her mother and tries, unsuccessfully, to rest her head on her mother's lap. Whether one interprets such moments in Freudian terms as the child's desire to regain the mother's love or in Kleinian terms as compensation for aggression against the mother who possesses what the daughter desires to possess for herself, a psychoanalytical interpretation of the film will eschew the "manifest" explanation proffered at the end of Marnie's heroic defense of her mother against a male villain. (This "recovered memory," which was described by the original screenwriter Evan Hunter as a patently false "screen memory," is dubious for a number of reasons to be discussed later.)[2] For Marnie's troubled relationship to the mother is primary, whereas the story of the sailor's attack—if that is what it was—is a "secondary revision" that fails to account for the search for a mother's love that permeates the entire film, as it does the entire Hitchcock oeuvre. As E. Ann Kaplan has written: "Marnie's terror is linked to a desperate need for the mother . . . felt also by Hitchcock," although, following Mulvey, Kaplan overstates the role of "patriarchal" power in the film.[3] In Hitchcock's preceding film, *The Birds,* there is a telling moment, understandably ignored in most interpretations of the film because of the first major bird attack that interrupts it, in which Melanie breaks down when telling Mitch about her mother's abandonment of her family. "You know what a mother's love is?" she tearfully asks. To which Mitch replies, as if startled by the strangeness of the question, "Yes I do." This scene, according to Spoto and others, was entirely rewritten by Hitchcock himself.[4]

The Purse

In the stunningly quiet opening scene of Hitchcock's *Marnie* (1964) the only sound is the clicking of a woman's high heels as she walks along the concrete platform of a deserted railroad station. The dark-haired female is seen only from behind, but the camera's close-up lingers on her bright, canary-yellow purse.

The dark hair will also soon turn to blonde when Marnie prepares for another con job, which again involves working as a secretary long enough to find a way to learn the combination of the company safe. Marnie's "m.o." is thus not unlike the theft of forty thousand dollars stolen by Marion Crane from her boss in *Psycho*—indeed, Marnie uses the pseudonym of *Marion* Holland for this particular heist.[5] Hitchcock's use of the same name and the comparable acts of stealing from the "officious," "stuffy" offices (as Norman Bates and Uncle Charlie, respectively, refer to them) where they work are indicative of a more profound similarity between these two Marions. For both women perversely steal in order to gain a respectability that will thus forever elude them. We will return to such comparisons between *Marnie* and

27. A rare "vaginal" symbol!

other of Hitchcock's films, such as *Psycho* and *Shadow of a Doubt,* later in this chapter. But for the moment our attention, like Hitchcock's camera, is drawn to Marnie's canary-yellow purse.

Although the symbolism seems quite obvious, critics of the film have frequently ignored this vaginal—or more correctly, vulval—image. For example, Cameron/Jeffery note only that the first shot is of "Marnie's conspicuously yellow handbag full of money forming a lozenge shape on the screen"; nor is it mentioned in the excellent article on the film (to which I shall refer numerous times in this essay) by Joseph McElhaney, "Touching the Surface: Marnie, Melodrama, Modernism." Even Bellour, who analyzes the same shot included here three times, (the shot actually occurs twice, being repeated shortly thereafter when Marnie goes to her hotel room) nowhere mentions its symbolism.[6] Nonetheless, even for the non-psychoanalytically inclined the purse will appear distinctly vaginal, and the fact that, as we soon learn, it is stuffed with the $9,967 that Marnie has just stolen only makes the sexual symbolism clearer. For, as we soon learn, Marnie is a frigid kleptomaniac, someone who steals from men rather than having sex with them. When the advances of her next boss Mark Rutland (Sean Connery) become particularly intense, this serves only to hasten the operation, and even later, after they are married, she prefers to steal what is now her own money from the large company safe than to have sex with her own husband. As Alexander Walker states in a review of the film, which is all the more remarkable for being contemporary with the first release, "And what are you to do when the only love interest in the film is the gratification that Marnie gets opening a safe door and fondling the dollar bills?"[7] The opening shot of the bulging vaginal yellow purse, then, is a wonderfully succinct way for Hitchcock to begin his psychosexual study of an otherwise respectable young woman who substitutes her ill-gotten gains for sexual satisfaction. But the opening shot, blatant as it may be to some, should also caution us against assuming that we already know "the whole story" about Marnie. Although the vaginal purse is clear evidence of the "psychological" nature of Hitchcock's film, the larger meaning of *Marnie,* involving as it does questions regarding Marnie's troubled relationship to her mother, is anything but clear.[8]

The Two Visits

Before beginning her next "heist" Marnie first performs two tasks that we can assume form something of a ritual that the young woman performs compulsively after each theft. First, flush with the excitement of her ill-gotten gains, Marnie goes to a stable where she rides her beloved horse Forio, whom she boards there. Second, Marnie returns to Baltimore to see her mother, Mrs. Edgar, to whom she gives gifts purchased with the money she has just stolen (recall Uncle Charlie's similar behavior in *Shadow of a Doubt*). Both of these actions, as we shall see, are manifestations of the pathological condition that causes Marnie to steal, and so are important clues in understanding both the compulsion to steal as well as the underlying state of Marnie's mental health.

Although the triple allusion to Mrs. Bernice Edgar's home in Baltimore is to Poe (an allusion surprisingly overlooked by many otherwise detailed discussions of the film, such as Moral's *Hitchcock and the Making of Marnie*), the situation encountered there is far more typical of the grotesque mother-child relations found throughout Hitchcock's own works.[9] Indeed, the nursery-rhyme that the children are singing in the street as Marnie exits her taxi, and that is repeated at the very end of the film, is a frighteningly apt description of Marnie's sickness, of her relationship to her mother as well as to the aforementioned purse:

> Mother Mother I am ill
> Call for the Doctor over the hill
> Call for the Doctor,
> Call for the Nurse,
> Call for the lady with the alligator purse . . .

Like the fairy tales that Freud explicitly describes as representative of an infantile consciousness that never fully escapes us, the nursery rhyme here reminds us of the importance of childhood in understanding the cause of Marnie's present condition.[10] Although, as we have seen throughout this work, mother complexes are commonplace in Hitchcock's films, *Marnie* is perhaps the most explicit of Hitchcock's films in sustaining Freud's view of childhood and of childhood's dependence on the mother. I will argue at the end of this chapter that Hitchcock's greater explicitness on this matter here may be why the film met with such a decidedly cold reception.

Marnie's own infantile behavior is made clear when the little girl who is visiting Marnie's mother answers the door. Jesse is evidently a frequent visitor, for Marnie has already acquired a deep dislike for the child who has taken her place at her mother's feet. Literally, because when Marnie tries to kneel down at her mother's feet and to lay her head in Mrs. Edgar's lap she is rebuffed ("Marnie, mind my my leg."), whereas Jesse is allowed just the sort of affection which Marnie is denied.

Marnie is not, it seems, unjustified in the resentment she feels for the other little girl, for Mrs. Edgar treats Jesse much better than she does Marnie, and knows exactly the sort of effect her announcement to Marnie that she is thinking of having Jesse and her mother move in with her will have on her daughter. Michael Walker notes that "whereas Mrs Edgar is quick to criticize Marnie she is kind and indulgent towards Jessie," but does not see how Jesse, who has no relation to the "plot" of the film, is clearly not a character in her own right, but is merely present in this scene in order to reveal Marnie's own infantile relationship with her mother.[11] We recall the moment, discussed earlier, when Melanie Daniels in *The Birds* unexpectedly breaks down when telling Mitch about how her mother abandoned her when she was a

28. Marnie's mother (Louise Latham) gives her rival the affectionate attention she desperately craves herself.

child. In all these cases we are dealing with the lack of a mother's love and affection and the traumatic effect it continues to have upon the grown-up child. The blame for Marnie's condition is placed squarely at her mother's feet, and the rather obnoxious presence of the "other daughter" Jesse is merely a projection of the resentment Marnie feels due to her mother's rejection; in other words, Marnie's own rejection is realized in the nightmarish phantasm of the other little girl's acceptance (in Winnicottian terms, the good mother/bad mother is represented here by the good daughter/bad daughter).[12] As such, this scene will support our contention that the other, more manifest explanation of the mother's rejection given later in the film (the murder of the mother's lover-client) is nowhere near "the whole story" about Marnie, but is rather the "screen memory" of Mrs. Edgar's rejection of her daughter and Marnie's resultant jealousy and obsession with regaining her mother's love.

The gift that Marnie presents her mother, a mink stole, is significant in a number of ways. Again we are reminded of a parallel between this gift-giving and *Shadow of a Doubt*, where Uncle Charlie, the "Merry Widow murderer," presents his motherly sister Emma with a similar mink. In that film we learn that the "stolen stole" belonged, like the other gifts he bestows upon the female members of the Newton family, to a widow whom he had married and eventually strangled. This is symbolized by the stole itself, which is constituted by a mink (no gentle creature), its head and feet intact, wrapped around the throat of its wearer. This does not mean, however, that either Marnie or Uncle Charlie is consciously hostile to the mother figures upon whom they are bestowing their larcenous largesse. Indeed, both characters are so eager to please their "mothers" and win their love that we can assume that any desire to strangle them would only be implied by the fact that, in both cases, their maternal love-objects can only be stolen, since to love them would violate not only a law but, as Freud insists, the law of laws.[13] Both Norman Bates and Uncles Charlie reveal, moreover, that this homicidal solution is not an unlikely alternative. Marnie, as we know from her childhood as well as from a comment she makes to her husband, is not incapable of killing anyone who comes between her and her mother; such jealousy could easily turn against Jesse, Mark, or even (as in *Shadow of a Doubt* and *Psycho*) against Marnie's mother herself. As Michael Walker has recently noted, "One senses that Marnie also feels an unconscious hostility—masked by an anxious seeking of love and approval—directed at Bernice."[14]

This rage is also indicated in the visually stunning scenes, scattered thoughout *Marnie* like the flashback of dancing couples that is interspersed throughout *Shadow of a Doubt,* when the entire screen is drenched in red as a result of something Marnie sees that reminds her of blood. The "manifest content" of the film, that is, the film's own overt explanation, would explain this solely as flashbacks to Marnie's murder of the sailor who was having sex with Marnie's mother. But as we have already begun to question this explanation as substituting an effect of Marnie's traumatic relationship with her mother for the cause of her neurosis, so we must also question this explanation of the famous "red diffusion" (Moral, *Making of Marnie*). When Kaja Silverman notes, in *The Acoustic Mirror,* that "The female subject's gaze is depicted as partial, flawed . . . she bangs into walls, or loses control at the sight of the color red" (31), she comes closer to the larger significance of Marnie's "female trouble."

The first such episode occurs when Marnie sees a large vase filled with red gladiolas while visiting her mother; with what little composure she can muster Marnie hastens to replace them with the white flowers she has brought with her to give her mother. Significantly, the argument that ensues over whether to replace the red with the white flowers is resolved when the little girl Jesse is told to take the red flowers with her to give to her mother. The two sets of flowers are thus representative, not just of the sailor's murder, but of the battle between Marnie and Jessie for Mrs. Edgar's love as well as of the need to replace the bouquet that, like Jesse, is already there in the house, with the one that she has brought. With regard to the latter Marnie wins a symbolic victory by sending both Jesse and the red bouquet back to her own mother. But the mere fact of having to fight this battle in order to regain a mother's love that has been redirected to Jesse means that Marnie has already lost, as she realizes later when her mother brings up the idea of Jesse coming to live with her.

The fact that this battle is fought over a bouquet of flowers—"female genitalia"—is also significant. Marnie, we later learn, has been brainwashed by her mother into hating men, and while homosexuality is only suggested it is similarly soft-pedaled in a significant number of Hitchcock's films such as *Rebecca, Strangers on a Train, The Paradine Case, Rope,* etc.[15] We are certainly justified in picking up where the film's censors leave off in positing Marnie's sexual attraction, if not for all women, then for the woman whose affection she so desperately craves—the large safes Marnie robs that "belong" to Strutt and Rutland are symbolic, in psychoanalytical terms, of the woman's body. The horror Marnie experiences with Jesse's red gladiolas, a shock so intense that it engulfs not only the entire screen but, in its repetition, the entire film, thus needs to be interpreted as more than just a memory of the sailor's murder. Cameron and Jeffery relate the motif to the blood of the sailor, but also note that the "image has further emotional extensions to the Victorian image of loss of virtue: blood on the sheet."[16] As Barbara Creed argues with regard to the "monstrous feminine," the association of women with menstruation is part of a larger association between the maternal and the abject (borrowing, of course, from Kristeva) which would explain the red diffusion as part of Marnie's love for her mother.[17] Moreover, we should also interpret the red flowers as a fairly obvious symbol of erotic female sexuality—not only Marnie's desire for her mother's love and the transgressive violence of that attraction but also the related fear of male penetration.[18] Pursuing this more complicated line of reasoning will lead us to posit a different sort of character from the one proffered by the more manifest content of the film. It will lead us to a Marnie whose bludgeoning of the sailor (with a "poker") who is making love to her mother is both an act of jealous rage against anyone who threatens to come between her and her "mama" as well as a symbolic denial of the sort of penetration that would accompany sex with a male. Despite the efforts of many of the film's critics recuperate at least the possibility of Marnie's relationship to Mark—to cure Marnie, as it were—it is important to remember that the film ends without any indication that Marnie is prepared to or even capable of returning Mark's love for her. "Oh, Mark, I don't want to go jail, I'd rather stay with you," indeed.

The other visit that Marnie makes after her heists is to her horse Forio. This act, as Hitchcock films it, is no less indicative of Marnie's precarious mental state than her visit to her mother was; indeed, it is important to see both parts of this "ritual" as related to each other. Notwithstanding all the usual clichés about women and horses—indeed, the clichés would argue against the "a-heterosexual" view of Marnie proffered thus far—this scene, and the importance Marnie places on her horse throughout the film, is distinctly sexual. Bellour refers to is as "orgiastic," while Joseph McElhaney notes that Marnie's horse riding scene is far more intimate and sexual than any of the other scenes involving her and Mark in the film.[19] Even the notes accompanying the various drafts of the screenplay refer to Marnie as "ecstatic" when riding. [20] This is the only time, including the later honeymoon and bedroom scenes, when Marnie literally and figuratively "lets her hair down." However, there is more to Marnie's relationship to Forio than just the ecstatic release of riding. Even before she climbs up on the horse to ride, Marnie replies to one of the stable's handlers who had complained that Forio was unmanageable and had tried to bite him: "Oh, Forio, bite me!" This statement, for anyone who has spent time with horses (as Marnie surely has), is extremely odd, for not even the most devoted horse lover would ever ask to be bitten by a horse; how, then, is one to understand such a comment? How, indeed, is one to answer the question Bellour poses, but leaves unanswered, about the riding scene: "What is a woman who can take such pleasure in herself? What is the nature of her pleasure?"[21]

Since Marnie makes it perfectly clear that she despises men or, more specifically, male penetration, it is necessary to begin by interpreting the statement "Oh, Forio, bite me!" as indicative of

29. Marnie's (Tippi Hedren) one moment of true happiness, riding her beloved horse Forio.

just the sort of male sexuality she abhors, and which she performs *on* men by robbing and penetrating them, by bludgeoning the sailor with a *poker* and, later, by her insistence on being the one who shoots her horse Forio. In asking Forio to bite her we have a brief but telling indication of what Klein described as the desire to penetrate the mother—to rob the large safe—that then becomes the fear of being herself penetrated.[22] This fear of being "robbed" is then itself denied by robbing, or penetrating, the one who would rob her—a contradiction that is later realized when Marnie insists on killing the object she loves most, the object that, as we have noted, gives Marnie her only moments of *jouissance.* If the true object of Marnie's desire—like that of many of Hitchcock's protagonists—is her mother, then the desire she expresses for Forio to bite her must be interpreted as precisely the sort of "oral" desire she so desperately craves from her mother. If, in Klein's analysis, female frigidity can be linked to a desire to penetrate the mother, then we can understand this desire to be bitten by her horse as part of this desire for the mother, and not as any desire to be penetrated by a male—a desire that is and remains abhorrent to Marnie throughout the film. (The closeness of the horse's name to "Florio" would also support this reading.)

It's not that the explanation of Marnie as a frigid kleptomaniac who steals because she cannot love is wrong, but simply that, like other "explanations" in Hitchcock's films (the end of *Psycho* being the most obvious example of this), it is inadequate and, as part of the manifest content of the film, itself needs further interpretation.[23] Such explanations, one might say, explain the character in the film, but not the film in the character. What the riding scene reveals, and what we are to deduce from Marnie's strange comment about Forio belies the film's depiction of Marnie as an innocent little girl. Despite the fact that the aforementioned "screen memory" of the film tries to depict Marnie as an innocent victim of the sailor who supposedly assaulted her, Marnie is in reality a much more aggressive character who intends to rob men of what they intend to take from her—the mother—because of her own desire (if Klein is correct) to penetrate the mother. Finally, because of this it is important to consider the possibility that we have frequently encountered in this work, namely, that the mother as depicted in the film is, like the little girl Jesse, just a phantasm of the protagonist's mother complex. If this is also the case here, then we would probably be right in assuming, yet again, the presence of a "Madonna/whore" complex in which the mother's depiction here as a former "harlot" who has become a sexless "Madonna" is, in reality, a function of Marnie's own forbidden desire for her mother, and the denial of same. To which we might also add, in this case, the contributing factor of the "Oedipal" father who tries to take the mother from the child and is thus transformed into someone who has no right to do so, and as such can be killed.

Mark Rutland

If there is more to Marnie than meets the eye, this will prove to be at least as true of the film's male protagonist, Mark Rutland (Sean Connery). From the very beginning of the film, when Mark is intrigued by the woman who robbed Strutt, Rutland's true motives are in question and, as is often the case with Hitchcock's male protagonists, his ostensibly heroic character in attempting to save Marnie is consistently undermined throughout the rest of the film. In his conversation with Truffaut Hitchcock complained of the fact that the "fetishistic" character of Mark's attraction to Marnie is harder to represent than "Jimmy Stewart's feeling for Kim Novak, [which] was clearly a fetishistic love": "To put it bluntly, we'd have had to have Sean Connery catching the girl robbing the safe and show that he felt like jumping at her *and raping her on the spot"* (italics mine).[24] This is another example of why I believe that Modleski goes a bit too far in claiming that "Hitchcock's fear and loathing of women is accompanied by a lucid understanding of—even sympathy for—women's problems in patriarchy."[25] Although her work is valuable in appreciating and unraveling the complexity of Hitchcock's characters, her notion of a certain "sympathy for women's problems" is belied by statements such as these and, more importantly, by the films themselves that, as Kaja Silverman argues with regard to *Marnie,* are "constructed through an identification with mastering vision, and with those male characters who might be said to embody that vision."[26]

Like "Mitch," the typologically parallel male figure in *The Birds,* which Hitchcock had just completed, "Mark" is another name which contains both the "M" which signifies a maternal obsession that engulfs both male and female characters (Margot, Melanie, Marion, Marnie, and all the M-names the latter uses as pseudonyms mentioned earlier) as well as the "guttural" sound which also twice ends Hitch-cock's own name—this as opposed to the appropriately "liquid" endings of all the women just mentioned. The close resemblance between the male characters' names in these two films is supported by the fact that the two men, Sean Connery and Rod Taylor, closely resemble each other physically as well as psychologically. So we will not be surprised to find that Mark reveals many of the same characteristics Mitch Brenner did in the preceding film, particularly the latter's transference of his mother complex onto his love interest and the catastrophe that, in both cases, results from this transference.

Recognizing Marnie during her interview for a position with Rutland Industries as the thief who stole close to ten thousand dollars from Strutt, the man who owns a company with which Mark does business, Mark insists that she be hired. But, before discussing Mark's own relationship with Marnie, one should consider the relationship of Marnie's two bosses to each other, a relationship that is initially suggested by their similar names ("Strutt" and "Rut-land"). Strutt is an important figure who provides a lengthy description of Marnie at the beginning of the film to two detectives who can't help snickering at the way he describes Marnie's physical attractiveness and who returns, at the end, to threaten Marnie after she has become the respectable wife of Mark Rutland. Strutt is a very distasteful figure, an officious little man whose nightmarish presence haunts the film. As such he seems the antithesis of the handsome Mark and the latter's efforts to save Marnie. But, as the similarity between their two names would suggest, we may in fact be dealing here with two sides of the same coin, and the efforts of the one to incriminate and the other to save Marnie may prove, on closer examination, to be one and the same. As we shall see, Mark Rutland is hardly different from the men he warns Marnie about, the bosses like Strutt who, if they catch her, will exact their vengeance "on her flesh." Indeed, Mark makes a very telling slip in this regard when he cautions Marnie that "Some *other* sexual blackmailer would have got his hands on you" if he had not been the one to catch her. Although Bellour does not mention this "slip," he reaches the same conclusion about the identification between Strutt and Rutland based on his own careful formal analysis: "The shot of Mark that ends segment two is almost identical to the shot of Strutt that opens it and recurs throughout the segment. . . . they [Strutt and Mark Rutland] are nothing but doubles, irregularly distributed along a trajectory at whose origin is Hitchcock, the first among all his doubles, a matrix that generates them as well as his own representation as duplicate image of himself."[27]

Shortly after Marnie begins working for him Mark tells Marnie that he will be needing her services in the office over the weekend. Thus the same man who will later warn Marnie about bosses taking advantage of her if they find out the truth about her is going to do exactly that himself! During the scene a storm arises outside in which lightening strikes a tree that breaks through the office window and in turn breaks a glass display case in which Mark keeps artifacts collected by his deceased wife. Like the earlier scene with the red gladiolas, the storm and lightening trigger another "panic attack" (ostensibly a memory of the night she murdered the sailor) in which the red filter is again used. While Marnie freezes in fear. Mark embraces her and even forces his lips upon hers, seemingly oblivious to the fact that she is more than just vulnerable at this moment, she is in fact unconscious. Despite all the controversy that continues to surround the later "rape scene" in which Mark forces himself on Marnie (Evan Hunter was fired as screenwriter of *Marnie* (despite his excellent work on *The Birds*) for disagreeing with Hitchcock

30. Hitchcock's send-up of a typical romantic embrace of a nearly catatonic Marnie (Tippi Hedren).

about this scene), the same thing has already happened here, replete with a tree symbolically breaking through a glass window, and Mark's embracing Marnie afterward and saying "It's all over." Bernard Hermann's lush romantic score and Hitchcock's own delight in discretely flaunting Hollywood stereotypes has caused many viewers—and male critics of the film, including Martin Scorsese—to mirror Mark's obliviousness to Marnie's pain and thus to miss the fact that Mark is already essentially raping Marnie here as well.[28] Mark Rutland is hardly the gallant gentleman he pretends to be, and which many critics take him to be. What, then, are we to make of this man who is sexually attracted to Marnie's criminality and wants to save her but is also not above raping her?

During this office scene, but before the aforementioned storm, Mark tells Marnie the story behind the photograph of the jaguarundi he has on his desk. The story is blatantly, even painfully symbolic of Mark's relationship to Marnie, but there is a more interesting side to the story of which even Mark is unaware. Mark proudly declares to Marnie that his accomplishment was not in killing the wild beast but in getting the jaguarundi to learn to trust him. As such this perfectly mirrors both Mark's attraction to Marnie's violence and criminality as well as his need to turn that violence into trust, which is its antithesis. I would agree with Pomerance's notion that "all the discussion of animals in this scene . . . is about Mark's dominance," but not that this dominance is defined strictly "in class terms."[29] Rather, we have yet another version of the male's attraction to two opposing types of women, a "loose woman" who can not be trusted and a trustworthy, respectable woman whom the man can marry, as Mark later does with Marnie. As we have frequently noted, behind this antithesis there is, according to Freud, a mother complex that splits the forbidden sexual attraction to the mother into two poles, that of a "loose woman" who represents the transgressive sensuality associated with the forbidden love for the mother and that of a respectable woman who, paradoxically, also represents the same forbidden love.

That Mark turns out to be the same sort of man he pretends to warn Marnie about, the boss who will use knowledge of her criminality to justify his own ("Some *other* sexual blackmailer would have got his hands on you") is due to the fact that, as their similar names would suggest, Mark has a mother complex that is every bit as strong as Marnie's. His desire to get a wild animal, and Marnie, to trust him is hardly gallant, but rather is part of a mother complex that seeks to dominate someone or something that is supposedly too wild to be tamed. The trusting part, which in psychoanalytical terms involves the splitting of the sensual into the tender in order to repress it, is in reality linked to the rape, for trust, understood as a version of the respectability associated with the mother, is simply the other half of the same complex that requires breaking that trust, just as Mark does when he later rapes a trusting Marnie after promising he wouldn't.[30]

We can now understand the broken display case and the destruction of its contents—artifacts belonging to Mark's dead wife. At the end of the scene, Mark picks up the only unbroken object from the floor and throws it to the ground to finish what nature had begun. This action functions like another parapraxis (*Fehlleistung*), a seemingly accidental, insignificant moment whose apparent insignificance masks its true importance. For why would Mark pick up the one unbroken object and throw it to the ground? The act, on closer examination, serves only to confirm the true nature of Mark's character, as well as giving us our only insight into Mark's earlier amorous relationship. The deceased wife is represented first by objects—pre-Columbian artifacts that are also symbols of the not-yet-conquered—and then by objects kept under glass. She thus represents, like the jaguarundi, what

Mark accomplishes through marriage: the taming of the wild sensual beast, now kept safely under glass, which stands in for the respectable—repressed—love of the mother. This is the essence of the mother complex as Freud defined it and as Hitchcock obsessively replays it, which is essential to understanding Mark's violence toward the very woman he is trying to save. Mark is simultaneously attracted to the transgressive object—either Marnie or the wild jaguarundi—and, at the same time, compelled to tame, domesticate, or otherwise "put it under glass" as a way of denying the transgressive, incestuous nature of this desire. Mark breaks the remaining object, instead of holding on to the one intact piece because, as his present attraction for the criminal shows, he has no need for that which has already been tamed and domesticated. This also explains Mark's insistence on buying Marnie a very expensive wedding-ring that "didn't belong to anyone before" despite having a "perfectly good" ring that belonged to his mother: the Oedipal mother, in other words, who has belonged to someone before must also not have belonged to someone before.[31]

Lil

It is no coincidence that the two dark-haired women in *The Birds* and *Marnie* both make themselves sexually available to male protagonists who reject their advances in favor of the less willing fair-haired criminal types they are pursuing. For Lil is part of a typological pattern that runs through a number of films from this period. In our earlier discussion of Annie Hayworth (Suzanne Pleshette) in *The Birds* we learned that Mitch's rejection of her was due to a desire that compelled him to seek out a figure who more closely resembled his own mother, a preference that of course fails to resolve anything because the fair-haired maternal figure is even less likely to satisfy the child than her more overtly sensual counterpart. Indeed, not only does the preference for the more maternal "Madonna" figure not resolve anything, but it in fact makes matters worse, for the remarkable physical resemblance between Melanie and Lydia, as well as the close physical proximity between the two caused by Melanie's breaking into the Brenner home, is precisely what precipitated the Oedipal plague of castrating birds that descended upon Bodega Bay.

Lil (Diane Baker) is the sister of Mark's dead wife, but her sisterly allegiance does not seem to inhibit her in the least from aggressively pursuing her own brother-in-law. Despite living in her dead sister's house with Mark and his father, she continues to treat theirs as a romantic relationship, replete with luncheon dates for which she picks him up at the office, requests for more spending money, and passionate embraces and kisses—even on the very day of Mark's wedding to Marnie. Her romantic attention to Mark, which we would better call a "crush" that plays like a young girl's immature romantic infatuation with an older man, is so strong that she is willing to risk her comfortable lifestyle by continuing her efforts to break up Mark's relationship with Marnie even after their marriage, culminating in the lavish dinner party to which she invites Strutt in an effort to destroy Marnie.

And yet, despite Lil's spying and plotting Mark reprimands her, if at all, with the gentlest of rebukes. Even the disastrous dinner with Strutt and all the damage control he is forced to do afterward does not provoke Mark to any action against Lil; Marnie, on the other hand, accuses her of the psychological equivalent of "murder." Mark's reluctance to act is inexplicable except in psychoanalytical terms. If, as we just discussed, Mark is attracted to the larcenous, frigid Marnie because of a mother complex in which he is acting out his transgressive, incestuous desire, he is secretly attracted to Lil for similar reasons. He tolerates her interference because he wants to, and he wants to because she too is an incestuous love object, another "jaguarundi" whose lack of trust(worthiness) is its real attraction. We saw, earlier, how Mark's repeated "rapes" of Marnie (one literal) are part of, and not an exception to, his attraction to her felonious nature. If Mark is remarkably tolerant when Lil does essentially the same thing, it is not really surprising given both his own attraction to Lil as well as the similarity between his and Lil's actions.

Finally, if Mark is destined to prefer the fair-haired Marnie to the darkly sensuous Lil, just as Mitch was destined to prefer the fair-haired Melanie to the darkly sensuous Annie in *The Birds,* it is because Marnie is largely disinterested in Mark while Lil is practically salivating whenever Mark is around. I would interpret Mark's preference for Marnie as well as his strange tolerance of Lil's bad behavior by the fact that since the "affairs" with dark-haired women in both *The Birds* and *Marnie* are preexisting conditions that precede the relationships with their fair-haired counterparts, they more closely resemble the "original mother" (Lil is even living in Mark's home "incestuously") and thus cannot be tolerated. Melanie and Marnie, on the other hand, in denying the male's sexual advances and thus fulfilling the "Madonna" role of virtuous attraction, are actually grateful for the existence of their more sensual counterparts. And the fact that, both here and in *The Birds,* Marnie and Melanie are also anything but virtuous themselves simply confirms the mother complex that is at the root of Mark's and Mitch's attraction to Lil and Annie, respectively.

Marnie's Fall

A number of events make up the film's first "ending," which occurs in the aftermath of the disastrous dinner-party at which Mr. Strutt recognized Marnie. During the foxhunt, which is meant to show off Marnie's expert horsemanship, Mark, is meeting with Mr. Strutt to try and discourage him from prosecuting Marnie. Meanwhile, at the hunt, the sight of the red hunting jackets and the gruesome killing of the fox causes another one of Marnie's disassociative episodes. She rides off alone in a panic, gaining momentum until she loses conrol of Forio, who breaks his leg attempting to leap over a stone wall. Although thrown from her horse Marnie is herself unhurt, and so she rushes into a nearby cottage demanding a gun to "put down" her horse. Lil arrives but is unwilling to shoot the horse, which Marnie does herself, muttering the "there, there now," which we will soon learn is what she says after remembering the sailor she bludgeoned to death. Returning to the house, Marnie retrieves a key she had secretly made and goes to the offices of Rutland Industries to accomplish her original goal of burgling the safe. She freezes, however, when attempting to reach inside the safe to take the cash. Mark arrives and insists on taking her to visit her mother in Baltimore, where we are given a second, *Psycho*-esque ending that purports to explain Marnie's problems.

The key to understanding the cluster of events that makes up the first ending of the film is, I believe, in understanding why Marnie freezes, unable to take the cash from Mark's safe. The film itself offers no explanation for this, and the casual explanation that Marnie has learned the error of her ways is not warranted by anything but the viewer's optimism, an optimism that is certainly not justified in any of Hitchcock's films. To understand the real reason for Marnie's reluctance one must remember what Marnie was accomplishing when she did steal. As we noted earlier, Marnie's thefts are sexual acts in which Marnie gratifies her need for forbidden sexual desire—both the desire for her mother as well as the desire for vaginal penetration of herself and the mother (Klein's thesis) that she both desires and fears. In classic psychoanalytical terms the "safe" is, like other boxes, caskets, etc., symbolic of the mother.[32] Before the moment she freezes instead of taking the money from the Rutland safe, Marnie has just killed the horse that, as we discussed earlier, provided her with her only other form of libidinal gratification. And Marnie has not just lost Forio, but she is also about to lose her freedom entirely, aware as she is of Strutt's meeting with Mark that transpired that very day. The reason Marnie cannot steal, then, is because Marnie cannot steal. That is, she has been caught; her real identity is known to her husband, her most recent victim has resurfaced, and her only other source of gratification is dead. The invisible hand that is restraining her, stopping her from reaching into the safe and stealing Mark's money, is due not to any sense of guilt or conscience that Marnie has acquired. It is the result of her being caught, as they say, "red-handed."

This darker, more sinister explanation of the penultimate ending will aid in understanding the darker, more sinister meaning of the film's other ending. As mentioned, Evan Hunter once described the story of the sailor's murder as only a "screen memory" (the term has particular relevance here) of the real motives that continue to underlie the characters of Marnie and her mother, as well as of Mark. Indeed, Hitchcock's sensitivity to these darker, more grotesque motives and qualities is evident in this very scene as correctives to the inadequacy of the film's supposed "solution." The relatively upbeat and even heroic screen memory depicts Marnie's prostitute-mother attacking a drunken sailor (Bruce Dern in one of his first screen roles) who was being, perhaps, too affectionate in trying to calm the crying child.[33] Mrs. Edgar strikes the sailor, who then turns against her, as a result of which the little girl Marnie then picks up a poker and ferociously bludgeons the sailor to death, ending with the now-familiar "there, there now."

This "screen memory" calls itself into question because the little girl is not initially crying because of the sailor, but because of her mother's moving her from the warmth of her own bed in order to service her client. In scattered memories that Marnie has throughout the film it is this frequent displacement, and coldness, that Marnie recalls in her nightmares. In this respect the sailor's affection in comforting the frightened, displaced child is somewhat ambiguous, as is the action itself, which may or may not have been abusive.[34] Similarly, the sailor's assault on Mrs. Edgar was provoked by her first breaking a bottle over his head and was certainly nowhere near as violent as Marnie's attack on him; as Michael Walker has recently stated, "although the sailor threatened to hit Bernice, what we see are his desperate attempts to control Bernice's own violence."[35] The story is, as one says, a little fishy, and becomes even more so when one realizes how little it tells us about Marnie's original and continued tortured relationship with her mother, and about the mother herself. As in *Spellbound,* a film that (according to Andrew Britton) bears a close resemblance to *Marnie* in combining therapy with a murder mystery, the film itself "works against the conclusion of the narrative . . . [and this] explicit solution is no solution at all."[36]

Marnie's mother tells us more through her own words and deeds about the cause of Marnie's current condition than does the problematic flashback sequence about the sailor. Just as horrifying, perhaps, is the story she tells of how, as a young girl "who didn't have nothing," she "let a boy do it" because she wanted his sweater. (This, as opposed to the murder, was considered questionable by the film's censors and producers.)[37] It is hard to agree with Pomerance's interpretation of this particular story as "touching" and "elegiac."[38] The grotesqueness of this scene is magnified considerably by the fact that she is telling Marnie about her own conception as a way of consoling her after she was told the horrific story of the murder! The seeds of Marnie's substitution of sex for money, it seems, were sown long before the murder; in fact, their sowing is what produced Marnie herself.[39] However, this history of Mrs. Edgar's prostitution begs the question of why such substitution occurs, of why, in other words, the sexual drive that is after all much stronger is diverted into the desire for money or a sweater.

The answer to this is given to us by Mrs. Edgar's actions in the final scene, not in the two stories she tells. Once again, as in the earlier scene when she visited her mother, Marnie kneels down at Mrs. Edgar's feet and attempts to rest her head on her mother's lap. Once again, and despite the highly emotional scene that has just occurred, Mrs. Edgar pushes Marnie away, complaining of her sore leg.[40] Reminiscent of Marnie's inability to reach into the safe to steal Mark's money, Mrs. Edgar here tries to reach out and stroke her daughter's head, but cannot, and instead pushes her away. This important gesture, or lack of one, tells us that Mrs. Edgar was probably subject to the same lack of maternal affection Marnie is now subject to, for they are both "blocked" from their desired love-objects and forced to find repressed, illicit objects of gratification—such as money or a sweater—which can substitute for the mother's love which both have been denied. Or, as we have seen, one might also interpret the whole story told by Bernice Edgar, and indeed her whole character, as simply a projection of Marnie's own experience. Understood thus, Marnie's inability to touch the money in the safe, rather than being indicative of any moral progress on her part, is to be understood as the same as the mother's inability to recreate the lost bond between the mother and child. As such, Marnie's condition at the end of the film is even worse than when she could at least touch something that would gratify her desires. Unfortunately, neither Marnie nor Mark understands any of this; all they understand is the "screen memory" of the murdered sailor that completely fails to address the issue of Mrs. Edgar's past and the continued effects her withholding of love from her daughter has on Marnie. On this basis one would have to disagree with George Toles, who sees at the end of Mrs. Edgar's speech a "measure of acceptance" between Marnie and her mother.[41] Despite the dogged optimism that certain critics find at the end of this and other Hitchcock's films,[42] there is little reason to be optimistic about Marnie's future married life with Mark,[43] a future that Hitchcock mocks by the final ironic spoken line of the film uttered as the couple leave the Edgar house ("Oh Mark, I don't want to go to jail; I'd rather stay with you"), by Mark's flippant reply ("Had you, love?"), by the fact that Marnie nowhere in the film demonstrates any real interest in Mark, and, finally, by the nursery rhyme which is repeated at the end just as it was chanted at the beginning.[44]

> Mother Mother I am ill
> Call for the Doctor over the hill
> Call for the Doctor,
> Call for the Nurse,
> Call for the lady with the alligator purse

Small wonder, then, that because of what Alexander Walker rightly perceived as the intense "cruelty" of *Marnie,*[45] the film encountered considerable critical resistance, as well as a poor box office.[46] Indeed, the poor reception of Marnie is often cited as the end of Hitchcock's "golden age" of filmmaking, and as a disappointment (according to Truffaut and others) from which Hitchcock never fully recovered.[47] The reason for this "failure" might be suggested by a comparison to the other, more successful films of Hitchcock, and by the interpretations of those films in this book. We have consistently argued that the "happy endings" of Hitchcock's films, like the ending of *Marnie,* are all ironic.[48] But if such endings are the rule rather than the exception, why "the trouble with *Marnie*"? What made the audience more uncomfortable with this film was not, as some have argued, the artificiality of the sets, but that in the other films the ideal of normalcy is more fully regained at the end, however ironically. In *The Birds* we are free to assume, as even many critics have done, that the attacks have now ceased, and that Mitch and Melanie will live happily ever after.[49] In *Psycho* we are gratified, however much we are also disturbed, by the fact that Norman is now tucked away safely in an insane asylum. In *Shadow of a Doubt,* we are hopeful, however unenthusiastic she may seem, that Young Charlie and Detective Graham will soon marry. Compared to these and the other endings of the films discussed in this book, Marnie's statement that "I don't want to go to jail, I'd rather go with you," and the chanting children who are still singing the exact same song that they were signing at the beginning, make it impossible to believe that the "neurosis" of the film has really been resolved. I am not suggesting, by this statement, that the "failure" of *Marnie* is due solely to its ending, but rather that this end is symptomatic of a film which deals even more explicitly than the others with a neurotic, infantile attachment to the mother that could never be resolved, and that as such *Marnie* was bound to make its audience more uncomfortable than the other films mentioned.[50] This discomfort, then, is really just a magnification of a certain discomfort that accompanies all these films, and so is why, in the end, *Marnie* has proven so remarkably influential among directors such as Truffaut, Buñuel, Oshima, and others, and has largely regained the position it deserves as one of Hitchcock's greatest films.[51]

9
Pota-toes: *Frenzy*

"The world has become darker than ever in *Frenzy*"
—Peter Bogdanovich

In her essay on "The Darker Side of Genius: The (Horror) Auteur Meets Freud's Theory," Linda Badley suggest that Donald Spoto's "definitive" biography of Hitchcock is part of a general tendency among biographers and critics to project their subjects' work onto their lives—particularly the lives of directors, like Hitchcock, who make such "dark" films.[1] In the following discussion of *Frenzy* I will indeed suggest a certain degree of correspondence between this particularly "dark" film, that signaled Hitchcock's return to England toward the end of his career, and the director's childhood as a source for the material of this as well as other films. But the important connections to Hitchcock's childhood that return in *Frenzy*, such as the fact that Hitchcock's father was, like the murderer in *Frenzy*, a "fruit importer" who set up shop in Covent Garden; the "running joke" about Hitchcock's notorious love of food—and especially, potatoes; and the film's numerous references to Christianity (Hitchcock's Jesuit education has been seen, since criticism of the late 1950s, as of critical importance to the man and his work), are neither the attempts decried by Badley to attribute falsely aspects of the work onto the man, nor are they the sort of "psychobiography" which, as E. Ann Kaplan points out in her survey of the various waves of psychoanalysis which have washed over film studies during the last 50 years, has been largely discredited for quite some time now.[2] If the present book is in part a return to the auteur-theory, it is not the theory as originally designed by Bazin, Rohmer/Chabrol, et al., but, rather, the rebirth of the theory that includes, according to Badley, the application of Freud's model as put forth in "The Poet and Daydreaming" in which the "auteur" explores, through the artwork, his (and our) unconscious dreams and desires.

The Beginning

During the last decades of the nineteenth century London gave birth both to Jack the Ripper, the first modern serial killer, and to Alfred Hitchcock, the first "modern" director.[3] Hitchcock's decision to return to his roots, both cinematic as well as cultural, with this film about another serial murderer stalking the women of London displays a sense of humor that is, like much in Hitchcock (who once referred to *Psycho* as a "black comedy"), as terrifying as it is jovial. That Hitchcock was deliciously aware of the black humor of *Frenzy* from the beginning is evident in the fact that he chose to replace the original, much more somber score written by Henry Mancini with the decidedly more upbeat composition of Ron Goodwin, whose glorious musical fanfare announcing the film's and Hitchcock's triumphant return to London ironically leads us to the discovery of a naked body floating in the Thames.

But *Frenzy* is more than a "self-conscious return to Hitchcock's origins," to the subject of his "breakout" film *The Lodger* of 1926, to the persistent "wrong man" theme, and to a childhood spent with his own "green grocer" father.[4] It is also, I shall argue in this chapter, the return to a number of the unconscious desires and their repressions—the "instincts and their vicissitudes"—that dominate the entire Hitchcockean corpus. (I will discuss, in an afterword following this chapter, how my thesis may be extended to a number of other Hitchcock films not directly included here, including *Rebecca, Notorious, Dial M for Murder,* and *The Man Who Knew Too Much.*) Perhaps it is not, then, insignificant that in this picture Hitchcock makes his celebrated cameo not once but twice, or that this "rare double cameo" occurs in the opening scene in which the aforementioned dead body is discovered floating in the Thames at precisely the moment when a high-ranking politician is proudly declaring how the stately river, once celebrated by Wordsworth, has been finally made "clear of the waste products of our society with which we have for so long poisoned our rivers and canals."[5] For in *Frenzy* the world's greatest director has returned to his roots, even if, as in these cameos, his return is marked as much by the crowd's morbid attention as by any official celebration.

The Jesuit Schoolboy

Hitchcock's Jesuit education, and the fact that one of the cinema's many great Catholic directors was also a marginalized figure in Protestant England, has been frequently noted by critics as well as by the director himself. Rohmer and Chabrol's groundbreaking studies of Hitchcock emphasized the director's formative religious influences, a theme picked up, in whole or in part, by practically all of the critics writing in the wake of their groundbreaking "auteur" theory of the director.[6] Yet, it is surprising that despite these many references to Hitchcock's Jesuit boyhood the critics of *Frenzy* have largely ignored the fact that this film contains a number of important references to religion, and specifically to Christianity—more, in fact, than any of the other films discussed here.[7] Modleski comes close in mentioning Hitchcock's Catholicism a number of times in her chapter on *Frenzy* ("Ritual of Defilement") in *The Woman Who Knew Too*

Much, but she does not make any specific connection to the references in the film itself. This is not surprising, for as numerous as these references to Catholicism are they are easily missed unless one is alert to the importance of such seemingly insignificant, "parapractic" details. As subtle as such references may be, they are some of the many important indications that *Frenzy* constitutes a more explicit return to the issues of Hitchcock's youth than any of his earlier films.

During one of their numerous dinner table conversations the chief inspector and his wife are discussing the fact that the murderer took something out of the clenched fist of his latest victim, the woman whose body was found by police after tumbling naked out of a truck carrying a load of potatoes.

> CHIEF INSPECTOR'S WIFE. "What do you think they held? A locket? A brooch? A cross? . . . Not a cross, I think."
> CHIEF INSPECTOR. I don't see why not. Religious and sexual mania are clearly linked.

What Babs, the victim in question, held was not a cross but the signature pin of the murderer Rusk. Nonetheless, Mrs. Oxford's conjecture is not unfounded, for during the gruesome scene in which Brenda Blaney, the wife of the "wrong man" Richard Blaney, is murdered by Rusk she utters, at the moment in which she realizes that she is to be the infamous "necktie murderer's" next victim: "Jesus help me." Also, during the scene in which Brenda recites the ninety-first Psalm as Rusk rapes her Sharff refers to Brenda's having "a martyr's look."[8] The inspector's wife is thus correct insofar as she associates the murderer's victims with religion, just as her husband is certainly right when he says that "religious and sexual mania are clearly linked." I would argue, however, that the association between the murders and religion is actually neither that of the murderer nor his victims; it is Hitchcock's. It is the director who first establishes the connection by virtue of the wife's incorrect conjecture, and then confirming it anyway through the earlier victim's final words. What then, is Hitchcock's point in adducing religion in this way? It is not an issue in *Shadow of a Doubt* or *Psycho,* both films featuring serial murderers. My contention is that the religious context, while no more relevant here than in the earlier films just mentioned, is brought in because Hitchcock has returned to "his roots," as it were, not only to England, but to the very part of his childhood—with which his own particular childhood is associated. We must consider, then, the connection between murder and religion in terms of Hitchcock's deep-seated conviction of a connection between the two based on his own religious background. As such, the explicit connection made here, in Hitchcock's penultimate film, is equally relevant to his earlier films; for this is just the sort of "reverse chronology" that is often found in psychoanalysis when the secrets of one's infantile unconscious are discovered later in life, far removed from when they actually occur.

In arguing for the importance of religion in *Frenzy* I am not suggesting that there is any uplifting religious message or meaning here or, as we have argued throughout this volume, anywhere in Hitchcock. For Hitchcock to invoke Christianity, and specifically the martyr's death in having his victim call out to Jesus and recite a Psalm in her death throes is hardly meant to infer a sense of redemption in the deaths of Brenda, Babs, or any of the victims of any of the serial murderers in Hitchcock's films. We are not dealing here with an overtly Catholic artist like Flannery O'Connor, a writer capable of every bit of gruesomeness as Hitchcock but one who always sought redemption for both her victims and their murderers.[9] Hitchcock's religious sense of these horrible sex crimes is based on his Jesuit upbringing, and on his childhood association between sex and crime, and the guilt that accrues to each. If sex outside of marriage is a crime, and sex within marriage is largely mitigated if it exists at all (there is evidence that for Hitchcock it did not), then sex is always seen, particularly by those brought up with the sort of strict Jesuit training as Hitchcock, as inherently "dirty" and thus criminal.[10] The association between "religious mania and murder" suggested here is to be understood, then, as the acting out of a strong sense of guilt due to the association between sex and crime. This is why, if anyone is to be redeemed in Hitchcock (and no one really is) it is much more likely to be the pathetic, artistic murderers (or suspected murderers) like the lodger, Uncle Charles, Norman Bates, or Bob Rusk than their "innocent" victims, because the murders are the result of an association between sex and crime from which Hitchcock would like to see the murderers absolved. And this is also why the figure in the film who is associated most closely with the figure of Christ turns out to be the very opposite of a savior.

I don't mean Rusk, the murderer who nonetheless seems genuinely concerned with the well-being of his friend Blaney ("Bob, I'm really grateful for all this. You know that"). Rusk is not, despite the greater sympathy that Hitchcock seems to lend his murderers than his victims, a Christ figure. The figure I am thinking of is the wife of the old friend who also tries to help Blaney, Hetty Porter. In the scene in which she and her husband are introduced Hetty cuts a most unusual figure, beginning with the ominous quick zoom up to the veranda on which she is standing, looking down from very high above on her husband as he speaks with "Old Dick-O" and Babs and learns of their situation. In Stefan Sharff's formal analysis of the film he notes that "since [this] is the strongest zoom in the film, it leaves me with an unanswered question as to Hitchcock's intention."[11] Although Sharff is understandably puzzled by the meaning of this shot of Hetty, whom he refers to as a "satanic madame," the answer is, I believe, to be found in the significance of one of the subsequent shots he discusses, but whose symbolic importance he does not recognize.

When the three enter the upstairs apartment, Hetty begins her harsh interrogation of Blaney:

> Yes, [she's dead] and you killed her.
> There's no spiteful act I would put past old Dick-O here.
> [He was guilty of] Both extreme mental and physical cruelty [towards his wife]. Depravity was mentioned, I think.

Throughout the scene Hetty delivers her lines in a slow, measured way which is meant to emphasize either her disgust with Blaney, who she is convinced murdered his wife, or the extreme sarcasm with which she dismisses the attempts by the other two present to exonerate him. But it is not so much her words, important as they are, in which I am interested as the odd way she is positioned throughout most of the scene. After her initial greeting Hetty goes to the sofa and sits with her arms outstretched and legs crossed, and maintains this striking, awkward position between Babs and Blaney ("a very symmetrical mise-en-scène") throughout the rest of the scene.[12]

Hitchcock, as is well known, was in charge of even the smallest visual details throughout his productions; he was certainly in charge of the odd position that Hetty maintained throughout the scene, and that she only relinquishes at the end when she stands

32. A severely judgmental Christ figure, Blaney's friend's wife Hetty (Billie Whitelaw).

up to leave. Now, the fact that Hetty is so mean-spirited throughout the film (she later refuses to provide the true alibi for Blaney that would have saved him) would seem to go against the obvious interpretation of Hetty's arms outstretched and/legs crossed in the canonical way, as that of a Christ figure. It is for this reason, I believe, that Sharff describes the striking pose as that "of a queen" (*Alfred Hitchcock's High Vernacular,* 202). I would agree that the powerful image here is "over-determined" and thus capable of being interpreted in different ways. But the image is so iconic that one should consider its primary significance to see if it makes sense. On reflection, there is a way in which the "satanic" Hetty very much works as a Christ figure, albeit a particular sort of one. It is certainly not the loving, charitable, forgiving Christ we are dealing with here. But within the history of Christianity, and particularly the part involving the Jesuit education that Hitchcock experienced as a child, the loving figure of Christ was often occluded by the harsher figure of a judge intolerant of any sin, even the most venial. Contrary to her husband's decision, despite evidence to the contrary, that "Of course we'll hide him," Hetty asks, in her typical slow and measured way, "*Why don't you go to the police and inform them?*" The Christ who is present in this scene, and I would suggest throughout Hitchcock, is the Christ who, like Norman's mother, "refuses to think of disgusting things." Specifically, Hetty is disgusted by a sexuality that makes everyone, even someone who is innocent like Blaney, guilty.

As she is leaving, Babs, Blaney's current girlfriend and chief defender of his innocence against both Hetty and her male counterpart Forsythe, assures Blaney that she won't say a word about their plan to escape England to anyone: "Cross my heart and hope to die." This is the last time Blaney will see her, for she is on the way to work at the pub, where she will meet Rusk, who will take her back to his apartment and murder her. The cross that the chief inspector's wife wrongly conjectured was in Babs' hand *was*, then, in a sense present at her death. The prevalence of all these Christian references in *Frenzy* is subtle yet important. And not just subtle in the sense of their unobtrusiveness, but also in the sense that Hitchcock's use of Christianity is based more on his own peculiar, "Jesuit school" association of Christianity with death, guilt, sex, and sin than on any conscious belief. Perhaps this is why it is not so shocking after all that, as Murray Pomerance has astutely noted with regard to the pastor of Ambrose Chapel in *The Man Who Knew Too Much* of 1956, "the religious man himself is evil."[13]

Rusk/Blaney

Love in Hitchcock, William Rothman suggests, has a peculiar way of recognizing innocence even when nothing or no one else does.[14] Babs, as mentioned, is Blaney's staunchest and only steadfast defender in *Frenzy*. Daisy befriends the man everyone wrongly believes is the Jack the Ripper murderer in *The Lodger*. *Rebecca*, *The Wrong Man*, *Dial M for Murder*, and *North by Northwest*, all offer further evidence of this pattern, even if, as Rothman wisely notes, the matter is often complicated by the question of whether the love itself is true (*Stage Fright*), or when, as in *North by Northwest*, jealousy rears it ugly head and causes one to doubt the beloved's innocence.

No so friendship. Same-sex relationships of friendship in Hitchcock tend to be as riddled with doubts and betrayals as love remains loyal and true. In *Rear Window*, for example, Doyle refuses to believe in Jeff, and even casts additional, unnecessary doubts concerning his sexual "dalliance" with Lisa; in *Vertigo*, the betrayal of Scottie's friendship with Gavin Elster cuts both ways, for Scottie is also in love with the woman he thinks is Elster's wife. Here, in *Frenzy,* the pattern continues with the betrayal of Blaney by Rusk, who pretends throughout the film to have Blaney's best interests in mind before turning him in to the police for the crimes he has himself committed. And yet, as with the case of love's belief in innocence, such matters are not simple. It would be a mistake not to believe in Rusk's genuine concern for Blaney as he packs up a "care package" of fruit for him after has lost his job, offers him money, and gives him a tip on a racehorse that ends up winning at twenty to one. Rusk, it turns out, is not all bad, just as Blaney, as we learn from the police and Hetty's accusations, is not all good. The relationship between the two, between the real necktie murderer and the man who is wrongly suspected of the crimes, can be best understood, not in terms of guilt/innocence, but in terms of an identity—like that of the two Charlies in *Shadow of a Doubt*—whose apparent differences are merely the result of varying degrees of repression. Evidence that we are dealing here with one person, rather than with two, is found in the simple fact that the two women whom Rusk murders in the film are Blaney's current lover Babs and his ex-wife Brenda.

We have seen how, in a number of his films, Hitchcock utilizes the traditional opposition between the fair-haired and the dark-haired woman, with the former seen as the "Madonna-figure" compared to the more sensual, "earthier" harlot figure (Judy in *Vertigo,* Annie in *The Birds,* Lil in *Marnie*). But, we have also seen how the opposition doesn't really hold; how the dark-haired woman can turn out to be virtuous, while the "Madonna-figure" can turn out to be something of a harlot (for example, Melanie in *The Birds*) due to the fact that, in psychoanalytical terms, the two women are really one woman, the "mother" figure who becomes a harlot because sex with her is forbidden just as the harlot becomes a Madonna because, originally, she *is* the mother figure.[15]

The women of *Frenzy*—Babs, Brenda, and others (including Rusk's "Mum") do not, for the most part, fit this pattern and so will be discussed later. The pattern is evident, however, in the two main characters, the fair-haired Rusk, the real necktie murderer, and the dark-haired Blaney, the man who is wrongly accused of his crimes. Just as the fair-haired/dark-haired women of Hitchcock are often two versions of the same woman, so, I would argue, are the fair-haired/dark-haired men of *Frenzy.* I am not, however, suggesting that "Old Dicko, the chivalrous knight of the skies" is guilty of the crimes Rusk commits. What I am saying is that Hitchcock did not see the two characters as opposites, or, if they are, they are the sort of opposites that, according to Freud, merge in the unconscious.[16] "Old Dicko" is one of the many examples of what we have referred to as the absence of true heroes in Hitchcock. They are largely absent, we have argued, because Hitchcock was highly suspicious of any idealization which ignores, by definition, the dark, hidden, unconscious truth that underlies every human being, and even (according to Freud) so-called heroism itself.[17] There is a moment in the film when Babs, sitting on a bench talking to her lover, says to Blaney that "I must be crazy letting a strangler put his hands on me," at which point Blaney jokingly puts his hands around her throat and pretends to strangle her. It is hard to imagine that Hitchcock, with his famously dark sense of humor, did not see himself in the same way, namely, as someone who is putting his imaginary hands around the throats of his victims and having a good laugh. (The relationship between the chief inspector and his wife, who discuss the former's work together every night at dinner, also seems to offer a rare bit of self-reflection on Hitchcock's own relationship with Alma.) It is not that Blaney, like the other "wrong men" of Hitchcock, is guilty, it's just that he is definitely not innocent, not even of the horrible crimes which he has not in fact committed.

The Fruit Cellar/Seller

There is a certain "accordion effect" that runs throughout the Hitchcockian oeuvre; that is, certain shots, scenes, themes, characters, actions, etc. are sometimes repeated in different films and (supposedly) different contexts, thus giving the oeuvre a unity all its own which provides the repeat "visitor" with a seemingly infinite array of delightful new connections to ruminate upon. This can take the form of certain "themes" or "motifs" that are repeated throughout the oeuvre, as cataloged in Michael Walker's excellent new work, although what I am referring to here is a subset of these in which there is a certain uncanny "return of the same."[18] There is, for example, the persistent dramatic and ominous use of staircases from *The Lodger* on; related to this is the way in which the scene of Ben McKenna leading Hank down the stairs in *The Man Who Knew Too Much* recalls the similar, climactic scene of *Notorious.*[19] Then there is the example of the incriminating keys in both *Notorious* and *Dial M for Murder,* or the persistent use of certain colors, such as the grey suits and dresses worn in *Dial M for Murder* and *Vertigo;* or the pre-*Psycho* appearance of a taxidermist in the 1955 remake of *The Man Who Knew Too Much;* or the stolen mink stoles that are bestowed on the two mother figures of *Shadow of a Doubt* and, more than twenty years later, *Marnie.* There are countless examples of this, and the "fruit seller" Rusk in *Frenzy* provides an unusual case of such unexpected connections: the murderer's occupation, which plays a very pronounced role throughout the film, creates a pun with the famous "fruit cellar" of *Psycho.* As we shall see, the pun is not without deeper significance, for, in both cases, concealed within both "cellars" is the murderer's mother.

In Donald Spoto's rich biography the author recounts how Hitchcock had a private laugh at *The Lodger*'s notoriously gay leading man by taking great pains to include a shot of Ivor Novello with a flowerpot "placed strategically on a shelf behind him."[20] Homosexuals are not only present in Hitchcock's films in fairly explicit ways (*Rebecca, The Paradine Case, Rope, North by Northwest*) but also, as Daniel Price has argued, implicitly (*Strangers on a Train*) as well by their general association with a realm of unconscious, sexual perversion.[21] There is, indeed, much to suggest that Rusk, while not gay, exemplifies this third sort of homosexuality. In addition to the aforementioned fondness for Blaney, Hitchcock seems to have attributed to this notorious "fruit seller" numerous other qualities associated with the gay male. He is extremely well coiffed and dressed throughout the film, including the signature gold tiepin that causes Rusk so much trouble in the end. But, most importantly, he resembles another example of this third sort of "gay" male, the decidedly less dapper Norman Bates, in demonstrating a strong love/hatred for women and a persistent fixation with his mother.

Although we see Rusk's mother only once in the film, she actually appears a number of other times in different forms. Rusk frequently refers to her in the film before and after her actual appearance. Early in the film, when Rusk is advising Blaney on how he should have his girlfriend Babs peel him the grapes he has just given him, he mentions how his mother used to have him do the same for her—a rather odd segué in that it suggests that Rusk identifies his relationship with his mother with Blaney's romantic relationship with Babs. Later in the film, Rusk mentions to Blaney that his mother, who frequently comes to stay with him in his apartment, "lives down in Kent, in the garden of England." During this same scene we see a framed photograph of Rusk's mother prominently displayed in Rusk's apartment, leading Michael Walker to note that "the flat, with mother's photograph on the mantelpiece, later becomes the centre of the film's chaos world."[22]

Common to all these references to Rusk's mother, including her one actual appearance in the film, is Rusk's good friend Blaney, leading one to suspect that, following the logic of the film, one should consider the three figures together as well as separately. The three occur together because, as we have just seen, Rusk and Blaney are not really two separate characters. Rusk, we have argued, is Blaney's unconscious, and as such it is perfectly fitting that the highly charged relationship between the serial murderer and his mother always includes Blaney. However, the latter's posi-

33. The murderer Rusk (Barry Foster), with the portrait of his beloved "Mum."

tion in all these scenes is significantly that of the uninvolved "third party," with Rusk insisting in talking about his mother to Blaney without much comment or enthusiasm on Blaney's part. This is important because it reveals that Rusk's murderous pathology is associated with a mother fixation that is totally absent in his more "heroic" friend Blaney. Moreover, the fact that Blaney is romantically involved with the two women whom Rusk just happens to murder further suggests that Blaney is the more normal of the two, having transferred his attention to the appropriate mother substitutes (one of whom was his wife), whereas Rusk, who is still attached to his mother, can only follow Blaney around, killing the women he—unlike Blaney—is incapable of loving. But the difference between the two men, as we have argued, is one of degree rather than of kind, for we recall that Blaney, it turns out, is also incapable of any lasting relationship with "Mrs. Blaney" or, presumably, with Babs, the woman he is temporarily (and rather unconvincingly) involved with during the film.

Just as in *Psycho,* where the reproduction of the painting of Susanna and the Elders provides a deliberate commentary on Norman's voyeurism, there are also a number of significant, if decidedly less impressive reproductions of paintings by the then-popular artist Vladimir Tretchikoff in Rusk's apartment.[23] All these paintings offer various depictions of gypsies, and particularly, of the notorious *femmes fatales* with whom, since Merimée's *Carmen,* such women are usually associated.

The fact that the notorious necktie murderer has chosen such images with which to adorn his apartment is significant. Such exotic women, like Carmen, are "fatal" not only to the men who love them but, just as often, to themselves, for in laughing at or toying with the men who love them they often end up being killed by the very men whom they sought to victimize.[24] There are, of course, no such *femmes fatales* in *Frenzy* (they are also significantly absent in Hitchcock), except, that is, in these pictures.[25] But these women are even more telling by their actual absence and their virtual presence. Like Norman, the "fruit seller" Rusk is faithful to that "great lady, my Mum" whose portrait dominates the other images of the room, and also like Mrs. Bates, Rusk's "mother" will make sure that she will continue her portrait's domination of all the "harlots" in the room who would seek to replace her.

34. Rusk (Barry Foster) framed by two images of gypsy women.

Babs, Brenda, and the Blaney Bureau

In a world of women dominated by maternal "M's" (Marnie, Margot, Melanie, Madeleine, Midge, Marion, et al.) why the sudden explosion of "B's"? If we are correct in our suspicion that all the "M"-names refer us back to the original female "M"-name, a suspicion that is compounded by the fact that Hitchcock's own mother Emma bore what is perhaps the ultimate maternal signifier ("M" "A"), then we may expect to find, by looking closely at the two female leads of *Frenzy,* a particular deviation from the maternal that distinguishes them from the other women just named.

One of the first things that confirms our suspicion that Brenda and Babs belong together is not only that they are the two main victims of the murderer in *Frenzy* but that, as we have mentioned, they are also the paramours—past or present—of the man who is wrongly accused of being the murderer, Richard Blaney. This, of course, is in service to the plot by increasing the likelihood that Blaney could be the murderer, but it also begs the question of why Rusk and Blaney should be so intimately connected. The other "B-word" which helps, I believe, to explain the dominance in *Frenzy,* of "B-women" is a word that figures strongly into this film and was of paramount concern to the director throughout his career: "*B*-usiness."

The scenes in which this word occurs are of particular importance in the film. After losing his own job as a bartender, Richard Blaney has gone to see his wife to ask her for some money. When climbing the stairs to the "Blaney Bureau," the highly successful matchmaking business established by his ex-wife after their divorce, Blaney encounters a middle-aged couple who are leaving the Bureau. The couple have been successfully "matched" by Brenda and are discussing their future wedding plans as they are leaving: "He would have cleaned the whole house, and never have waked me once," declares the rather bossy woman about her highly efficient previous marriage to her sheepish future husband. Commenting on the departing couple's future happiness during his conversation with his ex-wife, Blaney sarcastically compliments Brenda on the success of her business; later, when they go to dine at her club, he says to Brenda and the collective roomful of businesswomen: "You're good at business. They're all good at business here." The departing couple will, without doubt, run their marriage like a business, and the Bureau is itself in the business of establishing marriages, so Blaney's comment, while angry and sarcastic, is nonetheless true. Blaney himself, it turns out, is good at neither; he has lost his job, and he is there to ask his successful ex-wife for money. Rusk may be a successful businessman, but he too is unsuccessful at the sort of business run by the Bureau. As Brenda tells him in explaining why his application has been rejected, "[No] respectable agency would service you." Marriage is, it seems, a business at which neither the "right" nor the "wrong" man, Rusk nor Blaney, can succeed. Neither of them is "respectable" enough, and it is the relationship between business and respectability as announced by Brenda that is at the heart of the "matrimonial business" and, I will argue, the entire film.

The maternal women in Hitchcock, whether actual mothers or younger "Madonna-figures" such as Lisa in *Rear Window* or Madeleine in *Vertigo* are all "respectable" women. What distinguished the "B-Women" of *Frenzy* is that this "respectability," which was such an obsession with both Norman's mother and Marion in *Psycho* (Marion complains to her lover Sam, "You make respectability sound disrespectful"), has now completely taken over the love interests who are supposed to represent something—and someone—quite different. Marion Crane, we recall, was looking for respectability while, at the same time, representing the fallen, "loose woman" who is the sensual counterpart to the original mother fixation, not to mention her stealing the forty thousand dollars from the business at which she works.[26] In the run of films through Hitchcock's "golden age" (and including, earlier, women such as Alicia Huberman in *Notorious*), "fallen" female love interests like Eve Kendall, Melanie Daniels, Marnie Edgar and others were struggling—unsuccessfully, I have maintained—to resolve this tension by combining the two poles of the "Madonna-Whore" complex. Here, in *Frenzy*, things have gotten worse, not better, over time; as Peter Bogdanovich states: "The world has become darker than ever in *Frenzy*."[27] Brenda Blaney's insistence on running her marriage—and marriages in general—like a business will get her killed, in addition to having previously ruined her own relationship. The business-like "B-Women" of *Frenzy*, including the barmaid Babs (whose relationship with Blaney is hardly romantic), are all doomed because they represent the loss of whatever sensual component was previously left in the "mother-harlot" figures. As such, they are still maternal figures of a sort, but mothers who have taken their "respectability" to a degree of repression that leaves any sensuality far behind.

In the scene culminating in the horrible murder of Mrs. Blaney, which takes place, significantly, in Brenda's office at the aforementioned "Blaney Bureau," Rusk complains about the Bureau's failure to help him, and then tells Mrs. Blaney "I respect a woman like you and know how to treat you. . . . You're my type." When Brenda refuses to accommodate him, judging his "peculiar" needs a bad business risk, Rusk declares: "Women; they're all the same. Well, I'll show you." What Rusk means by women being "all the same" is the same thing meant by a number of other misogynistic comments directed against women in general throughout the film, comments such as the one by (of all people) the chief inspector who says that "These days ladies abandon their honor far more readily than their clothes," or by Blaney's kindly friend Porter who says "Mind you, there are some women who ask for everything they get." All these unfortunate comments are directed at women like Brenda who (according to Rusk) are hypocritical "whores" who can only pretend to be virtuous, women who are then punished, either verbally or physically, because they are unwilling to "deliver," not what men expect them to deliver, but what they expect such "respectable" women to withhold. Note how, in this scene, Rusk tells Brenda that she is his type, a "respectable" woman, but then becomes furious because she is unwilling to accommodate his "disrespectful" advances.

As we have seen, this paradigm—based on an original maternal figure—of avenging oneself on women who are "all the same" runs throughout the Hitchcockian oeuvre, going as far back as the "first" true Hitchcock film, *The Lodger,* where the so-called "Avenger" is "avenging" his anger at women in the same way that Rusk is here. (Hitchcock's *Vertigo* is of course the ultimate film about avenging oneself on women who are, in this case literally, "all the same.") What is different, in *Frenzy,* is that the murderer's frustration with this typical pattern of false respectability has reached a fever pitch. Unlike, say, Scottie Ferguson's murderous rage at finding out that the "harlot" Judy is not the more respectable "Madonna" Madeleine (or, rather, that she is), the respectable Brenda is all business, and so totally inaccessible to his desires. When Rusk utters, over and over again while raping Brenda, "lovely, lovely," it is as if he is commenting on the quality of a fine commodity, whether a fine piece of furniture, or even one of his fine pieces of fruit. It is the frustration of someone whose search for "love" has been replaced by the business of supplying things which are "lovely."

"Why Mr. Rusk—You're not wearing your tie"

Although Chief Inspector Oxford utters this, the last sentence of the film, in a "gotch'ya" moment of Aristotelian recognition that is a staple of the detective story genre, the statement is not really necessary at all. The chief inspector had already determined Rusk's guilt, and he now has the added evidence of Rusk's appearance with a large trunk to carry away the body of the naked strangled woman in his bed. And, as if to confirm the importance of the large trunk Rusk is carrying, the last shot—versus the last line concerning the necktie—of the film is of the selfsame closed trunk, which remains while the final credits roll on top of it. This trunk, and of course the necktie, are critical symbols in *Frenzy,* both separately as well as in their relationship to each other.

We might begin with the trunk, since it only appears in the film's final scene, whereas the necktie is important throughout. Why did Hitchcock choose the closed trunk as the last thing the viewers (versus either of the characters present) see, and then choose to emphasize this even more by leaving the camera close-up on the trunk as the final credits roll?

As we have discussed earlier in the analysis of *Psycho*, neatly disposing of things, and wrapping things up, is an obsession of both Hitchcock's "suave and seductive" villains as well as of the personally and artistically fastidious Hitchcock himself.[28] The "trunk" of the car into which the body of Marion Crane, wrapped up in a shower curtain in which forty thousand dollars has also been wrapped up in a newspaper is placed before being flushed down a local sinkhole comes to mind, as well as the trunk that contains the dead body of Brandon and Phillip's friend David in *Rope*. Like Hitchcock's other fastidious villains, Rusk, too, is trying to tidy things up before the police interrupt him, causing him to drop the aforementioned trunk.

Trunks, and the keys that open them, are an important part of the resolution of a number of Hitchcock films. In addition to *Rope* and *Psycho*, one recalls the keys which lock, or unlock, the denouements of *Notorious* and *Dial M*. Whereas one may dispute, as I have disputed throughout this book, the presence of "happy endings" in Hitchcock, there is certainly no disputing the importance of wrapping things up neatly and tidily in the end, however much the endings may also be problematic from an interpretive point of view. All of which is to say: the meaning of the trunk at the end of *Frenzy* is also the meaning of the end-as-trunk in *Frenzy*. The trunk is, first and foremost, the need to enclose, to wrap or "tidy up," which is certainly an essential feature of the end of every Hitchcock film. That the end of *Frenzy* is a sustained close-up of a trunk is thus a self-reflexive moment on Hitchcock's filmmaking in general, as well as on the "closure" of this particular film. But it is also much more.

To be a successful—or largely successful—murderer one must possess considerable organizational skills, particularly with regard to planning and execution. *One must, in a sense, be a director.* Perhaps this is why Hitchcock's villains are so likeable; at the end of *Dial M for Murder* the would-be murderer Tony (Ray Milland) offers everyone a drink before being taken off to prison. But it is not just their similar gifts for planning and "storyboarding" that relates Hitchcock to his murderers. There are numerous examples of other fastidious professionals (e.g. the police when they are not damnably incompetent) with whom Hitchcock seems to have no sympathy whatsoever. It is also their violence, usually directed against women that, from *The Lodger* on, is as much of a serial obsession with Hitchcock as it is with his serial murderers.

Which explains, I think, the aforementioned trunk. Hitchcock, not the other characters is the one staring at the trunk at the film's end. Yes, the trunk also refers to the end, the "wrapping up" of the film itself, and of the "classical" film itself. But it also refers, even more importantly, to the crime that is always contained *within* the classical confines of the Hitchcock film and narrative. As a director, Hitchcock, like his villains, tries to wrap up, to hide, to contain, to repress, to deny, the crime that, ultimately cannot be repressed or denied, cannot be hidden from view. The closed but empty trunk at the end of *Frenzy* is thus a symbol of what is not "wrapped up" at the end of this or at the end of any Hitchcock film. I am not just referring to the fact, as true and important as it may be, that Blaney, whose violent, sadistic tendencies have gone unexplained, is not simply "the wrong man" and Rusk the "right" one. I am also referring to the fact that the crimes committed in Hitchcock's films always escape the classical closure of the films themselves. In particular, the repeated violence against women, which has its roots, judging from the films we have studied, in a deep-seated mother complex (the so-called "labyrinth of the guilt-complex" referred to throughout *Spellbound*), cannot be easily contained, repressed, denied, or otherwise locked up in the guise of the murderer (the so-called "right man"), or in the guise of a director who is in a sense the real guilty party behind the crimes committed in all his films.

In *The Interpretation of Dreams*, as well as in his discussion in "The Theme of the Three Caskets" of the symbolism in Shakespeare's "The Merchant of Venice," Freud notes that boxes of all sorts are often symbols of the female and female genitalia.[29] And it is certainly the case that the trunk, in this particular narrative, is associated with the female despite a neat inversion in which the woman is placed in the box versus the box in the woman. The tie, however, seems decidedly phallic both in its appearance, its usual association with the male and, of course, the sexual use to which it is put by Rusk. As Modleski notes: "At the end of *Frenzy* the film brings together for the first time the three male protagonists—villain, 'wrong man,' and officer of the law. The chief inspector speaks on behalf of propriety, civilization, and sublimation when he observes wryly, 'Why, Mr. Rusk, you're not wearing your tie,' thereby restoring us to a world in which men are in control of themselves and their 'lusts' " (*Women Who Knew Too Much,* 110). But, if the necktie, like the trunk, represents a certain restoration of order and propriety, what does it mean that the "necktie murderer" uses a necktie as his signature in always leaving it around the women he has strangled?

An extraordinary thing, a necktie. It may be a rather obvious phallic symbol, but it is also a symbol of castration—the only other time, one might claim, that something is tied around the man's throat is when he is hanged. The fastidious Rusk is often shown wearing one, even when he is seen relaxing at home, whereas the "wrong man" Blaney, who begins the film by carefully putting on his tie as he prepares for work, gradually loses his. It is not irrelevant to recall in this regard that the equally fastidious Hitchcock always wore a tie at work; Herbert Coleman, the executive producer of the second *The Man Who Knew Too Much,* recalls how odd it was to see "Hitch" without a tie when filming in the blistering heat of Morocco. We begin, then, with the association of the necktie with work, with being gainfully employed. The tie is also associated with a certain sense of style; Rusk, after all, is something of a dandy, and if the tie is associated with work it is also associated with a sense of neatness, of not "getting one's hands dirty," something we never see Rusk (or Hitchcock) doing despite his particular line of work. Still, what does it mean when this symbol of castration, work, style and neatness is used to strangle women?

It would certainly not have escaped Hitchcock's famously dark sense of humor to have replied that the necktie is a horribly convenient means of strangulation; after all, the murderer is able to carry around his weapon openly, having it readily available whenever the appropriate occasion should arise. Moreover, the necktie is not only convenient, but efficient; the necktie becomes a weapon, a tool, an apparatus much as the camera is an apparatus applied to the mere act of seeing. Like his villain, Hitchcock eschewed the direct act of seeing by using a mediating apparatus that replaces brute, naked vision with something which is more elegantly framed and measured. Like the elegant Mr. Rusk, Hitchcock too does not "get his hands dirty" during the execution of his "dirty deeds."

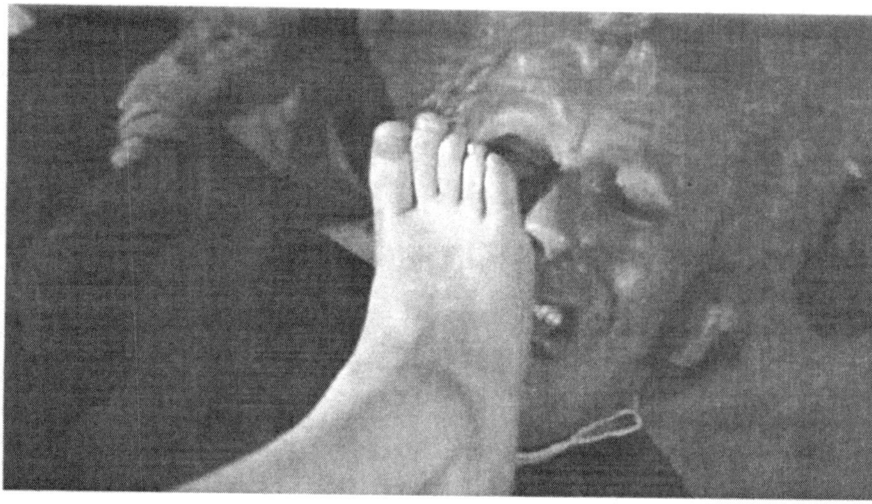

35. Another image of Hitchcock's devilishly delicious pun on "pota-toes."

Except, of course, that Rusk—and Hitchcock—*does* get his hands dirty. Rusk, as we know, is smudged and covered with potato dust when he has to climb into the truck to retrieve his pin from Babs's hand, at which time numerous potatoes, and "toes" (a deliciously dark visual pun) are thrust into his face.

And then there is the final scene of the film in which a dirty, sweaty and above all tie-less Rusk appears in his apartment. Like the trunk, the attempt to deny, or repress desire—to maintain, according to Modleski, one's sense of propriety—represented by the castrating necktie (a tie which is itself "castrated" by the signature tiepin) is ultimately a failure for the simple reason that what is denied, or repressed, is always stronger than, is indeed the cause of, the secondary acts of repression or denial. Neatness, tidiness, cleanliness, all of which were obsessions with Hitchcock and obsessions in his films, are ultimately deconstructed by the uncovering of an unconscious truth that the murderer tries to cover over even as it is being uncovered. The act of murder in all these cases and, here, in the actions of Rusk, is not about desire but about the impossibility of extinguishing—covering up—desire. As such, the idea of a "neck-tie murderer" is a perfect symbol of Freud's notion of "civilization and its discontents," of desire and the desire to deny desire that, like the necktie wound tightly around the neck, is close to murder.

In the horrifying final shot of the only murder we actually see in *Frenzy* the camera returns to show us Brenda Blaney after she has expired. Even more horrifying than the murder itself, which is certainly more gruesome than any scene in Hitchcock and perhaps, as Modleski states, in any film, is the final shot of the victim sprawled out half-naked with the necktie still wrapped tightly around her.[30] (Rothman refers to this memorable scene as "the most heartbreaking passage in Hitchcock's work" [*Murderous Gaze,* 250], but the sentiment—the heart that is broken—is, I believe, his and not Hitchcock's.) What is especially disturbing here is the fact that "She [Mrs. Blaney] stuck her tongue out, *exactly as Hitchcock asked her to.*"[31] Visually, the distended tongue parallels the necktie that is still wrapped around her, yet sticking one's tongue out, now as then, is certainly the very opposite of the sort of propriety that the tie is meant to represent. The two together represent, I think, exactly what Hitchcock wants to say about this murder, namely, that the very civilized tie, and the very uncivilized distended tongue, are one and the same. As such, the image is a variation on the neatly closed trunk with a body inside, as well on the opening scene in which the Minister, praising the progress in cleaning up the Thames and ridding London of its wastes and poisons, has instead produced a murdered, naked woman floating to its surface.

"It looks like a pig's foot"

Marriages, whether potential (as in *Rear Window, The Birds, Marnie*) or actual (*Mr. and Mrs. Smith, Rebecca, Suspicion, The Paradine Case, Dial "M" for Murder, Rear Window, The Man Who Knew Too Much,* etc.), are never really "happy" in Hitchcock. I have argued previously that even where potential marriages might be successful (as at the end of *Shadow of a Doubt* or *North by Northwest*) such inferences are largely wishful, conjectural, or ironic. This should not surprise us, for it would be hard to imagine the world of Hitchcock's films being "smoothed over" by a societal contract that is distinctly incompatible with the unruly perversions of a Freudian unconscious to which these films are remarkably faithful.[32] And, more specifically, the successful transference of one's original maternal desires onto a new love object (a new "mother," as it were) that is, according to

Freud, required of even a relatively happy marriage is prohibited both by the mothers who, like Sebastian's mother in *Notorious* or Mitch's mother Lydia in *The Birds,* block such a transference, or by potential love-objects who are, themselves, Madonnas, whores, or otherwise thinly disguised maternal figures.[33]

Throughout *Frenzy* we are treated to a "running gag" involving the chief inspector and his wife. During the film Chief Inspector Oxford is served various esoteric and decidedly unappetizing "continental" meals such as *soupe de poisson* (with various fish-heads and other viscous items floating on its surface), *caille aux raisins* (quail with grapes), and the aforementioned pig's feet (*pieds de porc*), all of which are deemed inedible by the dutiful husband who either secretly tosses them away or else finds ways to excuse himself from eating. Chief Inspector Oxford almost never complains to his wife about this state of affairs, choosing instead to make up for his secret fasts by eating out; at work we see him consume a very hearty breakfast of sausages, eggs, ham, and toast. At one point, however, the Chief Inspector can not help but blurt out, when telling his wife about the roadside diner where he obtained evidence against Rusk, that it was "a pull-in [i.e. truck-stop] where they serve humble food. Like bacon and egg sandwiches. Sausages and mashed potatoes." The husband's passionate description, which is mixed with equal parts longing and regret, makes a strong impression on his wife, who can only stare at the chief inspector, speechless and embarrassed.

One might have expected Mrs. Oxford to express anger, resentment or contempt at her husband's fantasy. Her expression of embarrassment, and even shame, is something of a surprise but, as such, is all the more important. The "coarse" fare mentioned by the chief inspector offends his wife because it is the sort of "steak and potatoes" meal that is meant to satisfy, versus the various concoctions served by the wife which all have exotic names but offer nothing substantial to eat. Indeed, the very word "eating" is conspicuously missing from the wife's vocabulary, who has replaced it with a "dining" experience replete with everything—exquisite settings, dim lighting, etc.—except the food itself. Dinner with the Oxfords is akin, in a way, to anorexia or other such disorders that replace the act of eating with more "spiritual" nourishment.

Freud identified sex and hunger as the two great libidinal drives, primary, "primitive" drives that are thus both subjected to a considerable degree of repression, albeit repression of different sorts.[34] The "humble fare" that the dignified chief inspector craves from his wife is not, one must imagine, just food. Their relationship has clearly become, as we are told in the Spoto biography (and confirmed elsewhere) Hitchcock's relationship to Alma was, one based on other concerns, and one in which the delights of gourmet dining have replaced those of sex.[35] This humorous motif is of considerable importance here and elsewhere in demonstrating, yet again, that Hitchcock's own obsession with the coarse, crude fare of sex, murder, and "pota-toes" is accompanied by—or even caused by—a correspondingly high degree of civilized culture and restraint. As such, the relationship between the inspector and his wife is not all bad: for one thing, their grisly nightly discussion of his cases is touching, and reminds us of Hitchcock's own close working relationship to Alma. For another, like Alma, the Inspector's wife is usually right; she knows, for example, that Blaney is innocent long before the inspector does.

In her discussion of *Frenzy* Tania Modleski discusses the importance of this running gag involving the chief inspector and his wife. I agree with her notion that, at the heart of the food=sex equation proffered throughout the film, there is a fear of women (i.e. the "vagina dentata" motif of being devoured by women) and, more specifically, a fear of the mother ("matrophobia") that "is central in much of Hitchcock's work, even where it is not apparent" (*Women Who Knew Too Much,* 107). This, I might add, is all the more important insofar as it is a woman who is constantly serving her husband inedible food. I would disagree, however, with Modleski's view of the wife's meals as "forcing the spectator into symbolically sharing the unholy feast with the Inspector" (109–10) since, for the most part, the inspector doesn't eat the meals and, moreover, the meals, while decidedly abject, are hardly "unholy." The meals may well represent, as Modleski argues, the devouring of the mother, but it is important to hear that phrase with the richly ambiguous "of" which refers both to the devouring *of* the mother—going back to the child's nursing at the mother's breast, the "first love object"—and the devouring *by* the mother—the separation from the "real food" that the chief inspector experiences nightly when his wife serves him highly civilized but inedible cuisine. In craving real, "humble" food like the potato the inspector's disdain for his wife's continental cuisine has also revealed a link with the brutal but dapper Rusk, for both men demonstrate the same desire for an original object of desire that, precisely because it is so basic, can only be denied, until it returns, sometimes in the most unusual ways and places. There is, in the end, precious little difference in Hitchcock's world between a body found floating on the Thames, a fish head peering out from a bowl of soup, and a woman's toe extruding from a heap of potatoes, for all reveal the director's signature concern with the horror underlying all civilized constraints, and with the desired mother whose frequent nightmarish persona is, as we have seen, a further function of this constraint. And if, as the Hitchcock scholar Ken Mogg has pointed out, "rusk" is an English term for breadstick, then the playful snapping of the latter by the chief inspector's wife in near unison with Rusk's snapping of Babs' finger can only further exemplify this equation of food with the mother's body. "Pota-Toes," indeed.

10
Afterword: Other Hitchcock Films

HITCHCOCK MADE OVER FIFTY FEATURE FILMS. OF THESE I HAVE DIS-cussed, at length, only eight. I deliberately chose six films from the so-called "golden age" of Hitchcock (from the mid-1950s to the mid-1960s) because, despite the fact that these are also his most frequently discussed films, there are remarkably few, if any, sustained Freudian, psychoanalytical interpretations of even one of these pictures.[1] It makes sense, then, to make one's case for the applicability of this approach to what are generally seen as Hitchcock's greatest films. Moreover, in order not to limit my argument to these films I have included two additional films from before and after the period in question: *Shadow of a Doubt,* from the early 1940s, and *Frenzy,* Hitchcock's penultimate film of 1972. But since I have focused, in the present work, on less than one-sixth of the Hitchcock oeuvre, it seems important to indicate how the Freudian interpretations offered here might be applied to a number of Hitchcock's other films. My hope is that the obvious shortcomings of these brief "minireadings" may be compensated for by their few merits, which are meant only to indicate ways in which such readings may proceed in including, *mutatis mutandis,* these as well as the majority of Hitchcock's films.

REBECCA

Critics' comments on *Rebecca* (1940) have often been directed at the story of the nameless protagonist's (Joan Fontaine's) life at Manderley, a forbidding estate that, for all its wealth, bears an uncanny resemblance to the Bates Motel in containing terrible secrets of sexual transgression, and even murder. The mother figure of the earlier film is clearly the evil Mrs. Danvers, a figure every bit as frightening, and dominating, as Norman's mother, although the absent Rebecca, the former Mrs. de Winter, is also a mother figure who "closes the narrative—spectrally—in a manner not unlike Mrs. Bates's final emergence as the voice and author of Norman's seeing."[2] I would like, however, to turn the reader's attention to the events preceding the nameless young woman's arrival at Manderley, as well as to yet another, third mother figure who dominates the earlier part of the film in which Max first meets his future bride. As is usually the case for such beginnings, the first part of the film establishes the essence of the narrative and presents us with characters who do not substantially change throughout the course of the film. In particular, the childlike figure to whom we are introduced will remain a child throughout most of the film; indeed, the rest of the story depends on it.[3]

Even before arriving at Manderley, where the dead Rebecca's "ghost" still rules the estate and everyone in it, the new Mrs. de Winter is already possessed by the ghosts and spirits of others. Indeed, if Hitchcock (and Daphne du Maurier) chose to leave the protagonist nameless, it is because she perfectly complements the figure of Rebecca, who is as lacking in a body as the new bride is lacking in a name. The nameless young woman is employed by a wealthy, obnoxious older woman to attend to her needs while the two are vacationing in Monte Carlo. The corpulent Mrs. Van Hopper, who makes herself detestable by constantly bossing her charge around ("Quick! Bring me some chocolates!") is not unlike a number of other mother figures encountered in Hitchcock. We recall the wife of Thorwald in *Rear Window,* who also demands to be waited on in bed, as well as the "necktie murderer's" mother in *Frenzy* who demanded that her son "peel me a grape." But as detestable as is our poor little Cinderella's "mother," her recently deceased father is just as beloved. The young woman becomes highly emotional in telling Max about the father she adored, an unsuccessful artist who painted the same tree over and over because "he had a theory that if you should find one perfect thing or place or person you should stick to it." The theory, which is certainly a questionable principle for a painter, is nonetheless highly relevant as a theory about the teller's own relationship to her adored, "perfect" father. It explains why she is and remains an infantilized figure whose relationship to the much older and much more mature widower Max is essentially that of a child to its parent: "The most urgent story question . . . has to do with whether the neglected, endlessly disappointing child bride can seduce her besotted, groggy 'father' away from the sorceress 'mother.' "[4]

"Eat it up like a good little girl," and "Stop biting your nails" are two of the comments Max makes to the woman he is courting; later, at Manderley, he will state, with regard to his new bride, that one "can't be too careful with children." The beloved father also explains why the first mother figure, Mrs. Van Hopper, is so repulsive. When Max and the young woman start seeing each other, and throughout their courtship, it is in secret, and behind Mrs. Van Hopper's rather large back. The reason for this, which is certainly not necessary on any narrative grounds, is the same reason why the beloved father is coupled with the detested mother: the daughter's relationship to the father is forbidden (in an unfilmed episode of the shooting script Joan Fontaine vomits onboard a ship because of Maxim's cigar), and the obstacle to that desired relationship is not only undesired, but undesirable.[5] If, as in the case of figures like Uncle Charlie, Norman Bates, and Rusk, it is the desired mother who represents this undesirable figure, that is because, although for the son the mother is turned into a repulsive figure in order to deny the very beginning of desire, for the daughter it is because of the mother's being an obstacle to the father's love. Finally, I should add that this version of the young woman's "positive Oedipal complex" (i.e., the daughter's desire for the father) would not preclude seeing this as the sort of "screen memory" of a "pre-Oedipal" desire for the aforementioned beloved mother described by Kaja Silverman in her extraordinary book on cinematic representations of female desire.[67]

It is not difficult to see how this "prestory" in Monte Carlo prefigures the main story at Manderley. The figure of Rebecca, Max's deceased first wife, would represent the original wife/mother whom the new Mrs. de Winter has replaced, a scenario discussed by Freud in his analysis of Ibsen's *Rosmersholm* (indeed, if anyone is as "wrecked by success" as Rebecca West in *Rosmersholm,* it is the new Mrs. De Winter).[8] This would explain why the new bride can not successfully take over as the new "lady of the manor," a point which is made painfully evident throughout the film, as when, for example, she must set the table with napkins monogrammed with the "RdW" of Max's first wife. It also explains the forbidding figure of Mrs. Danvers, the woman whose fierce devotion to Rebecca makes her into yet another detestable mother figure whose only goal is to deny the new Mrs. de Winter any comfort in her undeserved role. Finally, Max's scandalous wife can also be understood as based on the same fantasy of successfully overcoming the incest taboo by displacing the forbidden aspects of love onto the mother ("Rebecca [herself] is subjected to a brutal devaluation and punishment") rather than onto the daughter where they properly belong.[9]

Notorious

It is tempting to speak, albeit somewhat convolutedly, of the MacGuffin of Hitchcock's MacGuffin. By this I mean that the idea of the MacGuffin, which is not an invention of the critics but rather an idea authored by Hitchcock himself (discussed in his interviews with Truffaut), is itself a MacGuffin. The celebrated notion that a Hitchcock film, usually one of his espionage films, contains some artificial device that is meant to give the film its raison d'être (the radioactive material of *Notorious,* the microfilm of *North by Northwest,* etc.) is itself really artificial and of little or no importance. It is also possible to argue that the MacGuffin is itself a MacGuffin if one extends the notion beyond its usual limited reference to include more than merely a small artificial "plot device." One might consider (as I have here) the bird attacks of Hitchcock's *magnum opus* of 1963 a MacGuffin relative to the "real story" of Mitch and Melanie—a notion supported by Ken Mogg's recent discovery of another source for the film that emphasizes the human story more than does the du Maurier version.[10] Similarly, one might consider the entire espionage story, and not just the part about the radioactive dust, of Hitchcock's 1946 film *Notorious* a MacGuffin relative to the "real story" of Devlin's and Sebastian's love for Alicia Huberman, a woman who, in the words of Devlin, "is first, last, and foremost *not* a lady." By focusing, in this brief analysis, on the story of this "notorious" woman one realizes, yet again, how dark and disturbing is Hitchcock's view of romance, and why it was important to hide that story from view with the creation of various sorts of "MacGuffins."

No less a figure than J. Edgar Hoover was aware that *Notorious* had gone far beyond the boundaries of a good "spy story"—

and good taste—with the creation of the titular figure of Alicia Huberman (Ingrid Bergman). It is amusing to note that the head of the FBI was concerned, not with the politics of the film (which are always suspect for the intensely cynical Hitchcock), but with the "loose morals" of the main character.[11] The film does indeed make it very clear that, in today's parlance, Alicia Huberman is a "slut," or, more politely, a fallen, "loose" woman. After being introduced to her at a dinner party in which she agrees, in a drunken state, to go away with a much older (and equally inebriated) man, Devlin compliments Alicia when, a week later, she has "been sober for eight days, and, as far as I can tell, no new conquests." Realizing the sarcasm of such comments, Alicia replies, "Once a tramp, always a tramp." Such aspersions continue throughout the film, although they are sometimes softened to "We have no illusions about women of that kind," and "She's good at making friends with gentlemen." However, Alicia Huberman's "notorious" character is only a small but integral part of a much larger story (*not* the spy story), a story that includes her own desire for respectability, the two men who love her, and the mother of one of these who "has always been jealous of every woman I've (Sebastian/Claude Rains) ever shown any interest in." A larger story, in other words, that extends throughout Hitchcock's films.

Although, as Tania Modleski points out, "In a way, *Notorious* reverses the situation developed in *Suspicion,*" this is just as true of another of the "female Gothic" films of the 1940s.[12] Unlike the young woman of *Rebecca* who, as we just saw, adored her recently deceased father and is subsequently infantilized in her relationship with an older father figure, Alicia Huberman is at best ambivalent toward her own father, a Nazi sympathizer who is taken away from her at the beginning of the film when he is sentenced to twenty years in prison for treason. Alicia, we learn, had earlier refused to support her father's request for her to help him in his spying ("I'll see you all hang before I raise a finger against it [the United States]. . . . Don't ever come near nor speak to me again about your rotten schemes"), but she is now willing to do precisely that for Devlin and his FBI associates. Like many of the women discussed in this book (Judy in *Vertigo,* Eve in *North by Northwest,* Marion in *Psycho,* Melanie in *The Birds* and Marnie in *Marnie),* Alicia is also a fallen woman who is poised, and often eager, to gain respectability. But, unlike all those women, and certainly unlike the young woman in *Rebecca,* Alicia's betrayal of and by her own "treasonous" father has pushed her even further from the possibility of attaining respectability than any of the other women mentioned. Alicia, in a word, is a "fallen woman" because she has violated and been (symbolically) violated by her father. The fact that, in the cruelest moments of the film, she is ridiculed and rejected by the men for whom she is risking her life only really makes sense when viewed as a symbolical representation/repetition of her earlier mistreatment by the father, who also betrayed her allegiance to her true "father"-land. Modleski comes close to this reading of *Notorious* in her discussion of the relation of Alicia's "promiscuity" to the father's treason ("the father's lack of fidelity to the law causes his daughter's excessive sexuality," *Women Who Knew Too Much,* 58), although she does not relate this important "prestory" to Oedipal desire for the father that is then transferred on to the other Oedipal story of Sebastian and his domineering mother that, I would argue, is central to all aspects of the film and not, as Modleski argues, "very different" (64) from Devlin's relationship to Alicia.

Like the other "fallen women" of Hitchcock, Alicia also represents the mother whose sexuality with the father breaks the aura of her "purity" and makes of her a "whore." This is played out by the two men who love Alicia, the one a younger man who treats her sadistically (Devlin, played by Cary Grant), the other an older, wealthy, sophisticated man who nonetheless adores her to the point of being infantilized by his love. (Sebastian's [Claude Rains'] mother later tells him that she and the other Nazi spies "have been protected by the enormity of his stupidity" in falling in love with Miss Huberman.) Dev's cruel treatment of Alicia is the result of her "notorious" behavior and her involvement with the older men (her father, the man at the party, and Sebastian) who are, literally as well as symbolically, its cause. Devlin's own rather shocking mistreatment of Alicia is the result of his desire for a mother figure who is a "whore" because of her notorious involvement with older men, i.e., the father, just as Roger Thornhill's excessive mistreatment of Eve in *North by Northwest* ("Isn't everybody in her room?"), and Scottie's excessive mistreatment of Judy in *Vertigo,* is caused by their involvement with same. On the other hand, Sebastian's love for his domineering mother, like that of Norman in *Psycho,* will lead him to try and murder the very woman he adores precisely because she represents the impossible sexual-mother (hence his infantilized behavior around her). We thus realize a particularly gruesome irony in the fact that Devlin's hatred of Alicia ultimately saves her, while Sebastian's love for his young bride will ultimately cause him—with his mother's assistance, of course—to try and kill her.

The end of the film, in which Dev and Alicia drive off leaving Sebastian to die, hardly resolves the problems of their own previous troubling relationship; as we have seen, the endings of Hitchcock's films never do. One would have to disagree, then, with Stefan Sharff, whose brilliant formal analysis of this and other Hitchcock films (regarding *Notorious* he rightly claims that "Moving cinema is used . . . with a brilliance and originality hardly seen before") leads him to the surprising conclusion that, at the film's end, "love wins, as do the interests of the United States."[13] Not that Sharff is alone in reading the ending of this film in what I would claim are, for Hitchcock, impossibly upbeat terms. Commenting on Alisha's redemption Irving Singer argues that "she will be purged not only of the murderous fluids but also of the sexual past that has been poisoning her access to desirable marriage."[14] Modleski, however, is less sanguine about the end of the film, which she sees as a return to patriarchy with the taming of the "notorious" woman: "The fact is, Devlin has the full power of the law behind him, as Alicia has not. The inequality of power relations means that . . . the man—hero or spectator—gets to displace his masochistic urges onto a female victim and can therefore maintain a mastery which enables him to deny his suffering while at the same safely indulging it."[15] The "silver lining" that Modleski nonetheless finds in Hitchcock is that, in this case, the notorious woman may be tamed but she "can never be completely subdued or fully known" (*Women Who Knew Too Much*, 71), a view that I feel is less of a challenge to patriarchy when seen in the light of the mother figure who, in this Hitchcock film and others, holds all the keys.

Dial M for Murder

Although largely overshadowed by *Rear Window*, which was made in the same year (1954) as *Dial M for Murder*, the two films have more in common than the illustrious Grace Kelly. (Rothman is one of a number of important critics who believe that the 3D version of *Dial M* enhances, if not secures, its place as a major Hitchcock film.)[16] Both films feature, at their center, the murder (or attempted murder) by a husband of a wife. While the reason for Tony Wendice's (Ray Milland) attempt on Margot Mary Wendice's life is the adulterous affair between her and Mark Haliday (Robert Cummings), and we don't know what drove Thorwald to kill his wife in *Rear Window,* there is, in fact, a connection to be made between the motives for the two crimes. In talking with the "hit man" hired to murder his wife, Tony explains that "She tried to make me give up tennis and play husband instead." This must remind us of the similar situation in *Rear Window,* where not only is the murderer Thorwald seen caring for his wife at home but, more importantly, much time is spent discussing (and arguing over) Jeff Jeffries's reluctance to give up his career as a traveling international newspaper photographer and settle down with a rather insistent Lisa Fremont (Grace Kelly). Since, as we discussed in the earlier analysis of *Rear Window,* Jeff's interest in the murder of Thorwald's wife must, to some extent, be taken as a parallel to his own marked disinterest in, and resentment of, Lisa's attempt to run his life, we can not help but observe that both these films of 1954 deal with the murder of a beautiful wife who seeks to control her "husband's" independence. It is for this reason, perhaps, that Ray Milland's performance—and appearance—in *Dial M for Murder* resembles so closely the appearance of James Stewart in *Rear Window,* despite the fact that the latter is certainly a very different actor in both style and appearance. It is as if, in making *Dial M for Murder,* Hitchcock was already thinking about *Rear Window,* and vice versa.

Dial M for Murder is much more than a conventional story of a husband who attempts to kill his wife because of an affair. We don't really know, in watching *Dial M,* what to think of Tony, Mark, or Margot. Is Tony not a cold-blooded killer, despite the fact of being cuckolded by his wife over a period of many years? Is Margot not a sympathetic victim, despite her long-standing affair, which came after the aforementioned insistence that Tony give up his life as a professional tennis player and continues to the present day? Is Mark not a devoted lover, despite his continued attentions to another man's wife? The rich moral ambiguity of *Dial M for Murder* is best exemplified in the fact that, as numerous critics have noted, the murderous Tony is a much more interesting and sympathetic character than the boyfriend Mark. (Rothman notes how Robert Cummings's "blandness" is also a criticism of Americans' love of the cliché.)[17] What is one to think, after all, about a criminal who, when he is finally exposed in the end after having plotted and planned a murder so carefully throughout the film, has the good manners to offer everyone a drink before being taken away to jail?

These questions become less puzzling when applying the psychoanalytic pattern we have discovered in our analysis of Hitchcock's other films. The "nagging wife" syndrome that, we have noted, is a surprising but undeniable part of Grace Kelly's character here and in *Rear Window*, is less a function of her "real" character than it is of the male hero's (Ray Milland's/James Stewart's) Oedipal fear of the "respectability" that cannot, for Hitchcock, be reconciled with sexual desire. The wife's "nagging" is, in these terms, the repression of his own "nagging" sexual desire for a maternal object that he can only feel guilty for desiring. This is why the nagging is also found in more obvious mother figures like Mrs. Bates, who persistently nags Norman about his sexual desire because they are really directed *at*—not just *by*—her. It is for this reason that Norman's desires for Marion Crane are misunderstood when seen as the "disgusting" behavior Mrs. Bates is criticizing; they are, sadly, his own attempt at overcoming his Oedipal desires. This also explains the oddity about *Dial M for Murder*, namely, the fact that Mark and Margot's adulterous affair is never condemned in the film, but actually becomes virtuous when compared to the husband's desire to kill Margot. For the "adultery" of Mark and Margot, like Norman's voyeuristic desire for Marion in *Psycho*, is a "healthy" counterpart to Tony's desire to kill the mother figure who, because of the guilt imposed by the Oedipal complex, would deny him (and Jeff in *Rear Window*) his independence. Alas, the reason that such independence from the mother, a "healthy" romantic relationship, can never be achieved in Hitchcock is demonstrated by the fact that it is itself seen as perverse—adulterous or, for poor Norman, voyeuristic—relative to the "original," and in this sense, truly "normal" attraction to the mother.[18] M-argot M-ary . . . there really is, in Hitchcock, only one letter to be "dialed," and it is indeed synonymous, as it is almost homonymous, with "murder."

The Man Who Knew Too Much (1956)

Hitchcock only remade one film in his career, and I would like to consider, in this brief commentary, the possibility that the director's return to this particular film, where "once again at issue is a mother's determination to retrieve her lost son," was not as arbitrary as is generally believed.[19] The reason, I will argue, for Hitchcock's return to this particular film is that it is the only one in which the boy's separation from his mother, a "reality" that is only made manifest in a displaced or otherwise latent form elsewhere (as in Carlotta's search for her child in *Vertigo*), is here literally represented. The only film, then, to which Hitchcock returned, is a film in which the child—in this case, a son—is returned to its mother, a desire which, in all the other films, is hoped for but never achieved.

And yet the fulfillment of such a desire—of desire itself—is impossible, is "too much," even for a director who, by all accounts, certainly "knew too much" himself to accept such a fantasy.[20] One approach to *The Man Who Knew Too Much* would be to conflate the figures of Ben and Hank MacKenna, the father and the son who is kidnapped. This would entail, among other things, seeing Ben's story, the story of a father who accidentally learns too much about an assassination plot as the same story as Hank's separation from his mother. That the son's abduction is the cause, and not merely caused by, the "MacGuffin" story of international intrigue, can be briefly demonstrated here.[21]

The event which begins the plot "proper" is not, as it is often assumed to be, the moment early in the film when Louis Bernard, staggering through the Marakesh bazaar with a knife in his back, whispers his last words to Dr. Ben MacKenna. It is rather the moment even earlier when Ben's son Hank accidentally creates a disturbance on the bus that is taking the family to their hotel upon their arrival in Morocco.[22] Murray Pomerance is right when he notes that "all Ben MacKenna's woes ensue from the fact that he does not turn and use [the emergency exit off the bus]," but it is not the meeting with Henri Bernard that causes "all Ben MacKenna's woes," it is the event that precipitates the disturbance that in turn leads to the meeting with Bernard.[23] The accident that causes the riot is handled rather clumsily, leading one to suspect that there is more to it than just the accident itself, since the introduction of Bernard could certainly have been handled a hundred other ways. Indeed, this "accident" is highly significant, to which we even have Henri Bernard's odd comment regarding the scene that "The Moslem religion allows for few accidents."

"Your little boy," Henri Bernard tells the MacKennas, "accidentally pulled off his [the angry Arab who has confronted the family] wife's veil." For anyone who has traveled to a Moslem country, where the obligatory veil is even more common now than it was in 1956, it is hard to imagine how this could accidentally happen. It was evidently hard for Hitchcock to imagine too, since we don't actually see the "accident" occur. It is easier—albeit more disturbing—to imagine someone pulling off a veil, especially a little boy who would not be expected to understand the veil's religious significance, but who *would* be expected to see it as something playful, the way masks usually function in the West. Hank would also not have realized that the veil is worn to protect a woman—in this case, a wife—from uncontrolled, improper sexual attention. In the boy's removing the wife's veil, in thus violating the wife's sexuality, Hank has violated the taboo that is not only the "cornerstone" of this film, but—according to Freud—to all civilization.[24] His punishment will follow the biblical *lex talionis* in taking away from him the object of his original desire, in "veiling" from him the older married woman, the mother, whom he has here—albeit symbolically —attempted to violate.[25]

If young Hank MacKenna "knows too much" in unveiling the Moslem woman, it is for the older MacKenna to continue this story of "the man who knew too much." What happens, in other words, when the boy who "knows too much" becomes "the man who knew too much"? The notion that we are dealing here, as elsewhere in Hitchcock, with a "man-child" who wishes to unveil the taboo woman, i.e. the mother, is evident in a number of ways, only a few of which I will mention here. First, one must look closely at the relationship between Ben McKenna and his wife Jo. As the relationship with the overly-friendly Henri Bernard develops, it is the wife Jo who is quick to pick up on the fact that there is something wrong, while her husband appears completely clueless. Frustrated by his typically American forthrightness (one of the delights of the remake is the way Hitchcock thoroughly enjoyed dissecting the mannerisms of his new country) Jo complains, "You don't *know anything* about this man and he *knows everything* about you." For someone who supposedly knows too much, it appears that Dr. McKenna knows far too little while Jo, a former singer who retired to become a mother (another version of the Madonna/Harlot transformation we have seen so often in Hitchcock), seems to know everything. Similarly, we are reminded of the scenes, later in the film, when Ben wrongly thinks "Ambrose Chappell" is a person while Jo correctly goes to the church where the Draytons are keeping Hank; when Jo's scream saves the prime minister; and when her boisterous rendering of "Que sera sera" leads Ben to Hank.

If Ben McKenna does "know too much" it is tantamount, it seems, to knowing too little, whereas Jo's maternal knowledge seems able to undo the damage caused by Ben's excessive knowledge. Again, my main objection to Tania Modleski's brilliant work, which takes its title from the title of this film, is that "the women who knew too much" are the result of an infantile projection of a mother fantasy and not a reality. If, as we have suggested, Jo comes closest to representing the "original love object" that is the maternal matrix of many of Hitchcock's films, then Jo's knowledge, and Ben's lack of same, makes perfect sense, for Ben's attempt to know "too much," like Hank's attempt to unveil the Moslem woman, is forbidden, and can only end in failure. A point which Hitchcock drives home by Jo's two acts of "heroism" just mentioned. When Jo screams to save the prime minister, it is an act that is, at the time, a death sentence for her son—a disturbing fact often ignored by critics of the film such as Bill Krohn, who refers to the scene in Albert Hall only as the place "where Jo saves a man's life."[26] And when she sings the song that ultimately leads to Hank's rescue, it is not, as one might expect, a song of love and devotion, but rather the uncomforting story of a mother who (in the first and third stanzas) repeatedly fends off her child's questions about her/his future happiness in love by replying in a noncommittal way that "whatever will be, will be."

When I was just a little girl,
I asked my mother, "What will I be?
Will I be pretty, will I be rich?"
Here's what she said to me . . .

CHORUS:
Que sera, sera
Whatever will be, will be
The future's not ours to see
Que sera, sera
What will be, will be

When I grew up and fell in love,
I asked my sweetheart, "What lies ahead?
Will we have rainbows day after day?"
Here's what my sweetheart said . . .

CHORUS

Now, I have children of my own
They ask their mother, "What will I be?
Will I be handsome, will I be rich?"
I tell them tenderly . . .

CHORUS[27]

Michael Walker, in his wonderfully encyclopedic analysis of *Hitchcock's Motifs*, mentions that "the family reunion at the end of the remake seems genuinely happy, lacking the unease of the ending of the British version," but he is doubtless referring to the attempt at a lighthearted codicil that occurs when the MacKennas return to a long delayed party at their hotel.[28] More like the British version in its "unease" is the real end of the film, in which the father Ben leads Hank away from the "mother" who is willing to die for him. Murray Pomerance has written a fascinating essay concerning a close-up of this other mother—Lucy—during the sermon scene in Ambrose Chapel as indicating "the moment when we have the first inkling that Hank will be found and saved."[29] If Hitchcock's films, like those of Pedro Almodóvar, are "all about my mother," then being the "man who knew too much" will produce a director whose very greatness will often be marked, as in *Psycho* or *Vertigo*, by catastrophic failure or, as here, by a highly muted and very tenuous reunion between a mother and her child.

Notes

Chapter 1. Introduction

1. William Rothman, *Hitchcock: The Murderous Gaze* (Cambridge, MA: Harvard University Press, 1982), 246. Stefan Sharff, *Alfred Hitchcock's High Vernacular* (New York: Columbia University Press, 1991), 40.

2. See Jason Cangiolosi's study of the staircase motif in three of Hitchcock's British films (*Blackmail, Rich and Strange, The 39 Steps*): "Alfred Hitchcock's Stairways of Attraction." http://www.associatedcontent.com/article/12992/alfred_hitchcocks_stairways_of_attraction.html. See also Michael Walker, *Hitchcock's Motifs* (Amsterdam: Amsterdam University Press, 2005), "Staircases," 350–72. Laura Mulvey, *Fetishism and Curiousity* (Bloomington: Indiana University Press, 1996,), 64.

3. George Toles, "Mother Calls the Shots: Hitchcock's Female Gaze," in *A House Made of Light* (Detroit, MI: Wayne State University Press, 2001), 226.

4. Raymond Bellour, *The Analysis of Film* (Bloomington: Indiana University Press, 2000), 224.

5. Kaja Silverman, *The Acoustic Mirror* (Bloomington: Indiana University Press, 1988), ch. 6, "The Female Authorial Voice."

6. Elizabeth Cowie, *Representing the Woman* (Minneapolis: University of Minnesota, 1997), 216.

7. Toles, *House Made of Light*, 201–2.

8. Barbara Creed, *The Monstrous Feminine: Film, Feminism, Psychoanalysis* (London: Routledge, 1993), 143.

9. Bellour, *Analysis of Film*, 230. Bellour sees instead the m-names as "originating in a cultural fantasy arising from the ferment of his Catholic upbringing, M as in Mary." It is worth noting that Hitchcock's own mother Emma died during the making of *Shadow of a Doubt*.

10. Tania Modleski, *The Women Who Knew Too Much* (New York: Methuen, 1988), 107.

11. Michael Walker notes that the earliest instance of the type appears in *Easy Virtue* (1927). *Hitchcock's Motifs* (Amsterdam: Amsterdam University Press, 2005), 307. Rothman, *Murderous Gaze*, 146, 357.

12. Richard Allen, "Psychoanalytic Film Theory," in *A Companion to Film Theory* (Oxford: Blackwell, 1999), 142.

13. In a recent, encyclopedic survey of *Hitchcock's Motifs* by Michael Walker the author provides a schematic drawing of the "house" of Hitchcock themes and motifs which, without any psychoanalytic bias, supports my contention

about the centrality of this figure. Not insignificantly, the title of Walker's chapter on this particular motif is "Mothers and Houses."

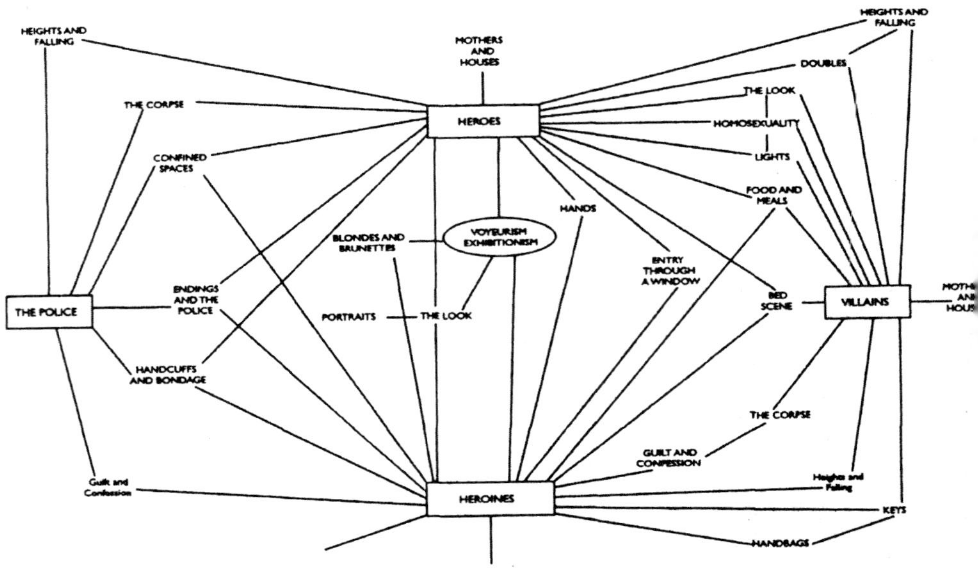

14. Jonathan Freedman and Richard Millington, eds., *Hitchcock's America* (Oxford: Oxford University Press,1999), and Richard Allen and S. Ishii-Gonzalès, eds., *Centenary Essays* (London: British Film Institute, 1999).

15. Richard Millington, "Hitchcock and American Culture," in *Hitchcock's America*, eds. Freedman and Millington, 136.

16. Margaret Horoitz, "*The Birds:* A Mother's Love," *Wide Angle* vol.5, no. 1 (1982): 44.

17. David Spoto, *The Art of Hitchcock* (New York: Anchor, 1976) continues: "nothing in the final analysis is analyzable at all. The madness is inscrutable" (326). I respectfully disagree, however, with the notion that, because the psychiatrist is wrong, "nothing is analyzable at all," and hope to convince the reader of this in the chapter on *Psycho* included in this volume.

In a clear exception to the abovementioned "dearth" of Freudian readings of Hitchcock Andrew Britton has explores the important Oedipal complexes in *Spellbound* of *both* Ballantyne and Constance. See "Hitchcock's Spellbound: Text and Counter-Text," *cineAction* 3–4 (1986): 72–83. My thanks to X (reader) for this important reference.

18. Daniel Spoto's astute comment about the motif of "covering up" in *Psycho* ("Everyone in the story has something to hide"), like his equally astute comment about the importance of mirrors in the film, is a good example of how one critic's endpoint can provide an excellent beginning for a psychoanalytic discussion of the same motif. Spoto, *Art of Hitchcock*, 316, 320.

19. In "Alfred Hitchcock and Therapeutic Culture in America" (*Hitchcock's America*, eds. Freedman and Millington. Jonathan Freedman discusses Hitchcock's skepticism and ambivalence about the popularity of psychoanalysis among Selznick and others among Hollywood's elite. The argument of the present volume agrees with this overt skepticism, but deals with the psychoanalytic interpretation of the films, the validity of which is not affected by this ambivalence.

Ian Cameron and Richard Jeffery, "The Universal Hitchcock," in *A Hitchcock Reader*, eds. Deutelbaum and Poague (Ames: Iowa State University Press, 1986), 265–78.

20. William Paul, "Ultimate formlessness: Cinema, Horror, and the Limits of Meaning," in *Horror Film and Psychoanalysis*, ed. Schneider (Cambridge: Cambridge University Press, 2004), 159.

21. André Green, *The Dead Mother* (London: Routledge, 1999), 24

22. Kaja Silverman, *The Acoustic Mirror* (Bloomington: Indiana University Press, 1988), 120.

23. Sarah Kofman, *The Childhood of Art* (New York: Columbia University Press, 1988). Freud's various essays on art and art-related matters are collected in *Creativity and Unconscious* (New York: Harper, 1958) and, more recently, in *Writings on Art and Literature* (Stanford, CA: Stanford University Press, 1997).

24. "Yet, although it is clear that psychoanalysis does not trust the visible . . . neither does the cinema." Mary Ann Doane, "Veiling over Desire," *Feminism and Psychoanalysis*, ed. Richard Feldstein and Judess Roof (Ithaca, NY: Cornell University Press, 1989), 107.

25. Sharff, *Alfred Hitchcock's High Vernacular*, 3.

26. Samuel Slipp, *The Freudian Mystique* (New York: New York University Press, 1993) 15, 47. In *Psychoanalyses/Feminisms* (New York: SUNY, 1995, 12) Madelon Sprengnether writes that "In Freud's rough sketch of patriarchal social organization, mother goddesses, mother-right, even mothers themselves quietly disappear." However, as J. C. Smith and Carla Freseman, the authors of *The Castration of Oedipus*, note: "Freudian Oedipal theory, which privileges the father and the phallus, presupposes the primacy of the mother" (New York: New York University Press, 1996), 139. D. N. Rodowick, *The Difficulty of Difference* (London: Routledge, 1991), 4.

27. Sigmund Freud, *Introductory Lectures on Psychoanalysis* (New York: Norton, 1966), 389.

28. Silverman, *Acoustic Mirror*, 73, 122.

29. D. W. Winnicott, "Mirror Role of Mother and Family in Child Development," in *Playing and Reality* (New York: Basic Books, 1971), 111–18.

30. Michelle Ballif, *Seduction, Sophistry, and the Woman with the Rhetorical Figure* (Carbondale: Southern Illinois University Press, 2001), 130.

31. Rodowick, *Difficulty of Difference*, 4, 13.

32. For this as a defining characteristic of primary narcissism see Freud's "A Special Difficulty of Psychoanalysis," in *Creativity and the Unconscious*.

33. Sigmund Freud, "A Special Type of Object-Choice Made by Men," in *Creativity and the Unconscious*.

34. Walker, *Hitchcock's Motifs*, 71.

35. Although, as I discuss in the relevant chapters, many of the endings of the films discussed in this book (*Shadow of a Doubt, Rear Window, North by Northwest, The Birds, Marnie*) are often interpreted as unironically "happy," Robin Wood notes the "perfunctory nature of so many Hitchcock happy endings . . . without much evidence of enjoyment or conviction." Robin Wood, "Plot Formation," in *Perspectives on Hitchcock*, ed. Davd Boyd (New York: G. K. Hall, 1995), 48.

36. Rothman, *Murderous Gaze*, 55.

37. Cameron and Jeffery ("The Universal Hitchcock," 265–78) agree with Penelope Houston, who "pointed out gleefully that almost any interpretation would fit *The Birds*" (266).

38. Modleski, *Women Who Knew Too Much*.

39. Rothman, *Murderous Gaze*, 249.

40. Rothman, *Murderous Gaze*, 248.

41. Stanley Cavell, *The World Viewed (Reflections on the Ontology of Film)*, (Harvard University Press, 1979), 85.

42. Toles, *House Made of Light*, 183.

43. Murray Pomerance, *An Eye for Hitchcock*, (New Brunswick: Rutgers University Press, 2004), 5.

44. Robin Wood, *Hitchcock's Films*, (New York: Barnes, 1966), 137–38.

45. Bellour, *Analysis of Film*, 224.

46. Malcolm Turvey, "Philosophical Problems in Psychoanalytical Theories of the Horror Film," in *Horror Film and Psychoanalysis*, ed. Schneider (Cambridge: Cambridge University Press, 2004), 68.

47. As Michael Grant has pointed out, Lacan dominated the important journal *Screen* throughout the 1970s. "Freud's worst nightmare: dining with Dr Hannibal Lector," in *Horror Film and Psychoanalysis*, 180.

48. E. Ann Kaplan, ed., *Psychoanalysis and Cinema*, (London: Routledge, 1990), 8.

49. Robin Wood, "Introduction," in *Horror Film and Psychoanalysis*, xv; Murray Pomerance, *Eye for Hitchcock* (New Brunswick: Rutgers University Press, 2004), 5.

50. Steven Jay Schneider, "The Question of Horror-Pleasure—'What's the matter with Melanie?': reflections on the merits of psychoanalytic approaches to modern horror cinema," in *Horror Film and Psychoanalysis*, 13.

51. Matt Hills, "The Darker Side of Genius: The (Horror) Auteur Meets Freud's Theory," in *Horror Film and Psychoanalysis*, ed. Schneider, 208.

52. E. Ann Kaplan, "Introduction," in *Psychoanalysis and Cinema*, 5.

53. Mary Ann Doane, "Remembering Women: Psychical and Historical Constructions in Film Theory," in *Psychoanalysis and Cinema*, ed. Kaplan, 56.

54. David Bordwell and Noël Carroll, *Post-Theory: Reconstructing Film Studies* (Madison: University of Wisconsin Press, 1996).

55. Slavoj Žižek, "The Hitchcockian Blot," in *Centenary Essays*, eds. Allen and Ishii-Gonzalès, 123.

56. "At the very end of the film, Mitch's mother 'accepts' Melanie as her son's wife, gives her consent, and abandons her super-ego role" (as indicated by the fleeting smile she and Melanie exchange in the car), ibid., 137.

57. Jane Wagner, *Dangerous Dames* (Athens: Ohio University Press, 1999), 6.

58. Gaylyn Studlar, *In the Realm of Pleasure* (Urbana: University of Illinois Press, 1998), 11. Rodowick, *Difficulty of Difference*, 4.

59. Michael Grant, "Ultimate Formlessness: Cinema, Horror and the Limits of Meaning," in *The Horror Film and Psychoanalysis*, ed. Schneider, 180.

60. Feldstein and Roof, eds. *Feminism and Psychoanalysis* (Ithaca, NY: Cornell University Press, 1989), 3.

61. Juliet Mitchell, *Psychoanalysis and Feminism* (New York: Macmillan, 1982), xiv. Elizabeth Wright, *Psychoanalytic Criticism: A Reappraisal* (Cambridge, MA: Polity Press, 1998), 173.

62. Mary Ann Doane, "Veiling over Desire," *Feminism and Psychoanalysis*, in ed. Feldstein and Roof.

63. Laura Mulvey, "Visual Pleasures and Narrative Cinema," *Screen* 10, no. 3 (1975), 6–18.

"I would ask, instead, if there *is* a gaze." Quoted by Mary Ann Doane, "Psychical and Historical Constructions in film theory," *Psychonalysis and Cinema*, ed. E. Ann Kaplan, 52. See also Elizabeth Cowie, *Representing the Woman* (Minneapolis: University of Minnesota, 1997), 170, and Rodowick, *Difficulty of Difference.*

64. See Marian Keane, "A Closer Look at Scopophilia: Mulvey, Hitchcock and *Vertigo*," in *A Hitchcock Reader*, eds. Marshall Deutelbaum and Leland Poague, 231–48, and Susan White, "Allegory and Referentiality: *Vertigo* and Feminist Criticism," *MLN*, 106/5 (1991): 310–32.

Toles, *House Made of Light*, 197. Marian Keane also agrees that "Mulvey describes the Stewart figure as possessing . . . a position of active power, but the truth is that he suffers throughout *Vertigo*" "Closer Look," (236).

65. Modleski, *Women Who Knew Too Much*, 3. Bellour, *Analysis of Film.*

66. Silverman, *Acoustic Mirror*, 211.

67. In their excellent essay on *Rear Window* Robert Stam and Roberta Pearson argue strongly for the early Jefferies as "a serious case of psychosexual pathology" ("Hitchcock's *Rear Window*," in *A Hitchcock Reader* ed. Deutelbaum and Poage [Ames: Iowa State University Press, 1986] 198), a view that I would extend, to varying degrees, to many if not all of the protagonists discussed in this book.

68. Molly Haskell, *From Reverence to Rape: The Treatment of Women in the Movies* (Harmondsworth: Penguin, 1974), 349. To call, for example, brunettes like Lil in *Marnie* "good" is clearly mistaken.

69. Vicky Lebeau, *Psychoanalysis and Cinema* (London: Wallflower, 2001), 41. Creed, *Monstrous Feminine*, 7.

70. Creed, *The Monstrous Feminine*, 144.

71. E. Ann Kaplan, *Motherhood and Representation in Literature and Film, 1830–1960* (London: Routledge, 1988); and "Motherhood and Representation: From Postwar Freudian Figurations to Postmodernism," in *Psychoanalysis and Cinema* (London: Routledge, 1990), 128–42.

72. In *The Acoustic Mirror* Silverman expresses considerable chagrin at the extent to which Kristeva herself seems to accept the "patriarchal" system.

73. Tom Cohen, *Hitchcock's Cryptonomies* (Minneapolis: University of Minnesota, 2005).

74. Jane Gallop, "The Monster in the Mirror," in *Feminism and Psycho-*

analysis, ed. Feldstein and Roof. 21. Gallop is quoting the important work of Nancy Chodorow on motherhood here.

75. Gilles Deleuze, *Coldness and Cruelty*, (New York: George Braziller, 1971).

76. Cohen, *Hitchcock's Cryptonomies*, 2:97.

77. Millington, "Hitchcock and the American Culture," 136.

78. "The attitude toward marriage is remarkably bleak and skeptical. This may account for the perfunctory nature of so many Hitchcock happy endings . . . without much evidence of enjoyment or conviction." Wood, *Perspectives on Hitchcock*, 48.

79. Maurice Yacowar, "Hitchcock's Imagery and Art," in *A Hitchcock Reader* eds. Deutelbaum and Poague (Ames: Iowa State University Press, 1986), 16–26.

80. Joseph McElhaney, "Touching the Surface: Marnie, Melodrama, Modernism," in *Centenary Essays*, eds. Allen and Ishii-Gonzalès (London: British Film Institute, 1999): 87–105.

81. "Hitchcock on Hitchcock: an Interview" in *Perspectives on Hitchcock*, ed. David Boyd (New York: G. K. Hall, 1995), 19. My italics.

82. Rothman, *Murderous Gaze*, 7.

83. Actually, Hitchcock merely regarded it as his favorite, but I think this might with some justice be parleyed into the view that he thought it was his best. John Michael Hayes, the screenwriter for *Rear Window*, relates in a documentary included with the recently released DVD that he received the nod to work with Hitchcock after agreeing with the director about his preference for the 1943 film.

84. Sharff, *Alfred Hitchcock's High Vernacular*, 168.

85. Yacowar, "Hitchcock's Imagery and Art," 16.

86. Theodore Price, *Hitchcock and Homosexuality* (Metuchen, NJ: Scarecrow Press, 1992).

87. Schickel, *Perspectives on Hitchcock*, in Boyd, ed. 18.

88. Jean Douchet, "Hitchcock and his Public," in *A Hitchcock Reader*, eds., Deutelbaum and Poague, 14.

89. Pomerance, *Eye for Hitchcock*, 68.

Chapter 2. *Shadow of a Doubt*

An early version of this essay appeared in *Literature/Film Quarterly*, 1991, vol. 19, no. 4.

1. William Rothman, *Hitchcock: The Murderous Gaze* (Cambridge: Harvard, 1982), 246.

2. Ibid., 194.

3. George Toles, "Mother Calls the Shots: Hitchcock's Female Gaze," in *A House Made of Light* (Detroit, MI: Wayne State University Press, 2001), 226.

4. Robin Woods, "Ideology, Genre, Auteur: *Shadow of a Doubt*," in *Hitchcock's Films Revisited* (Columbia University Press: New York, 1989), 288–302.

5. Sigmund Freud, "Uber einen besonderen Typus der Objektwahl beim Manne," 1910. "A Special Type of Object-Choice Made by Men," in *Creativity and the Unconscious* (New York: Harper, 1958), 162–72.

6. Francois Truffaut, *Hitchcock*, (New York: Simon and Schuster, 1967), 64.
7. Toles, *A House Made of Light*, 227.
8. Freud's famous statement that "Sometimes a cigar" is just a cigar' should obviously not he taken as a denial of sexual symbolism. For a defense of such symbols see "Representation by Symbols in Dreams," section 6, *The Interpretation of Dreams*.
9. James McLaughlin. "All in the Family," in *A Hitchcock Reader*, eds. Deutelbaum and Poague (Iowa State University Press, 1986), 141–52. As I mentioned in the introduction, Tania Modleski *The Women Who Knew Too Much* (New York: Methuen, 1988) interprets such "knowing," powerful women as less of a projection of the films' male protagonists than I do here.
10. Rothman, *Murderous Gaze*, 235.
11. Ronnie Scheib, "Charlie's Uncle," *Film Comment* Vol 12, no. 2; Raymond Durgnat, *The Strange Case of Alfred Hitchcock* (Cambridge, MA: MIT Press, 1974).
12. Rothman, *Murderous Gaze*, 179.
13. Lindsay Anderson, "Alfred Hitchcock," in *Focus on Hitchcock* (Englewood Cliffs, NJ: Prentice Hall, 1972), 48–59) notes another connection between the two films, namely, Hitchcock's use of the "overlapping conversation" technique featured in *The Magnificent Ambersons*, while James Naremore ("Hitchcock at the Margins of Noir") discusses other affinities between the two directors (in *Centenary Essays* [London: British Film Institute, 1999], 263–78). But neither discusses the connection between *Ambersons* and the "Merry Widow Waltz" sequence.
14. Toles, *House Made of Light*, 226.
15. Wood, "Ideology, Genre, Auteur, 288–302. Rothman, *Murderous Gaze*, 198.
16. Donald Spoto, *The Dark Side of Genius* (Boston: Little, Brown and Co., 1983), 261.
17. The same amount of money that Marion Crane steals from her job in *Psycho*, providing yet another clue to the palimpsest of unconscious truth that underlies the films and unites its main characters and their actions.
18. Charles Samuels, *Mastering the Film and Other Essays* (University of Tennessee Press, c1977), 84.
19. Gavin Miller, "Hitchcock vs. Truffaut," *Sight and Sound* vol. 38, no. 2 (Spring, 1969): 87. Speaking of the "rather clever and unconvincing façade's of the two Charlies" Albert LaValley says: "These repetitions finally have a vertiginous and nihilistic effect on us instead of establishing rigorous moral and intellectual patterns . . . the real strength of the film lies elsewhere." *Focus on Hitchcock* (Englewood Cliffs, NJ: Prentice Hall, 1972), 5–6.
20. Paula Cohen, as mentioned in my introduction, sees the father-daughter relationship as essential to this and other of Hitchcock's films (*Alfred Hitchcock: The Legacy of Victorianism* [Lexington: University of Kentucky, 1995], 74). Although this argument is based on rather suspect biographical versus psychoanalytical analyses, it is not incompatible with the explanation of the relationship between the two Charlies offered here.
21. Rothman, *Murderous Gaze*, 244.
22. Among the critics who accept, in part or *in toto*, this view of young Charlie as sharing her uncle's murderous intentions are McLaughlin, "All in the

Family," 141–52); Rothman, *Murderous Gaze,* and Wood, "Ideology, Genre, Auteur, 288–302.

23. Rothman, *Murderous Gaze,* 238.

Chapter 3. *Rear Window*

1. Whether an intentional "inside joke" or not, it is worth noting that Stewart's name in 1950s *Broken Arrow* is "Jeffords."

2. Tania Modleski, *The Women Who Knew Too Much* (New York: Methuen, 1988), 75; John Fawell, *Hitchcock's "Rear Window": The Well-Made Film* (Carbondale: Southern Illinois University Press, 2001), 52. It is surprising that Laura Mulvey, in her brilliant discussion of voyeurism and castration in "Visual Pleasures and Narrative Cinema" (*Screen* 10 no. 3 (1975): 6–18), does not mention the symbolism of Jeff's leg in her discussion of *Rear Window.*

3. For a general discussion of cinema as voyeurism see Christian Metz's famous essay on "The Fiction Film and its Spectator," in *The Imaginary Signifier* (Bloomington: Indiana University Press, 1982); for an excellent discussion of this idea in *Rear Window* see Robert Stam and Roberta Pearson, "Hitchcock's *Rear Window,*" in *A Hitchcock Reader,* eds. Deutelbaum and Poague (Ames: Iowa State University Press, 1986).

4. Modleski, *Women Who Knew Too Much,* 75.

5. Jane Wagner, *Dangerous Dames* (Athens: Ohio University Press, 1999), 8.

6. Fawell, *Hitchcock's "Rear Window,"* 51.

7. George Toles, "Mother Calls the Shots: Hitchcock 's Female Gaze," in *A House Made of Light* (Detroit, MI: Wayne State University Press, 2001), 227.

8. Fawell, *Hitchcock's "Rear Window,"* 127. See also Jean Douchet's classic discussion of the film as metacinema in "La troisième clef de Hitchcock," *Cahiers deu Cinéma* no. 113 (November, 1960), and Stam and Pearson, "Hitchcock's *Rear Window,*" 193–206. Toles, *House Made of Light,* 159.

9. Mary Ann Doane, "Veiling over Desire," in *Feminism and Psychoanalysis,* eds. Feldstein and Roof, (Ithaca, NY: Cornell University Press, 1989).

10. Robin Wood, "Ideology, Genre, Auteur," in *Hitchcock's Films Revisited,* (New York: Columbia University Press, 1988), 102: "From the first, a clear link is established between [Jeff's] relation with Lisa and his spying on his neighbors."

11. Modleski, *Women Who Knew Too Much,* 76.

12. The screenplay also notes in describing Lisa's first appearance, that she "recalls the positive image on the cover of the magazine" www.filmsite.org/rear.html.

13. Freud himself uses this analogy in one of his "metapsychology" papers: "A rough but not inadequate analogy to this supposed relation of conscious to unconscious activity might be drawn from the field of ordinary photography. *The first stage of the photograph is the 'negative'*; every photographic picture hs to pass through the 'negative process', and some of these negatives which have held good in examination are admitted to the 'positive process' ending in the picture." "The Unconscious of Psychoanalysis," in *Collected Papers* (London: Hogarth, 1955), 4:27, italics mine.

14. Modleski's thesis (*Women Who Knew Too Much*) about a heroic woman who is discernible between the lines of Hitchcock's films might be understood more cynically as a function of a mother complex that elevates as well as denigrates the desired and denied object of desire.

15. Sigmund Freud, "The Medusa's Head," in *Collected Papers* (London: Hogarth, 1955), 5:105.

16. Sigmund Freud, "The Most Prevalent Form of Degradation in Erotic Life," in *Creativity and the Unconscious* (New York: Harper, 1958), 178.

17. Modleski, *Women Who Knew Too Much*, 78.

18. Wood's comment, quoted as the epigraph of this paper ("The attitude towards marriage is remarkably bleak and skeptical. This may account for the perfunctory nature of so many Hitchcock happy endings . . . without much evidence of enjoyment or conviction"), demonstrates the need for a psychoanalytic explanation of *why* this should be the case. See also my quotation/discussion, in the introduction, of Maurice Yacowar's refutation of "happy endings" in Hitchcock.

19. Fawell, *Hitchcock's "Rear Window,"* 385.

20. Ibid., 193–206. Wood, "Ideology, Genre, Autuer," 104.

21. Sigmund Freud, "The Poet and Daydreaming," in *Creativity and Unconscious* (New York: Harper, 1958), 50–51.

22. Freud discusses the relation of psychoanalysis to the "Copernican Revolution' in "A Special Difficulty of Psychoanalysis," in *Creativity and the Unconscious* (New York: Harper, 1958). Jean Laplanche discusses this discussion in his essay on "The Unfinished Copernican Revolution," in *Essays on Otherness* (New York: Routledge, 1999).

23. Freud, "Poet and Dayreaming," 49.

24. I agree, in this sense, with Lesley Brill's nonpsychoanalytic theory of the presence of the "romance" in Hitchcock's work. See "*North by Northwest* and Romance," *Perspectives on Alfred Hitchcock*, ed. Boyd (New York: G. K. Hall, 1995), 128–43.

25. A point well argued in Stam and Pearson, "Hitchcock's *Rear Window*," 193–206.

26. Fawell, "*Hitchcock's Rear Window*," 60.

27. Modleski, *Women Who Knew Too Much*, 84.

28. Quoted in Tony Lee Moral, *The Making of Marnie* (Lanham: The Scarecrow Press, 2002), 186.

29. "What is called sexuality outside psychoanalysis relates only to a restricted sexual life, which serves the purpose of reproduction and is described as normal." Sigmund Freud, "The Sexual Life of Human Beings," lecture 20, in *Introductory Lectures on Psychoanalysis* (New York: Norton), 319.

30. Toles, *House Made of Light*, 167.

31. www.filmsite.org/rear.html

32. Sigmund Freud, "On Narcissism," in *Collected Papers*, vol. 4 (London: Hogarth, 1955).

33. Ibid., 4:30.

34. For example, Rothman, *Murderous Gaze*, 178.

35. Toles, *House Made of Light*, 166.

36. Douchet argues that the "jokingly ineffectual" flashbulbs refer to the

entrapment of many Hitchcock protagonists. In a typically brilliant essay, which is no less so for being a foray outside his usual area of expertise, Fredric Jameson (*Signatures of the Visible* [New York: Routledge, 1990]) notes, in "Allegorizing Hitchcock," that the camera is used similarly, in *Shadow of a Doubt* and *Rear Window*, as a "gun" (122). This ignores, however, its ineffectiveness here.

37. Murray Pomerance, *An Eye for Hitchcock* (New Brunswick, NJ: Rutgers University Press, 2004), 240.

CHAPTER 4. *VERTIGO*

1. Laura Mulvey, *Visual and other Pleasures* (Bloomington: Indiana University Press, 1989), 24.

2. D. N. Rodowick, *The Difficulty of Difference* (London: Routledge, 1991), 10.

3. Tania Modleski, *The Women Who Knew Too Much* (New York: Methuen, 1988), 92.

4. Sigmund Freud, *Introductory Lectures on Psychoanalysis* (New York: Norton, 1966), 389.

5. Mary Ann Doane, *Femmes Fatales: Feminism, Film Theory and Psychoanalysis* (New York: Routledge, 1991).

6. Charles Barr, *Vertigo* (London: British Film Institute, 2002), 15. Wood briefly discusses the title sequence as referring to "the impossibility [of knowing] what goes on beyond the mask" (*Hitchcock's Films Revisited* [New York: Columbia University Press, 1989], 110). I think, though, that this is less impossible than he claims, given (for example) the comparison to *Psycho*.

The influence of Freud's discoveries on "New Critics" such as I. A. Richards is undeniable, although the implications of this relationship have yet to be explored.

7. I discuss Marion Crane's nervous looks in the chapter on *Psycho*.

8. See Heidegger's *Der Satz vom Grund* (Pfullingen: Neske, 1957), for what is surely the most important modern discussion of the epistemological importance of "the law of the ground," and of the abyss that threatens it. Freud, in his essay on "The Unconscious" and throughout his writings emphasized the essential groundlessness of the unconscious versus the essential grounding of the conscious.

9. Sigmund freud, Lecture 2, in *Introductory Lectures on Psychoanalysis* (New York: Norton), 36.

10. Modleski, *Women Who Knew Too Much*, 90.

11. Modleski sees as this central thesis the "deconstruction" of the male spectator by a fascination with femininity which "throws masculine identity into question" (ibid., 87). I agree, but attempt in this chapter and elsewhere to offer a psychoanalytic explanation of this "identity crisis" that goes further in identifying its underlying causes.

12. Modleski identifies this important association between the bra and the issue of weightlessness and vertigo but does not do more than state that "it seems clear that the film is humorously linking his condition to femininity" (ibid., 91).

13. Robin Wood, "Ideology,Genre, Auteur: *Shadow of a Doubt*," in *Hitchcock's Films Revisited* (New York: Columbia University Press, 1988), 110.

14. Sigmund Freud, Lecture 10, "Symbolism in Dreams," in *Introductory Lectures on Psychoanalysis* (New York: Norton), 155.

15. Royal Brown ("*Vertigo* as Orphic Tragedy," in *Perspectives on Hitchcock*, ed. Boyd [New York: G. K. Hall, 1995]) interprets Scottie's obsession with saving and losing his love-object in terms of the myth of Orpheus, but acknowledges, at the end of his essay, its compatibility with a more overtly "sexual" explanation: "*Vertigo* transforms the sexual content expressed on diverse levels of the cinematic language into hierophantic content" (126).

16. Although it may seem as though I am making too much out of this detail, there is certainly no director who is known to have been more in control of all the details of his pictures than was Hitchcock. If, however, it was an unintentional "slip," all the better.

17. Sigmund Freud, "The Unconscious," in *Standard Edition* (London: Hogarth Press, 1957, 14:186–87.

18. Charles Barr, *Vertigo* (London: British Film Institute, 2002), 12. Murray Pomerance, *An Eye for Hitchcock* (New Brunswick, NJ: Rutgers University Press, 2004), 225.

19. Freud explains the particular appeal of Sophocles' play as the result of its veiled rendering of the "Oedipus complex" and the related incest-theme, something that can be related to the other "universally" acclaimed works just mentioned. "The Development of the Libido," in *Introductory Lectures on Psychoanalysis* (New York: Norton, 1966), 330.

20. Dan Aulier, *Vertigo: The Making of a Hitchcock Classic* (New York: St Martins Press, 1998), 68.

21. This pattern, with particular reference to Freud's essay on "A Special Type of Object Choice," is discussed in the first chapter of the present work dealing with Hitchcock's *Shadow of a Doubt*, a film in which the serial murderer marries and then kills widows exclusively.

22. Modleski, *The Women Who Knew Too Much*, 94.

23. Freedman attributes the ambiguity of the psychoanalytic explanation (a pattern, by the way, that is also found in *Psycho* and *Marnie*) to Hitchcock's ambivalence about psychoanalysis, but that I would attribute to the necessarily veiled—repressed—nature of the unconscious.

24. Modleski, *Women Who Knew Too Much*, 93.

25. Modleski is, I believe, only partly right when she states that "Madeleine represents the lost child whom the 'mad Carlotta' had sought everywhere" (ibid., 93). For there is little evidence in this film that the Madeleine/Judy/Carlotta trinity is anything other than a projection of the main character's own neurosis—in this case his vertigo, which elsewhere Modleski rightly identifies with Scottie's "fascination with these women" (91). This failure to identify Scottie with the child is especially surprising given Modleski's comment that Scottie (not Madeleine) wanders the streets of San Francisco looking for Madeleine the way that Carlotta had (96).

26. Andrè Green, *The Dead Mother:* London: Routledge, 1999.

27. In Wood, Modleski, and all the other critics mentioned here there is no discussion of this important line, an omission that, I would suggest, is part and parcel of the very obsession (and its denial) that the film is about.

28. Michael Walker, *Hitchcock's Motifs* (Amsterdam: Amsterdam University Press, 2005), 82. Pomerance, 231. *Eye for Hitchcock*, Robin Wood, in *Perspectives on Hitchcock*, (Ed. Boyd, New York: G. K. Hall, 1995), 124 also refers to this hairstyle as "arranged in a spiral."

29. Freud's most explicit discussion of what was to be known as the "Madonna/Whore Complex" is found in his essay on "A Prevalent Form of Abjection Found Among Men," in *Creativity and the Unconscious* (New York: Harper, 1958).

30. Freud is referring here to his earlier essay on "The Antithetical Sense of Primary Words" (1910). I have written elsewhere on the importance of this essay to all aspects of Freud's thought in "Freud's 'Uber den Gegensinn der Urworte' : Psychoanalysis, Art, and the Antithetical Senses." *Style* vol. 24, no. 2, (Summer 1990).

Sigmund Freud, "A Special Type of Object-Choice Made by Men," in *Creativity and the Unconscious* (New York: Harper, 1958), 167–68.

31. Paula Cohen, "Hitchcock's Revised American Vision," in *Hitchcock's America*, ed. Freedman and Millington, (Oxford: Oxford University Press, 1999), 170.

32. Charles Barr, *Vertigo* (London: British Film Institute, 2002), 77.

33. Francois Truffaut, *Hitchcock* (New York: Simon and Schuster, 1967), 189.

34. See chapter 1 of the present work on *Shadow of a Doubt*.

35. According to Edith Head's recollection of having to convince Kim Novak to wear the "uncomfortable" "gray suit which made me stand so straight." Aulier *Vertigo*, 68–69.

36. Freud, "A Special Type of Object Choice," 172.

37. Wood, "Hitchcock's Films Revisited," (New York: Columbia University Press, 1989), 128.

38. Marian Keane, "A Closer Look at Scopophilia: Mulvey, Hitchcock and *Vertigo*," in *A Hitchcock Reader*, ed. Deutelbaum and Poague (Ames: Iowa State University Press, 1986), 245.

39. In *The World Viewed (Reflections on the Ontology of Film*), (Cambridge, MA: Harvard University Press, 1979), Stanley Cavell argues that "The Hitchcock heroine is, as it were, a defrocked nun" (87), a notion that is one of many statements by Cavell that approach a psychoanalytic reading without, however, proffering one.

40. William Rothman, *The "I" of the Camera* (Cambridge: Cambridge University Press, 1988), 166.

41. I agree with Royal Brown's notion that the film ultimately asserts a male "Apollonian" view over that of a female "Dionysian" one ("*Vertigo* as Orphic Tragedy") although the death of the mother is here seen in Freudian terms that are more melancholic than triumphant.

Chapter 5. *North by Northwest*

1. William Rothman, *Hitchcock: The Murderous Gaze* (Cambridge, MA: Harvard University Press, 1982), 178.

2. In the following chapter I will argue that the closest we can come to knowing the real Mrs. Bates is in fact the beautiful young Marion Crane (Janet Leigh), whom Norman also kills.

3. Murray Pomerance, *An Eye for Hitchcock* (New Brunswick, NJ: Rutgers University Press, 2004), 21.

4. Ibid., 57.

5. William Rothman, "Some Thoughts on Hitchcock's Authorship," in *Centenary Essays*, ed. Allen and Ishii-Gonzalès (London: British Film Institute, 1999), 31.

6. Thomas Elsaesser, "The Dandy in Hitchcock," in *Centenary Essays*, ed. Allen and Ishii-Gonzalès (London: British Film Institute, 1999) relates the polish of Thornhill's character to the idea of the dandy, whose definitional indifference to definitions is a common characteristic of not only many Hitchcock's heroes and (especially, I would add) his villains but also of the director himself.

7. Dan Williams, *North by Northwest* (Essex: York Press, 2000), 32. William Rothman, *The "I" of the Camera* (Cambridge: Cambridge University Press, 1988), 177.

8. Stanley Cavell, "*North by Northwest*," in *A Hitchcock Reader*, ed. Deutelbaum and Poague Ames: Iowa State University Press, (1986), 249–64.

9. *An Eye for Hitchcock* (New Brunswick: Rutgers University Press, 2004), 14–57.

10. Modleski, *The Women Who Knew Too Much*, 91.

11. Richard Millington, "Hitchcock and American Character," in *Hitchcock's America*, ed. Freedman and Millington (New York: Oxford University Press, 1999), 137

12. I also discussed this "upbeat" view of the ending of *North by Northwest* in the introduction to the present volume. Similar readings of the end of *Rear Window* (Stam and Pearson, "Hitchcock's *Rear Window*," in *A Hitchcock Reader*, ed. Deutelbaum and Poague [Ames: Iowa State University Press, 1986]) *Vertigo* (Brown, "*Vertigo* as Orphic Tragedy") and *Marnie* (Cameron and Jeffery, "The Universal Hitchcock," in *Perspectives on Hitchcock*, ed. Boyd [New York: G. K. Hall, 1995], 277) support this tendency to read the endings in more positive terms than I do here, which one might counter with Maurice Yacowar's statement that "almost all Hitchcock's films end on an uncertain image, from the new lovers in *The Pleasure Garden* to the mass of abiding doom at the end of *The Birds*" ("Hitchcock's Imagery and Art," in *A Hitchcock Reader*, ed. Deutelbaum and Poague [Ames: Iowa State University Press, 1986], 16–26).

13. Robin Wood, *Hitchcock's Films* (New York: Barnes, 1965), 134.

14. "Hitchcock is so little interested in his spies as spies . . . that it becomes very easy to accept them as simply the embodiment of the forces of disorder and subversion," ibid., 135.

15. Ibid.

16. Deborah Knight and George McKnight, "Suspense and its Master," in *Centenary Essays*, ed. Raymond Allen and Sam Ishii-Gonzalès (London: British Film Institute, 1999) correctly identify *North by Northwest* as one of Hitchcock's many "innocent man on the run" films, but just as there are, from a psychoanalytical perspective, no innocent men, I would urge, as here, a reconsideration of the so-called "innocence" of these characters.

17. Michael Walker, *Hitchcock's Motifs* (Amsterdam: Amsterdam University Press, 2005), 312–13.

18. Dan Williams, *North by Northwest* (Essex: York Press, 2000).

19. Sigmund Freud, *Jokes and their Relation to the Unconscious* (New York: Norton, 1960).

20. Wood continues: "The parallel is emphasized by Hitchcock's having the two women (who look very much alike) stand in similar postures, hands folded before them," *Hitchcock's Films*, 135.

21. Freud's most explicit discussion of what was to be known as the "Madonna/ Whore Complex" is found in his essay on "A Prevalent Form of Abjection Found Among Men," in *Creativity and the Unconscious* (New York: Harper, 1958).

22. Wood, *Hitchcock's Films*, 135.

23. Stanley Cavell has crafted an entire reading of *North by Northwest* in relation to *Hamlet*, beginning with the title of the film itself (i.e., Hamlet's reference to his own madness as only "north-northwest"), to which I would add my Freudian interpretation of Thornhill's mother as comparable to Gertrude. "*North by Northwest*," *A Hitchcock Reader*, ed. Deutelbaum and Poague (Ames: Iowa State University Press, 1986), 249–64.

24. Pomerance, *Eye for Hitchcock*, 27.

25. Wood, *Hitchcock's Films*, 136.

26. See Freud's essay on "A Prevalent Form of Abjection Found Among Men," in *Creativity and the Unconscious* (New York: Harper, 1958).

27. Williams, *North by Northwest*, 28–29.

28. *Hitchcock's Films*, 138.

29. Cavell, "*North by Northwest*," 256.

30. Leslie Brill's literary notion of romance in Hitchcock , in which the "ordinary constraints of natural law are loosened," is certainly compatible with, if different from, the psychoanalytic view of fantasy offered here. See Lesley Brill "*North by Northwest* and Romance," in *Perspectives on Alfred Hitchcock*, ed. Boyd (New York: G. K. Hall, 1995), 128–43.

31. I discuss this and other aspects of *Notorious* in the afterword of this volume.

32. See Brill, "*North by Northwest* and Romance," 128–43.

33. Yacowar, "Hitchcock's Imagery and Art," 16–17.

34. Rothman, *"I" of the Camera* refers to the film's "perfectly happy ending," 174. Millington, "Hitchcock and American Character," 149. Cavell, "*North by Northwest*," 262.

35. Cavell, "*North by Northwest*."

36. Brigitte Peucker, "The Cut of Representation," in *Centenary Essays*, ed. Allen and Ishii-Gonzalès (London: British Film Institute, 1999), 145–46.

Chapter 6. *Psycho*

1. George Toles, "If Thine Eye Offend Thee: *Psycho* and the Art of Infection," in *Centenary Essays*, eds. Allen and Ishii-Gonzalès (London: British Film

Institute, 1999), 164. Raymond Bellour, "Psychosis, Neurosis and Perversion," in *The Analysis of Film* (Bloomington: Indiana University Press, 2000), 238.

2. William Rothman, *Hitchcock: The Murderous Gaze* (Cambridge, MA: Harvard University Press, 1982), 255.

3. Elsewhere in this volume I have referred to the important Freudian psychoanalytic work of André Green, *The Dead Mother* (London: Routledge, 1999).

4. I agree, partially, with Žižek's notion that *Psycho* represents the "psychotic reverse" of Hitchcock's other films, and of the first part of *Psycho* itself, but not that these two worlds are unrelated "reversals" of each other. Slavoj Žižek, *Everything You Always Wanted to Know about Lacan (but Were Afraid to Ask Hitchcock)* (London: Verso, 1992), 276–77. If, as Žižek maintains (following Lacan), the "psychotic clings to the mother's desire" (228), then all of the films discussed in this book are related to the psychotic's—i.e., Norman's—desire (or "drive").

5. Maurice Yacowar, "Hitchcock's Imagery and Art," in *A Hitchcock Reader*, eds. Deutelbaum and Poage (Ames: Iowa State University Press, 1986), 16–26.

6. Barbara Klinger, "*Psycho:* The Insistutionalization of Female Sexuality," in *A Hitchcock Reader*, eds. Deutelbaum and Poague (Ames: Iowa State University Press, 1986), 332.

Bellour's essay on "Psychosis, Neurosis and Perversion" in *Psycho* nonetheless notes many structural (versus thematic) similarities between the two parts of the film. *A Hitchcock Reader*, Ames: Iowa State University Press, 1986, 311–31.

7. Barbara Creed, *The Monstrous Feminine: Film, Feminism, Psychoanalysis* (London: Routledge, 1993), 141

8. Yacowar, "Hitchcock's Imagery and Art," also argues for the connection between the two parts of *Psycho* when he writes: "In *Psycho* we have a pervasive feeling of parental oppression, by Marion Crane's mother, Sam's father, and the happiness-buying Texas daddy; but in the main thrust of the film, it is the sick son that projects his guilt and inhibitions upon his parental image," 20.

9. The one exception to this in the films just mentioned might appear to be *Shadow of a Doubt*. But, here too, the exception proves the rule. Emma may be Charlie's sister but in the films she serves as a mother figure who smothers her son/brother in affection, which he returns by trying to kill her daughter and calling her friends "fat, wheezing animals."

10. Barbara Klinger ("*Psycho*") places appropriate emphasis on the split between Marion's sexuality and the "respectability" of the family but does not emphasize, as I do here, the conflict as taking place, like Norman's, within her own conflicted desires.

11. Sigmund Freud, Lecture 21, "The Development of the Libido," in *Introductory Lectures on Psychoanalysis* (New York: Norton,1966).

12. Sigmund Freud, "On 'the Uncanny,'" in *Creativity and the Unconscious* (New York: Harper, 1958), 122.

13. Robin Wood, in *Perspectives on Hitchcock*, ed. David Boyd (New York: G. K. Hall, 1995), 48.

14. Rothman, *Murderous Gaze*, 301.

15. The character's name in the original story was Mary, not Marion. One

might also note the choice of spelling—"o" for "a"—which emphasizes the connection.

16. Toles, "If Thine Eye Offend Thee" discusses the eye motif in Hitchcock with reference to Bataille.

17. Rothman, *The Murderous Gaze*, 298.

18. Creed, *Monstrous Feminine*, 149.

19. Ibid., 142–3.

20. The specific term is not Freud's, although he speaks of certain related characteristics (parsimoniousness, orderliness, and obstinacy) that function as the repression of anal desire (see "Character and Anal Eroticism" (1908) and "The Transformation of Instincts with Specific Regard to Anal Eroticism" (1916) in *Collected Papers*, vol. 2 (London: Hogarth, 1949). This pun is more than justified in Freudian terms because the "analytic" character type is explicitly related to the "anal" character type described in Freud's essay.

21. Toles, "If Thine Eye Offend Thee" notes Hitchcock's famous detachment from and control over his actors and characters, "his refusal to be engaged or *soiled by* his transactions with suffering," 161, italics mine.

22. Reported in Tony Lee Moral, *Hitchcock and the Making of Marnie* (Lanham, MD: The Scarecrow Press, 2002), 2.

23. Creed, *Monstrous Feminine*, 142.

24. Freud, "Character and Anal Eroticism," in *Collected Papers*, 2:50.

25. See my discussion of this in Freud's "On the Antithetical Sense of Primary Words: Psychoanalysis, Art, and the Antithetical Senses," *Style* vol. 24, no. 2 (1990).

26. Freud, "Transformation of Instincts," in *Collected Papers*, 2:168.

27. Freud discusses the antithetical relation of beauty and the abject in his essay on "The Theme of the Three Caskets," in *Creativity and the Unconscious* (New York: Harper, 1958).

28. Sigmund Freud, "Parapraxes," in *Introductory Lectures on Psychoanalysis* (New York: Norton, 1966).

29. Murray Pomerance, *An Eye for Hitchcock* (New Brunswick, NJ: Rutgers University Press, 2004), 142.

30. This could be seen as symptomatic of all the other problems of this needless remake, which was almost universally (and I think rightly) denounced by its critics as aesthetically, if not morally, bankrupt. For an even harsher denunciation of the film, see William Rothman, "Some Thoughts on Hitchcock's Authorship," in *Centenary Essays*, eds. Allen and Ishii-Gonzalès (London: British Film Institute, 1999), 28–42. A less vitriolic but equally damning discussion is in Irving Singer, *Three Philosophical Filmmakers* (Cambridge, MA, MIT, 2004), 16–22.

31. "This [sensual] sucking involves making the mother's breast the first object of the sexual instinct. I can give you no idea of the important bearing of this first object upon the choice of every later object, of the profound effects it has in its transformations and substitutions even in the remotest regions of our sexual life." Sigmund Freud, *Introductory Lectures on Psychoanalysis* (New York: Norton, 1966), 389.

32. See Freud's discussion of breast/bird imagery in the famous essay on Leonardo da Vinci (*Standard Edition*, vol. 11, London: Hogarth, 1955).

33. I discuss this further in my chapter on *The Birds*. I would disagree, then, with those who insist that one should not attempt to understand the "supernatural" significance of the birds' attacks on Bodega Bay, e.g., Lee Edelman's comment that "The film is quite insistent that the explanation [for the attacks] for the attacks is unknown." "Hitchcock's Future," in (*Centenary Essays*, eds. Allen and Ishii-Gonzalès (London: British Film Institute, 1999), 243.

34. Quoted (correctly) in Marnie.

35. The potentially rich comparison of Norman to Hamlet has not, I believe, been explored elsewhere, although Stanley Cavell develops a reading of *North by Northwest* in terms of Shakespeare's play in *The Hitchcock Reader*, ed. Deutelbaum and Poague, (Ames: Iowa State University Press, 1986), 249–64.

36. There are notable exceptions to this "absent Father" idea in some of the very films where, as in *Marnie* and *The Birds*, the figure is also noticeably occluded. Melanie Daniels, for example, talks to her father on the phone, but it is her absent mother that she grows hysterical about, while Mitch Brenner's father is present only in his large portrait.

37. This is the meaning of the pun I discuss in my chapter on *Vertigo* dealing with the bra that is designed on the principle of the "can't-I-leave-her" (cantilever) bridge.

38. Creed, *Monstrous Feminine*, 142. Creed does, however, consider the thesis proferred here that "we have no way of knowing what she [Mrs Bates] was like in reality," (143).

39. Kaja Silverman, *The Acoustic Mirror* (Bloomington: Indiana University Press, 1988), 71. As one would expect, Silverman does speak of Mrs. Bates's voice elsewhere in her study, (48).

40. Freud, "On the Uncanny."

41. *Dead of Night, Magic, Poltergeist, Child's Play,* and a memorable 1963 episode of *The Twilight Zone* entitled *The Living Doll.*

42. It is indicative of the privileged role of women in Hitchcock's films that in both these films the female is able to accomplish what, earlier, a man could not. This would support Tania Modleski's view of women's roles in Hitchcock, to which she ascribes a higher knowledge without, however, viewing this as part of Hitchcock's abiding mother complex. *The Women Who Knew Too Much* (New York: Methuen, 1988).

43. Freud, "On the Uncanny."

44. In "The Sandman" loss of the eyes is also a prominent feature of Nathaniel's fantasy.

45. Žižek emblematizes this shot as Hitchcock's surpassing the imaginary or symbolic orders with a (typically Žižekian) paradoxical subjectivity: "Yet the crucial feature of *Psycho* is that Hitchcock precisely does not accomplish this step towards subjectivization: when we are thrown into the 'subjective' gaze of the Thing, the Thing, although it 'becomes subject,' does not subjectivize itself, does not 'open up,' does not 'reveal its depth' . . . we look through its eyes, and this very coincidence of our view with the Thing's gaze intensifies its radical Otherness to an almost unbearable degree," (*Everything You Wanted to Know about Hitchcock*, 252). The reading offered here differs in its less mystifying notion of the mother's skeleton as nothing more nor less than the internalization of Norman's mother within his own psyche.

CHAPTER 7. *THE BIRDS*

1. I would argue that *The Birds* owes, at least in part, its origin to the popularity of the British, American and Japanese monster/science-fiction films of the 1950s and 1960s. Indeed, the lunchroom scene where a stock science-fiction discussion takes place of how to deal with the bird attacks (a plan for using smoke with a local town hero that is quickly forgotten) seems to indicate some degree of self-consciousness in this regard.

2. Ken Mogg, "The MacGuffin Web Page," "Two Discoveries," (http://www.labyrinth.net.au/~muffin/).

3. Quoted in Tony Lee Moral, *The Making of Marnie* (Lanham, MD: The Scarecrow Press, 2002), 27.

4. Slavoj Žižek, "The Hitchcockian Blot," in *Centenary Essays*, ed. Allen and Ishii-Gonzalès (London: British Film Institute, 1999), 136. Barbara Creed, *The Monstrous Feminine: Film, Feminism, Psychoanalysis* (London: Routledge, 1993), 143.

5. Malcolm Turvell, "Philosophical Problems in Psychoanalytical Theories of the (Horror) Film," in *Horror Film and Psychoanalysis* (Cambridge: Cambridge University Press, 2004), 75.

6. Lee Edelman, "Hitchcock's Future," in *Centenary Essays*, ed. Allen and Ishii-Gonzalès (London: British Film Institute, 1999), 243.

7. "The Universal Hitchcock," *A Hitchcock Reader* (Ames: Iowa State University Press, 1986), 266.

8. Margaret Horowitz, "*The Birds:* A Mother's Love," *Wide Angle* vol. 5, no. 1 (1982), 42.

9. William Rothman, *Hitchcock: The Murderous Gaze* (Cambridge, MA: Harvard University Press, 1982), 146.

10. Donald Spoto, *The Dark Side of Genius* (Boston: Little, Brown and Company, 1983), 449.

11. Edelman,"Hitchcock's Future."

12. Ibid., 245. Edelman's excellent "queer reading" of the film, and its use of children in particular, leads him to conclusions about the "reproductive rites of heterosexual lovebirds" that are very different from the psychoanalytical points proffered here.

13. "It may be remarked in passing that they [incest and parricide] are also the two great crimes proscribed by totemism, the first socio-religious institution of mankind." Sigmund Freud "The Development of the Libido," lecture 21, in *Introductory Lectures on Psychoanalysis* (New York: Norton, 1968), 335.

14. Michael Walker, *Hitchcock's Motifs* (Amsterdam: Amsterdam University Press, 2005), 359. This recent work was brought to my attention after my own, Oedipal interpretation of staircases in Hitchcock had been written.

15. "What is called sexuality outside psychoanalysis relates only to a restricted sexual life, which serves the purpose of reproduction and is described as normal." Sigmund Freud, "The Sexual Life of Human Beings," lecture 20, in *Introductory Lectures on Psychoanalysis* (New York: Norton, 1968), 319.

16. Camille Paglia, *The Birds* (London: British Film Institute, 1998), 20.

17. Ken Mogg, "Will and Wilfulness: Recent Commentary on Hitchcock's *The Birds*," *Screening the Past*, online journal, (March 2001). One of the author's

many useful links is to an article on the affinities between "Schopenhauer and Freud" by Christopher Young and Andrew Brook.

18. See the discussion of this important motif in my chapter on *Vertigo.*

19. Freud is referring here to his earlier essay on "The Antithetical Sense of Primary Words" (1910). I have written elsewhere on the importance of this essay to all aspects of Freud's thought in "Freud's 'Uber den Gegensinn der Urworte' : Psychoanalysis, Art, and the Antithetical Senses," *Style* vol. 24, no. 2, (Summer 1990). Sigmund Freud, "A Special Type of Object-Choice Made by Men," in *Creativity and the Unconscious* (New York: Harper, 1958), 167–68.

20. Walker, *Hitchcock's Motifs,* 69–86.

21. Edelman, "Hitchcock's Future," 243.

22. Sigmund Freud, "The Poet and Daydreaming," in *Creativity and the Unconscious* (New York: Harper, 1958).

23. Horwitz, "A Mother's Love."

24. Among the few other critics of the film who mention this, such as Theodore Price (*Hitchcock and Homosexuality* [Metuchen, NJ: Scarecrow Press, 1992], 198) and Tania Modleski (*The Women Who Knew Too Much* [New York: Methuen, 1988], 5), there is little attention given to the significance behind this striking similarity.

25. Modleski, *Women Who Knew Too Much,* 5.

26. "All dreams are to be interpreted bi-sexually, as a confluence of two currents described as a masculine and feminine one." Sigmund Freud, "Uncertainties and Criticisms," lecture 15, in *Introductory Lectures on Psychoanalysis* (New York: Norton, 1968), 237.

27. Modleski, *The Women Who Knew Too Much.* Robert Samuels, *Hitchcock's Bi-Textuality* (New York: SUNY Press, 1998).

28. Spoto, *Dark Side of Genius,* 462–63.

29. Although Barbara Creed does not identify the birds with the maternal breast as I do here, she does make nearly the same identification in her study of *The Monstrous-Feminine* (144).

30. "During the filming of the last attack scene, Hedren became exhausted to the point of sitting down on the middle of the set and crying. A week's rest was ordered by a doctor at that time of completing the film. "For a first film, it was a lot of work," Hedren mused (Lavender Vroman. "Tippi Hedren Airs Out Her Early Acting Days, Wildlife Preservation," Antelope Valley Press September 30, 2004).

31. See Jason Cangiolosi's study of the staircase motif in three of Hitchcock's British films (*Blackmail, Rich and Strange, The 39 Steps*) in "Alfred Hitchcock's Stairways of Attraction," http://www.associatedcontent.com/article/12992/alfred_hitchcocks_stairways_of_attraction.html

32. Maurice Yacowar, "Hitchcock's Imagery and Art," in *A Hitchcock Reader,* eds. Deutelbaum and Poague (Ames: Iowa State University Press, 1986), 16–26.

33. Joseph McElhaney, "Touching on Suspense," *Centenary Essays,* 88. George Toles, "Mother Calls the Shots: Hitchcock's Female Gaze," in *A House Made of Ligh*t (Detroit: Wayne State University Press, 2001), 228.

34. Nowhere in the film except for the decidedly ambiguous "fleeting smile" illustrated above, does Lydia "accept" Melanie or "give her consent." In a departure from his usual Lacanian subtlety Žižek ("Hitchcocian Blot," 137) inter-

prets the end rather conventionally as the sort of successful resolution of the Oedipus complex, which I have argued, here and elsewhere, does not occur in Hitchcock.

35. Horwitz, "A Mother's Love," 47–48, neatly compares the end of the film to a family drive, with the *pater familias* at the wheel, and the mother seated between her two children in the back seat. I agree that the rivalry between the mother and the love interest has been decisively won by the former, but I disagree with Horwitz's contention, which is the thesis of her essay, that the central conflict is between Lydia and Melanie, for to argue thus is to miss the deeper point of Hitchcock's films, which is that of the parent/child relationship in general, not that of the boy or girl respectively.

Chapter 8. *Marnie*

1. Melanie Klein, "The Effects of Early Anxiety-Situations on the Sexual Development of the Girl," in *Female Sexuality*, ed. Bassin (London: Jason Aronson Inc., 1999) 288.

2. Tony Lee Moral, *Hitchcock and the Making of "Marnie,"* (Lanham, MD: The Scarecrow Press, 2002), 29–30.

3. E. Ann Kaplan, "Motherhood and Representation: From Postwar Freudian Figurations to Postmodernism," in *Psychoanalysis and Cinema* (London: Routledge, 1990), 137.

4. Daniel Spoto, *The Dark Side of Genius* (Boston: Little, Brown and Company), 462–63.

5. As another indication of the importance of M-names in Hitchcock (which I have linked to the predominance of the mother theme in these same films), the three other pseudonyms Marnie has identification (social security cards) for are Martha, Margaret, and Mary.

6. Cameron and Jeffery, "The Universal Hitchcock," in *A Hitchcock Reader* (Ames: Iowa State University Press, 1986, 265–78. Joseph McElhaney, "Touching the Surface: Marnie, Melodrama, Modernism," in *Hitchcock's America*, Ed. Freedman and Millington, (Oxford: Oxford University Press, 1999) 87–105). Raymond Bellour, "To Enunciate (on *Marnie*)," in *The Analysis of Film* (Bloomington: Indiana University Press, 2000), 218, 222, 224.

7. Quoted in *Moral, Making of "Marnie,"* 179.

8. Melanie Klein's notion of the girl's fear of being robbed as fear of vaginal penetration, and Karen Horney's notion of the girl's "fear of rape and injury by the large penis of the father" ("The Denial of the Vagina" in *Female Sexuality*, 190) are developments of Freud's theories that are particularly useful in explaining Marnie's fear of penetration, her protecting her vagina "as if it were a national treasure," her obsessive riding, etc.

9. Dana Brand, "Rear-View Mirror: Hitchcock, Poe and the Flaneur in America," in *Hitchcock's America*, eds. Freedman and Millington (Oxford: Oxford University Press, 1999) discusses the importance of Poe in Hitchcock's work, but surprisingly does not mention *Marnie*. The most Poeian moment in Hitchcock's most explicitly Poeian film is doubtless the tapping of Mrs. Edgar's

cane as she walks down the stairs after Marnie's nightmare, where the silhouette of her slow descent down the stairs is as frightening as the silhouette of Norman's mother in the window of the Bates Motel.

10. Sigmund Freud, "The Occurrence in Dreams of Material from Fairy Tales," in *Collected in Writings on Art and Literature* (Stanford, CA: Stanford University Press, 1997).

11. Michael Walker, *Hitchcock's Motifs* (Amsterdam: Amsterdam University Press, 2005), 101.

12. D. W. Lannicott, "Transitional Objects and Transitional Phenomena," in *Psychoanalysis and Gender*, ed. Minsky (London: Routledge, 1996).

13. "It may be remarked in passing that they [incest and parricide] are also the two great crimes proscribed by totemism, the first socio-religious institution of mankind." Sigmund Freud, "The Development of the Libido," lecture 21, in *Introductory Lectures on Psychoanalysis* (New York: Norton, 1966), 335.

14. Walker, *Hitchcock's Motifs*, 41.

15. Theodore Price, *Hitchcock and Homosexuality* (Scarecrow Press, 1992) is one of the few critics to deal with this important theme in Hitchcock.

16. Cameron and Jeffrey, "The Universal Hitchcock," 274. Michele Piso's Marxist interpretation of the film (discussed elsewhere) also notes that "At the center of *Marnie* is the virginal hymen." Michele Piso, "Mark's Marnie," in *A Hitchcock Reader*, 298.

17. Barbara Creed, *The Monstrous Feminine: Film, Feminism, Psychoanalysis* (London: Routledge, 1993).

18. Klein, "Effects of Early Anxiety-Situations."

19. Bellour, *Analysis of Film*, 236. McElhaney, "Toucing the Surface," 93.

20. Dan Auiler, in *Hitchcock's Notebooks* (New York: Avon, 1999) Marnie is referred to as "ecstatic" when riding Forio in this scene.

21. Bellour, "To Enunciate (on *Marnie*)," 236.

22. Klein, "Effects of Early Anxiety-Situations."

23. In his discussion of dreams (see, for example, lectures 5–15 in the *Introductory Lectures on Psychoanalysis*) Freud insists that, with the exception of infantile dreams, the manifest content of a dream is never the same as its real, i.e., latent content.

24. François Truffaut, *Hitchcock* (New York: Simon and Schuster, 1984), 277.

25. Modleski, *The Women Who Knew Too Much*, 112.

26. Silerman, *Acoustic Mirror*, 218.

27. Bellour, *Analysis of Film*, 223–24.

28. "Not only is this moment highly sensual, it also marks the beginning of the healing process for Hedren's character." *Moral, Making of "Marnie"*, 188

29. Pomerance, *Eye for Hitchcock*, 136.

30. Discussed in Freud's essay on "The Most Prevalent Form of Degradation in Erotic Life," in *Creativity and the Unconscious* (New York: Harper, 1958), 173–86.

31. In *Shadow of a Doubt*, this is evident in Uncle Charlie's attraction to mother figures—widows—whom he subsequently murders—not, I would argue, something different from what Mark is doing here with Marnie. Also like *Marnie*, in *Shadow of a Doubt* Uncle Charlie gives his niece a wedding ring that

belonged to one of his victims and ultimately incriminates him. I.e., the "slip" is actually Charlie's desire to marry his mother, a desire that is compulsively repeated in Charlie's repeated act of marrying widows.

32. Sigmund Freud, "The Theme of the Three Caskets," in *Writings on Art and Literature* (Stanford, CA: Stanford University Press, 1997).

33. In Dan Aulier's *Hitchcock's Notebooks,* 413–14 we learn that, in the original screenplay by Evan Hunter, the "primal scene" is actually one of Marnie's jealousy over her mother's lover, whom she confuses with her father (also a sailor in the original treatments), and the mother's subsequent murder of the sailor-father. This confirms my insistence, here, of not taking the film's explanation at face value, and of interpreting Marnie as herself a more aggressive figure than she is shown to be in the scene's "recovered memory."

34. According to Evan Hunter's notes (in ibid.) the scene is an affectionate one between Marnie and the sailor who is comforting her during a storm (repeated, interestingly, in the later scene in Mark's office).

35. Walker, *Hitchcock's Motifs,* 40.

36. Andrew Britton, "Hitchcock's Spellbound: Text and Counter-Text," *cineAction* 3–4 (1986): 72–83, 74.

37. According to Moral, the film's distributors sought to delete this scene from certain versions of the final film.

38. Pomerance, *Eye for Hitchcock,* 151.

39. Michele Piso offers a strong Marxist interpretation of the film that takes this notion of economic exchange much further, and is, like the present essay, relentlessly suspicious or attempts to recuperate the film's darker message. "Mark's Marnie," 288–304.

40. Kaplan, "Motherhood and Representation," 135.

41. *A House Made of Light,* 228.

42. Moral, *Making of "Marnie,"* 176. Although Moral notes the irony of Mark's reply "Had you, love?" he insists on "the possibility, not the certainty, of him and Marnie having a real life together."

43. Richard Schickel, "Hitchcock on Hitchcock: An Interview," in *Perspectives on Hitchcock,* ed. David Boyd (New York: G. K. Hall, 1995), 37, agrees: "I'm sure that even though they went off to get married, she'd [Marnie] probably steal his nightshirt on their wedding night." Like Moral, however, Cameron and Jeffrey, see in the end "signs of hope" ("Universal Hitchcock," 277). Moreover, confirmation of this less optimistic ending is found in the original story on which the screenplay was based.

44. In his entry on "Children" Michael Walker (*Hitchcock's Motifs*) who offers (as we saw) astute comments about the little girl Jesse in *Marnie,* nonetheless fails to mention the important role of these chanting children

45. Moral notes Alexander Walker's remarkably "perceptive" contemporary review of the film, in which the author noted "I can't think it will be widely popular . . . it's too cruel." Moral, *Making of "Marnie,"* 179.

46. "With both the production and reception of *Marnie* Hitchcock seemed to suffer both a private and public humiliation, one in which his integrity and relevance as a film artist was called into question." McElhaney "Touching the Surface," 87–105 discusses the issue of *Marnie*'s poor reception, and the question of whether the film belongs among Hitchcock's best (to which he reaches an ambivalent conclusion).

47. "I am convinced Hitchcock was never the same after *Marnie.*" Truffaut, *Hitchcock,* 1984), 327.

48. I discuss these ironic endings throughout this book, and, in particular, in the introduction, note 35, and in the chapter on *North by Northwest,* note 12.

49. For example, Slavoj Žižek, "The Hitchcockian Blot," in *Centenary Essays,* eds. Allen and Ishii-Gonzalès (London: British Film Institute, 1999), which is discussed in my chapter on *The Birds.*

50. I thus agree with Donald Spoto's explanation of the film, referred to by McElhaney, as "having a psychological intimacy to it unusual in Hitchcock, 'a naked feeling he had never allowed in his films before.'" McElhaney, "Touching the Surface," 89–90.

51. Moral discusses the "film influence" of *Marnie* (*Making of "Marnie,"* 184–89), but does not include Buñuel's *Belle de Jour,* perhaps the greatest of the homages to *Marnie.*

Chapter 9. *Frenzy*

1. Linda Badley, "The Darker Side of Genius: The (Horror) Auteur Meets Freud's Theory, in *Horror Film and Psychoanalysis* (Cambridge: Cambridge University Press, 2004), 222–40.

2. hitchcock@tdfilm.com. There is a touching story, included in the "making of" documentary included in the Special Edition DVD, of how an older gentleman approached Hitchcock while *Frenzy* was being filmed in Covent Garden claiming to remember his father. Hitchcock's assistants were ready to shoo the man away, but Hitchcock insisted on giving the man a seat next to him and talking at some length, as well as buying the man lunch. E. Ann Kaplan, *Psychoanalysis and Cinema,* 5.

3. "If there is a modernist cinema it begins with Hitchcock." William Rothman, *Hitchcock: The Murderous Gaze,* (Cambridge, MA: Harvard University Press, 1982) 6. Both Rothman and Deleuze (*Cinema I/II*) acknowledge the genius of Hitchcock as the need "to acknowledge, at every moment, not only what is on view within the frame but the camera itself" (Rothman, *Murderous Gaze,* 7). Of course, it is perhaps even more important to note that Hitchcock was born only three years after the first films were shown in Paris.

4. Ibid., 249.

5. Stefan Sharff, *Alfred Hitchcock's High Vernacular* (New York: Columbia University Press, 1991), 170. Hitchcock's presence with the others in the crowd, as well as his own famous morbid curiosity, argues against Modleski's notion that the director's "contempt for the tourists" gathered in this scene is evident. Moreover, they are not really tourists, but native Londoners.

6. Claude Chabrol and Eric Rohmer, *Hitchcock* (Paris: Editions Universaires, 1957).

7. The obvious exception, among Hitchcock's "lesser films," is the underrated *I Confess* of 1953, writing about which Murray Pomerance (*An Eye for Hitchcock* [New Brunswick, NJ: Rutgers University Press, 2004]) notes that, at the time he made the film, Hitchcock's life was "certainly vitally connected to

the Catholic Church" (182). Among the so-called "major films," *The Wrong Man* also contains important references to Christianity.

8. Sharff,*Alfred Hitchcock's High Vernacular,* 191.

9. See, for example, O'Connor's celebrated story of another murderer, "A Good Man is Hard to Find."

10. Tony Lee Moral, *The Making of "Marnie"* (Lanham, MD: The Scarecrow Press, 2002), 23.

11. Sharff, *Alfred Hitchcock's High Vernacular,* 202.

12. Ibid., 203.

13. The Alfred Hitchcock Scholars/"MacGuffin" webpage, "Why Hides the Sun in Shame?: Ambrose Chapel and The Man Who Knew Too Much." www .labyrinth.net.au/macguffin/

14. Rothman, *Murderous Gaze,* 40–41.

15. Freud's most explicit discussion of what was to be known as the "Madonna/ Whore Complex" is found in his essay on "A Prevalent Form of Abjection Found Among Men," in *Creativity and the Unconscious* (New York: Harper, 1958).

16. I have written elsewhere on the importance of Freud's essay on "The Antithetical Sense of Primary Words" (1910) to all aspects of Freud's thought in a volume of *Style,* "Freud's 'Uber den Gegensinn der Urworte' : Psychoanalysis, Art, and the Antithetical Senses," *Style* vol. 24, no. 2 (Summer 1990).

17. Sigmund Freud, "The Poet and Daydreaming," in *Creativity and the Unconscious* (New York: Harper, 1958).

18. Michael Walker, *Hitchcock's Motifs* (Amsterdam: Amsterdam University Press, 2005).

19. See the Jason Cangiolosi study of the staircase motif in three of Hitchcock's British films (*Blackmail, Rich and Strange, The 39 Steps*): "Alfred Hitchcock's Stairways of Attraction," http://www.associatedcontent.com/article/ 12992/alfred_hitchcocks_stairways_of_attraction.html. See also Walker, *Hitchcock's Motifs,* 350–72.

20. Spoto, *Dark Side of Genius,* 86.

21. See Theodore Price, *Hitchcock and Homosexuality:* His 50-year Obsession with Jack the Ripper and the Superbitch Prostitute: A Psychoanalytic View (Metuchen, NJ: Scarecrow Press, 1992).

22. Walker, *Hitchcock's Motifs,* 312.

23. Credit to Michael Walker, ibid., 319 for his identification of these paintings.

24. See Mary Ann Doane *Femmes Fatales: Feminism, Film Theory and Psychoanalysis* (New York: Routledge, 1991).

25. I discuss the surprising absence of the important figure of the *femme fatale* in Hitchcock in my chapter on *Vertigo.*

26. This contradiction is discussed in my analysis of *Psycho* (chapter 6).

27. From an interview included with the DVD features of *Frenzy.*

28. Irving Signer, *Three Philosophical Filmmakers* (Cambridge, MA: MIT, 2004), 231.

29. Sigmund Freud, "The Theme of the Three Caskets," *Creativity and the Unconscious* (New York: Harper, 1958).

30. "It is infinitely sad, pathetic, among the most disturbing scenes cinema has to offer." Modleski, *The Women Who Knew Too Much,* 113.

31. The screenwriter (and celebrated playwright) Anthony Schafer in the DVD commentary of *Frenzy.*

32. Freud discusses the relationship of marriage to the larger realm of sexual perversion in "The Sexual Life of Human Beings," in *Introductory Lectures on Psychoanalysis* (New York: Norton, 1966).

33. Freud, "Prevalent Form of Abjection Found Among Men."

34. Sigmund Freud, "A Special Difficulty of Psychoanalysis," collected in *Creativity and the Unconscious* (New York: Harper, 1958).

35. Corroborating Spoto's account is the statement by Hitchcock's screenwriter/collaborator Joseph Stefano, who stated that "Hitchcock was strongly attracted to women and told me one time that he was celibate." Moral, *Making of "Marnie,"* 23.

Chapter 10. Afterword

1. The only book which I have found that comes closest to a "Freudian" reading of Hitchcock is Theodore Price's insightful *Hitchcock and Homosexuality: His 50-year Obsession with Jack the Ripper and the Superbitch Prostitute: A Psychoanalytic View* (Metuchen, NJ: Scarecrow Press, 1992). I should mention, however, Michael Walker's study of *Hitchcock's Motifs* (Amsterdam: Amsterdam University Press, 2005) as making occasional use of psychoanalysis and, in essay form, Andrew Britton's excellent study of *Spellbound:* "Hitchcock's *Spellbound:* Text and Counter-Text," *cineAction* 3–4 (1986), 72–83.

2. George Toles, "Mother Calls the Shots: Hitchcock's Female Gaze," in *A House Made of Light* (Detroit, MI: Wayne State University Press, 2001), 204.

3. "The story emphasizes the heroine's childishness," Tania Modleski, *The Women Who Knew Too Much* (New York: Methuen, 1988), 47. I would agree with those who claim the young woman does assert herself strongly in defense of her husband when he is on trial, but not that this signals a real change in her character; moreover, the defense of her husband's impropriety *against* the law supports my Oedipal reading of the film.

4. Toles, "Mother Calls the Shots," 204.

5. According to Modleski, (*Women Who Knew Too Much,* 43) Selznick insisted Hitchcock delete this scene.

6. Kaja Silverman discusses both variations in "The Fantasy of the Maternal Voice," in *The Acoustic Mirror* (Bloomington, Indiana University Press, 1988), 122–24.

7. Modleski, *The Women Who Knew Too Much,* 33, 46.

8. Sigmund Freud, "Character-Types Met with in Psychoanalytic Work: Those Wrecked by Success," *Creativity and the Unconscious* (New York: Harper, 1958).

9. The studio was required to soften or otherwise change the du Maurier version, in which Max does murder Rebecca. Modleski, *Women Who Knew Too Much,* 53.

10. Ken Mogg, "Two Discoveries," on "The MacGuffin Web Page," http://www.labyrinth.net.au/~muffin/

11. The fascinating story of the correspondence between Selznick, Breen (from the production code office that had to approve the film), Hoover and others is told in the supplementary materials to the Criterion DVD.

12. Modleski, *Women Who Knew Too Much*, 57.

13. Stefan Sharff, *Alfred Hitchcock's High Vernacular* (New York: Columbia University Press, 1991), 3, 14.

14. Irving Singer, *Three Philosophical Filmmakers* (Cambridge, Mass.: MIT, 2004), 241.

15. Modleski, *Women Who Knew Too Much*, 70.

16. *Hitchcock: The Murderous Gaze*, 248.

17. Ibid., 177.

18. And, if Freud is right, anywhere. See "A Prevalent Form of Degradation," in *Creativity and the Unconscious* (New York: Harper, 1958), where Freud discusses the difficulty of sexually degrading the idealized love object.

19. Toles, "Mother Calls the Shots," 194.

20. Anecdotes about Hitchcock's total, unparalleled control of the filmmaking process are numerous. One recalls, in particular, the comment by James Stewart, who told Doris Day not to worry about working with Hitchcock, for she was in the hands of a master. Herbert Coleman, the executive producer of the film, recalls seeing Hitchcock immersed in thought on the set one day. He assumed there was a problem with *The Man Who Knew Too Much*, but Hitchcock answered that he was merely "thinking about his next film."

21. Following the earlier discussion of *Notorious* I am using the term in a different, expanded sense.

22. Tom Cohen has commented upon the importance of the M-R names in Marakesh and Morrocco. *Hitchcock's Cryptonomies* (Minneapolis: University of Minnesota Press, 2005).

23. Murray Pomerance, *Eye for Hitchcock* (New Brunswick, NJ: Rutgers University Press, 2004), 267.

24. Sigmund Freud, *Introductory Lectures on Psychoanalysis* (New York: Norton, 1966), 335.

25. Shortly after writing this "minireading" I discovered the following reference to *The Man Who Knew Too Much* hidden among the footnotes of Rothman's classic study of *The Murderous Gaze:* "The wife's fainting spell in the early version of *The Man Who Knew Too Much* is closely related to this, as is the structurally central moment early in the later version when the young son, *suffering oedipal pangs on board a bus*, immerses himself in the view of the Moroccan landscape and then precipitates the narrative by accidentally pulling the veil from a Moslem woman's face," (362, italics mine)

26. Bill Krohn, *Hitchcock at Work* (London: Phaidon, 2000), 178.

27. According to songfacts (www.songfacts.com): This was written by Ray Evans and Jay Livingston. The phrase came from a movie called *The Barefoot Contessa*, where the character Rossano Brazzi's family motto was "Che Sera, Sera." The motto in the film was Italian, but Evans and Livingston switched the "Che" to "Que" because more people spoke Spanish in the US. Doris Day sang this in the Alfred Hitchcock movie *The Man Who Knew Too Much. In the film, she was putting her young son to bed.* She was a little reluctant to release it because she felt it was a children's song. (italics mine)

It is also worth mentioning, in this regard, that Hitchcock and his mother long maintained their nightly ritual of recounting his day's activities at bedtime.

28. Walker, *Hitchcock's Motifs*, 104.

29. "Why Hides the Sun in Shame?: Ambrose Chapel and The Man Who Knew Too Much," on the "MacGuffin" webpage, http://www.labryinth.net.au/macguffin/.

Bibliography

Allen, Richard. "Psychoanalytic Film Theory." In *A Companion to Film Theory.* Oxford: Blackwell, 1999.

Allen, Richard, and S. Ishii-Gonzalès, eds. *Centenary Essays.* London: British Film Institute, 1999.

Anderson, Lindsay. "Alfred Hitchcock." In *Focus on Hitchcock.* Englewood Cliffs, NJ: Prentice Hall, 1972.

Aulier, Dan. *Hitchcock's Notebooks.* New York: Avon, 1999.

———. *Vertigo: The Making of a Hitchcock Classic.* New York: St Martins Press, 1998.

Badley, Linda. "The Darker Side of Genius: The (Horror) Auteur Meets Freud's Theory." In *Horror Film and Psychoanalysis.* Cambridge: Cambridge University Press, 2004.

Ballif, Michelle. *Seduction, Sophistry, and the Woman with the Rhetorical Figure.* Carbondale: Southern Illinois University Press, 2001.

Barr, Charles. *Vertigo.* London: British Film Institute, 2002.

Bellour, Raymond. *Analysis of Film.* Bloomington: Indiana University Press, 2000.

Bordwell, David, and Noell Carroll, *Post-Theory: Reconstructing Film Studies.* Madison: University of Wisconsin Press, 1996.

Boyd, David. ed. *Perspectives on Hitchcock.* New York: G. K. Hall, 1995.

Brand, Dana. "Rear-View Mirror: Hitchcock, Poe and the Flaneur in America." In *Hitchcock's America,* ed. Jonathan Freedman and Richard Millington. Oxford: Oxford University Press, 1999.

Brill, Lesley. "*North by Northwest* and Romance." In *Perspectives on Hitchcock,* ed. Boyd. New York: G. K. Hall, 1995.

Britton, Andrew. "Hitchcock's *Spellbound:* Text and Counter-Text." *cineAction* 3–4 (1986):72–83.

Brown, Royal. "*Vertigo* as Orphic Tragedy." In *Perspectives on Hitchcock,* ed Boyd. New York: G. K. Hall, 1995.

Cameron, Ian, and Richard Jeffrey. "The Universal Hitchcock." In *A Hitchcock Reader,* eds. Deutelbaum and Poague. Ames: Iowa State University Press, 1986.

Cangiolosi, Jason. "Alfred Hitchcock's Stairways of Attraction." http://www.associatedcontent.com/article/12992/alfred_hitchcocks_stairways_of_attraction.html.

Cavell, Stanley. "*North by Northwest.*" In *A Hitchcock Reader,* eds. Deutelbaum and Poague. Ames: Iowa State University Press, 1986.

———. *The World Viewed (Reflections on the Ontology of Film).* Cambridge, MA: Harvard University Press, 1979.

Chabrol, Claude, and Eric Rohmer. *Hitchcock.* Paris: Editions Universaires, 1957.

Cohen, Paula. *Alfred Hitchcock: The Legacy of Victorianism.* Lexington: University of Kentucky, 1995.

Cohen, Tom. *Hitchcock's Cryptonomies.* Minneapolis: University of Minnesota Press, 2005.

Cowie, Elizabeth. *Representing the Woman.* Minneapolis: University of Minnesota, 1997.

Creed, Barbara. *The Monstrous Feminine: Film, Feminism, Psychoanalysis.* London: Routledge, 1993.

Deleuze, Gilles. *Coldness and Cruelty.* New York: George Braziller, 1971.

Deutelbaum and Poague, eds. *A Hitchcock Reader.* Ames: Iowa State University Press, 1986.

Doane, Mary Ann. *Femmes Fatales: Feminism, Film Theory and Psychoanalysis,* eds. Feldstein and Roof. New York: Routledge, 1991.

———. "Veiling over Desire." In *Feminism and Psychoanalysis,* eds.

Douchet, Jean. "Hitchcock and his Public." In *A Hitchcock Reader,* eds.

———. "La troisième clef de Hitchcock." *Cahiers deu Cinéma,* no. 113 (November, 1960.

Durgnat, Raymond. *The Strange Case of Alfred Hitchcock.* Cambridge, MA: MIT Press, 1974.

Edelman, Lee. "Hitchcock's Future." In *Centenary Essays,* eds. Allen and Ishi-Gonzalès. London: British Film Institute, 1999.

Elsaesser, Thomas. "The Dandy in Hitchcock." In *Centenary Essays,* eds. Allen and Ishi-Gonzalès (London: British Film Institute, 1999).

Fawell, John. *Hitchcock's "Rear Window": The Well-Made Film.* Carbondale: Southern Illinois University Press, 2001.

Feldstein, Richard, and Judith Roof, eds. *Feminism and Psychoanalysis.* Ithaca, NY: Cornell University Press, 1989.

Freedman, Jonathan. "Alfred Hitchcock and Therapeutic Culture in America." In *Hitchcock's America,* ed. Freedman and Millington. London: Oxford University Press, 1999.

Freedman, Jonathan, and Richard Millington, eds. *Hitchcock's America.* Oxford: Oxford University Press, 1999.

Freud, Sigmund. *Collected Papers.* London: Hogarth, 1957.

———. *Creativity and the Unconscious.* New York: Harper, 1958.

———. "Das Medusahaupt." In *Gesammelte Werke.* Frankfurt: Fischer, 1999.

———. *Introductory Lectures on Psychoanalysis.* New York: Norton, 1968.

———. *Jokes and their Relation to the Unconscious.* New York: Norton, 1960.

———. *Writings on Art and Literature.* Stanford, CA: Stanford University Press, 1997.

Gallop, Jane. "The Monster in the Mirror." In *Feminism and Psychoanalysis,* eds. Feldstein and Roof.

Green, André. *The Dead Mother.* London: Routledge, 1999.

Haskell, Molly. *From Reverence to Rape: The Treatment of Women in the Movies.* Harmondsworth: Penguin, 1974.

Heidegger, Freidrich. *Der Satz vom Grund.* Pfullingen: Neske, 1957.

Horney, Karen. "The Denial of the Vagina." In *Female Sexuality,* ed. Bassin. London: Jason Aronson Inc., 1999.

Horwitz, Margaret. "*The Birds:* A Mother's Love." *Wide Angle* vol. 5, no. 1 (1982).

Jameson, Fredric. *Signatures of the Visible.* New York: Routledge, 1990.

Kaplan, E. Ann. "Motherhood and Representation: From Postwar Freudian Figurations to Postmodernism." In *Psychoanalysis and Cinema,* ed. Ann E. Kaplan. London: Routledge, 1990.

———. *Motherhood and Representation in Literature and Film, 1830–1960.* London: Routledge, 1988.

———, ed. *Psychoanalysis and Cinema.* London: Routledge, 1990.

Keane, Marian. "A Closer Look at Scopophilia: Mulvey, Hitchcock and *Vertigo.*" In *A Hitchcock Reader, Ed. Deutelbaum and Poague. Ames: Iowa State University Press, 1986.*

Klein, Melanie. "The Effects of Early Anxiety-Situations on the Sexual Development of the Girl." In *Female Sexuality,* ed. Bassin. London: Jason Aronson Inc., 1999.

Klinger, Barbara. "*Psycho:* The Insistutionalization of Female Sexuality." In *A Hitchcock Reader,* ed. Deutelbaum and Poague. Ames: Iowa State University Press, 1986.

Knight, Deborah, and George McKnight. "Suspense and its Master." In *Centenary Essays,* eds. Allen and Ishii-Gonzalès. London: British Film Institute, 1999.

Kofman, Sarah. *The Childhood of Art.* New York: Columbia University Press, 1988.

Krohn, Bill. *Hitchcock at Work.* London: Phaidon, 2000.

Laplanche, Jean. "The Unfinished Copernican Revolution." In *Essays on Otherness.* New York: Routledge, 1999.

LaValley, Albert. ed. *Focus on Hitchcock.* Englewood Cliffs, NJ: Prentice Hall, 1972.

Lebeau, Vicky. *Psychoanalysis and Cinema.* London: Wallflower, 2001.

McElhaney, Joseph. "Touching the Surface: Marnie, Melodrama, Modernism." In *Hitchcock's America,* ed. Freedman and Millington. Oxford: Oxford University Press, 1999.

McLaughlin, James. "All in the Family." In *A Hitchcock Reader,* eds. Deutelbaum and Poague. Ames: Iowa State University Press, 1986.

Metz, Christian. "The Fiction Film and its Spectator." In *The Imaginary Signifier.* Bloomington: Indiana University Press, 1982.

Miller, Gavin. "Hitchcock vs. Truffaut." *Sight and Sound* vol. 38, no. 2. Spring, 1969.

Millington, Richard. "Hitchcock and American Culture." In *Hitchcock's America*, eds. Freedman and Millington. Oxford: Oxford University Press, 1999.

Mitchell, Juliet. *Psychoanalysis and Feminism*. New York: Macmillan, 1982.

Modleski, Tania. *The Women Who Knew Too Much*. New York: Methuen, 1988.

Mogg, Ken. "Will and Wilfulness: Recent Commentary on Hitchcock's *The Birds*." *Screening the Past*. Online journal (March 3, 2001).

Moral, Tony Lee. *Hitchcock and the The Making of "Marnie"*. Lanham, MD: The Scarecrow Press, 2002.

Mulvey, Laura. *Fetishism and Curiousity*. Bloomington: Indiana University Press, 1996.

———. "Visual Pleasures and Narrative Cinema." *Screen* 10 no. 3 (1975):6–18.

Naremore, James. "Hitchcock at the Margins of Noir." In *Centenary Essays*, eds. Allen and Ishii-Gonzalès. London: British Film Institute, 1999.

Paglia, Camille. *The Birds*. London: British Film Institute, 1998.

Peucker, Brigitte. "The Cut of Representation." In *Centenary Essays*, eds. Allen and Ishii-Gonzalès. London: British Film Institute, 1999.

Piso, Michele. "Mark's Marnie." In *A Hitchcock Reader*, eds. Deutelbaum and Poague. Ames: Iowa State University Press, 1986.

Pomerance, Murray. *An Eye for Hitchcock*. New Brunswick, NJ: Rutgers University Press, 2004.

———. "Why Hides the Sun in Shame?: Ambrose Chapel and The Man Who Knew Too Much." The Alfred Hitchcock Scholars/'MacGuffin' webpage.

Price, Theodore. *Hitchcock and Homosexuality: His 50-year Obsession with Jack the Ripper and the Superbitch Prostitute: A Psychoanalytic View*. Metuchen, NJ: Scarecrow Press, 1992.

Rodowick, D. N. *The Difficulty of Difference*. London: Routledge, 1991.

Rothman, William. *Hitchcock: The Murderous Gaze*. (Cambridge, MA: Harvard University Press, 1982.

———. *The "I" of the Camera*. Cambridge: Cambridge University Press, 1988.

———. "Some Thoughts on Hitchcock's Authorship." In *Centenary Essays*, eds. Allen and Ishii-Gonzalès. London: British Film Institute, 1999.

Samuels, Charles. *Mastering the Film and Other Essays*. Knoxville: University of Tennessee Press, c1977.

Samuels, Robert. *Hitchcock's Bi-Textuality*. New York: SUNY Press, 1998.

Sarris, Andrew. "Hitchcock." In *Focus on Hitchcock*.

Scheib, Ronnie. "Charlie's Uncle." *Film Comment* vol 12, no. 2.

Schneider, Steven Jay. *Horror Film and Psychoanalysis*. Cambridge: Cambridge University Press, 2004.

Sharff, Stefan. *Alfred Hitchcock's High Vernacular*. New York: Columbia University Press, 1991.

Silverman, Kaja. *The Acoustic Mirror*. Bloomington: Indiana University Press, 1988.

Singer, Irving. *Three Philosophical Filmmakers*. Cambridge, MA: MIT, 2004.

Slipp, Samuel. *The Freudian Mystique.* New York: New York University Press, 1993.

Smith, J. C., and C. S. Ferstman. *The Castration of Oedipus.* New York: New York University Press, 1996.

Spoto, Daniel. *The Art of Hitchcock.* New York: Anchor, 1976.

———. *The Dark Side of Genius.* Boston: Little, Brown and Company, 1983.

Stam, Robert, and Roberta Pearson. "Hitchcock's *Rear Window: Reflexivity and the Critique of Voyeurism.*" In *A Hitchcock Reader,* ed. Deutelbaum and Poague. Ames: Iowa State University Press, 1986.

Studlar, Gaylyn. *In the Realm of Pleasure.* Urbana: University of Illinois Press, 1998.

Toles, George "If Thine Eye Offend Thee: *Psycho* and the Art of Infection." In *Centenary Essays,* eds. Allen and Ishii-Gonzalès. London: British Film Institute, 1999.

———. "Mother Calls the Shots: Hitchcock's Female Gaze." In *A House Made of Light.* (Detroit, MI: Wayne State University Press, 2001.

Truffaut, François. *Hitchcock.* New York: Simon and Schuster, 1967.

Turvey, Malcolm. "Philosophical Problems in Psychoanalytical Theories of the Horror Film." In *Horror Film and Psychoanalysis,* ed. Schneider. Cambridge: Cambridge University Press, 2004.

Vroman, Lavender. "*Tippi Hedren Airs Out Her Early Acting Days, Wildlife Preservation.*" *Antelope Valley Press* (September 30, 2004).

Wager, Jane. *Dangerous Dames.* Athens: Ohio University Press, 1999.

Walker, Michael. *Hitchcock's Motifs.* Amsterdam: Amsterdam University Press, 2005.

White, Susan. "Allegory and Referentiality: *Vertigo* and Feminist Criticism." *MLN* 106/5 (1991):310–32.

Williams, Dan. *North by Northwest.* Essex: York Press, 2000.

Winnicott, D. W. "Mirror Role of Mother and Family in Child Development." In *Playing and Reality.* New York: Basic Books, 1971.

———. "Transitional Objects and Transitional Phenomena." In *Psychoanalysis and Gender,* ed. Rosalind Minsky. London, Routledge, 1996.

Wood, Robin. "Plot Formations" in *Perspectives on Hitchcock,* ed. Boyd. New York: G. K. Hall, 1995.

———. "Ideology, Genre, Auteur: *Shadow of a Doubt.*'" In *Hitchcock's Films Revisited.* Columbia University Press: New York, 1989.

Wright, Elizabeth. *Psychoanalytic Criticism: A Reappraisal.* Cambridge: Polity Press, 1998.

———. *Writings on Art and Literature.* Stanford: Stanford University Press, 1997.

Yacowar, Maurice. "Hitchcock's Imagery and Art." In *A Hitchcock Reader,* eds. Deutelbaum and Poague. Ames: Iowa State University Press, 1986.

Žižek, Slavoj. *Everything You Always Wanted to Know about Lacan (but Were Afraid to Ask Hitchcock.* London: Verso, 1992.

———. "The Hitchcockian Blot." In *Centenary Essays.*

Index